On Time, Causality, and the Block Universe

Scientific answers to our deepest questions

Anthony C. Proctor

Published by Clink Street Publishing 2022

Copyright © 2022

First edition.

First in the Parallax View series.
Author contact via parallaxview@proctor.net
Website https://parallax-view.com

© Anthony C. Proctor
Cover design, "Nexus of Life-Time" © Anthony C. Proctor

ISBN:
978-1-913136-43-7 - hardback
978-1-913136-44-4 - paperback
978-1-913136-45-1 - ebook

Dedicated to my father, Stanton (1934–2018),
who would argue black-and-blue on everything in
order to test the depth of my understanding.

*I believe in intuitions and inspirations. I sometimes
feel that I am right. I do not know if I am.*

Albert Einstein,
G. S. Viereck interview, 26 October, 1929,
reprinted in his Glimpses of the Great (1930).

*To see a World in a Grain of Sand
And a Heaven in a Wild Flower
Hold Infinity in the palm of your hand
And Eternity in an hour*

. . .

William Blake,
Auguries of Innocence (1863).

Contents

How are our thoughts, perceptions, and even emotions, relevant to a description or interpretation of reality?

What is the true nature of the wave function, especially in a block universe? Does it bias one direction in time?

What underpins the apparent flow of time from past to future? Where is the asymmetry in the laws of physics?

Why are computers not intelligent or conscious? Can we learn anything by looking more deeply at them?

What is the relationship between mathematics and the physical universe?

Figures

Preface

Ever since my teens in English secondary school, I have been in awe of the concept of time. As a science student, I was aware of Einstein's perspective, and was attempting to learn tensor calculus in order to see a little further, but it was clear that there was a gulf between the mathematical descriptions and the real world. It seemed that time was the mainstay of both physics and experience, and yet it remained very poorly understood.

A more profound — even sad — feeling concerned the way that time was both giver and taker in equal measure. In particular, that it gave us new memories but gradually took our older ones. To quote a line from actor Rutger Hauer in the film *Blade Runner*: "All those moments will be lost in time, like tears in rain."[1] Most people will understand this feeling, but may be surprised to find such an angst-ridden subject pursued in a rational way.

Following an unconventional educational route, I graduated in the *wrong type of physics*, and so had to abandon any hopes of theoretical research, instead embarking on a successful career in computer software. This change was fortunate as it allowed me to pursue my own research — still important in order to answer my own questions — without having to chase research grants in fields deemed by others to be productive.

I have always been convinced that the universe is fundamentally static and unchanging, and that this accounts for its close relationship with mathematics, but subjects such as quantum theory, thermodynamics, and consciousness seemed, initially, to present obstacles to a fuller explanation. Physics has a goal of explaining everything around us, but this is primarily the universe as we see it, and not the universe as it really is. To what extent can physics achieve a wholly objective measurement, and to what extent can any measurement provide an insight into things as they really are, in our absence? It seemed that this gulf constantly widened as I made progress, and it became evident that the repertoire of concepts in physics (such as velocity or energy) had interpretational issues associated with their history.

On 6 April 1922, German-born theoretical physicist Albert Einstein accepted an invitation to the Société française de philosophie, in Paris, to attend a forum discussing his theories of relativity. One of the many intellectuals there was celebrated French philosopher Henri-Louis Bergson. The pair clashed over the nature of time, and their heated debate turned in a lifelong disagreement on the subject. Bergson was interested in many of the same subjects to be covered here, including time, free will, perception, identity, change, memory, consciousness, and the foundation of mathematics, but his arguments will not be covered as they are the antithesis of those to be put forward. Like many readers opening this book, he believed in the sanctity and fundamentality of experience, and the presence of a single universal time. Einstein had shown that space and time could be treated orthogonally by mathematics, and that they were not absolute since their measurement depended upon the observer. But Einstein never bridged the gap between his mathematics and our experience of time.

The approach taken here in order to resolve this is one of deconstruction based on the initial premise of a timeless universe. This premise can be justified even though it feels unnatural in the face of experience. Assuming it to be true then it is necessary to deconstruct various fields in order to understand their true nature, and to reimagine them in such a universe. This includes the nature of time, quantum mechanics, the nature of measurement, consciousness, experience, free will, probability, causality, the second law of thermodynamics, and mathematics.

Such was my obsession with the subject of time that when I started dating my eventual wife, Dorothy, in 1990, I mistakenly introduced her to some of my ideas on time, only to see her cringing and visibly thinking 'this is not going work' (luckily, it did!).

In 2004, I ventured into the world of genealogy to solve a family mystery surrounding my mother's adoption: she and her five siblings were removed from the family home in 1947, and separated from each other. At nine years old, she was the oldest of the children when this happened, but she could only just recall their names and ages. I eventually found and reunited the siblings for her 70th birthday, an emotional and life-changing event for everyone. I continued this research in order to uncover the reason for their removal, and so succeeded in giving them closure on a dark episode in their past.

I found that trying to reconstruct the past, and to preserve both images and documents, became another obsession that stemmed from the same feelings about time. I was tailor-made for historical and genealogical research, despite having hated history at school, and I continue to indulge in my spare time by recovering lost lives and events, and by solving further mysteries.

Winding down from my contract software work, I found more time to correlate the various ideas that I'd formed over the years. As things began to gel, and the overall picture began to make more sense to me, I realised that my understanding of the world around us was significantly different from the mainstream one of science. But in order to make it known, my original goal of a mere magazine article would have been far too restrictive in terms of size, and an academic paper would have been too restrictive in terms of interdisciplinary scope. My scope had reached beyond the world of physics, and into topics of metaphysics such as existence and consciousness, all of which had to be addressed in order to make a coherent argument. A book was the logical alternative.

The book represents a personal understanding, but in trying to tread a path that is both rational and self-consistent the content will inevitably differ from the accepted wisdom in several fields; wisdom that has failed to yield an overall description free of conflicts, contradictions, or simply unexplainable phenomena. The epigraph to this book contains two quotations: the first (by Albert Einstein) describes my current state of mind, but the second (by William Blake) describes where I would like it to be.

Touching on philosophical issues would, on its own, place this book in a category along with some rather fanciful notions, but this is not the intention here. They are addressed on equal terms with the scientific and mathematical issues, hopefully delivering a rational, informed, and insightful interpretation of our reality. The content tries, as best I can manage, to be accessible to people of a broad range of backgrounds since the main topics, and the associated questions, are relevant to all of us; however, the subjects are deep and the problems hard. The Notes section includes helpful information and source citations. Some knowledge of physics would help in several of the chapters but the mathematical content is low, partly as a consequence of this accessibility goal, but also because the applicability of mathematics to an understanding of our universe will be examined. The initial chapters will gradually introduce the relevant topics, and so it will be common to encounter forward references to where the analysis becomes more in-depth.

Depending upon the fate of this book, it may be followed by another that devotes a little more time and space (so to speak) to build up an easier understanding of the topics. Constructive suggestions may be sent to the email address below.

People of a religious disposition may be especially interested in the final conclusions chapter. I have always been, and ever will remain, an atheist, but having demonstrated that there are questions that we simply cannot ask then it has left me with a sense of there being an intangible *more*, and yet rendering all attempts to comprehend any rationale for existence as simply head-wrecking.

If asked whether this understanding has helped me personally, I would have to say that it has been profoundly helpful and reassuring in matters such as our short existence, goals and aspirations, relationships, life around as well as life within, the fragility of life, death and grief, and generally separating what's important in life from the inconsequential trivia.

Somewhat unusually, this work is presented from the viewpoint of both a feeling person and a thinking person. Expressing my personal thoughts as a series of logical arguments is one thing; expressing the depth of their profound impact on me is quite another. Despite the best intentions of my old English teacher (who was actually Welsh), it has taken me until recent years to finally understand the need for concepts such as poetry. In the epilogue, I include my attempts at utilising this unfamiliar medium to express my feelings, not because they add anything to the body of the work but because they say something more about the mind of the author.

My special thanks to Nigel Rickard and Susan Lethbridge for their invaluable time in proofreading my drafts and making helpful suggestions on their readability.

Stylistic Matters

Because the worlds of science, philosophy, and mathematics have many technical terms, these pages see them divided into two categories (admittedly with some subjective assessment). Established and well-defined terms are italicised, while weaker or informal terms are placed in single quotes. Single quotes are also used for internal dialogue (thoughts) and for hypothetical quotations, while double quotes are reserved for direct quotations and for titles in citations. When making use of more-common terms, the book strives to identify the context of its particular usage in order to avoid ambiguities.

The text employs British-English spelling, logical quotes, serial (Oxford) commas, and padded em-dashes. The citation format is a variant of that used in the *Chicago Manual of Style* since that is less cryptic than those more commonly used in the sciences, and it allows them to be placed in endnotes along with any discursive notes associated with the text. The particular variant used here is that by E. S. Mills (*Evidence Explained: Citing History Sources from Artifacts to Cyberspace*, 2nd ed. (Baltimore, Maryland: Genealogical Pub. Co., 2009)) as it treats material published in print and online in a consistent way (https://www.evidenceexplained.com/node/1521), as well as unpublished material and many other source types. It also accommodates citation layering for such detail as provenance, derivation, or quality assessment.

When persons are mentioned, the first ever reference will include their nationality, occupation, and full name. The first reference in subsequent chapters will just include their given name and surname. Subordinate references in all chapters will just include their surname. Selected German names will identify their chosen *Rufnamen* (or 'call names') by the standard mechanism of underlining. Some non-English names have also been given pronunciation hints for readers who might be less familiar with them.

Anthony C. Proctor
parallaxview@proctor.net
March 2021

— 1 —

Time for Change

*What is the fundamental distinction between physics
and metaphysics? Why should they be distinct?*

In a book of this nature, you may be expecting to read about 'string theory', 'multiverses', 'quantum gravity', 'supersymmetry', and the like. There are several fashionable fields of theoretical research that appear to be getting further and further away from testable verification, and some of these could rightly be classified more as mathematics than physics. We will examine this distinction in later chapters, but before we can do that, we need to go back to basics and take a fresh look at what we think we know. What are we missing?

It is well known that fundamental physics has failed to yield a significant prediction for more than 40 years (the Higgs boson, discovered in 2012, was actually predicted back in 1964), which means that the latest theories are either unverifiable or have failed experimental verification. This hiatus is compounded by experimental physics which, as well as not verifying these new theories, has not yielded much that we did not already know during this time.

There are a number of cornerstones in fundamental physics — including *general relativity, quantum mechanics,* the *standard model* of particle physics, and the *lambda-CDM* model of cosmology — upon which great effort has been expended to unite them within a single theoretical framework, but with little or no success. There is huge reluctance to question any of these given the evidence for them individually, and radical alternatives are usually viewed as heresy, but the lack of progress strongly suggests that something is wrong at the lowest levels; our theoretical foundations may be wrong, we may not be looking for the right things, or we may not have access to the next levels of scale.

American science journalist John Horgan, who has long been disillusioned with fundamental physics, recently argued that pure science has run its course, and that the vision of total knowledge is "a laughable delusion".[2] There may be some truth in this implied limit, based upon whether all aspects of reality are accessible to us, and whether our concept of measurement is superficial or deeper, but fresh clarity is required for a serious appraisal of his argument. It could also be that physics has been extrapolating too far from a weak core.

What would the universe look like without us, and without any other conscious entities? If you think that it would still consist of stars and planets, and fundamental particles, all whizzing around then you are probably wrong. Mathematics cannot capture our experience of anything, it being deadpan and inexpressive to a surprisingly large extent. But as we dig deeper, and into fundamental physics, then neither metaphysics nor anything else stemming from our own experience can be relevant, leaving mathematics as our only reliable tool. How, then, can we have a complete theory of reality that genuinely explains consciousness and free will — goals that are necessary if we accept that we do not possess any privileged status within the universe?

With all due respect to current researchers, some reorientation of our perspective is needed to ensure the future progress of our understanding, but it is evident that the answers cannot come solely from physics, mathematics, or metaphysics as there are areas of explanation to which each is inapplicable. That is, each of these fields has their areas of relevance, but also their areas of irrelevance where they are unable to address the associated subjects at all. Accepting and understanding these boundaries would help answer a wider range of questions, and also avoid inappropriate crossovers.

The goal of this book is to explore an alternative perspective on both physics and metaphysics, including our own relationship to the real world around us, and yet one that remains consistent with both mathematical physics and our perceived reality. This must entail stepping around some pervasive examples of group-think resulting from a cognitive bias, so please be prepared to follow some different lines of reasoning. We are so often hampered by baggage from our everyday perceptions that we can misinterpret both evidence and the mathematics that we have constructed to help explain that evidence.

So is this book presenting a 'theory of everything' (TOE)? No, it is not, since this term means something quite specific within physics, and it is less far-reaching than non-physicists would expect. The book covers a wider range of issues related to the nature of reality, but the treatment is neither in-depth enough to be considered a complete theory nor is it falsifiable. Its value rests in that it is an adjustment to our understanding — a rather large adjustment — that adds clarity to what we think we know, and signposts a different direction to the one we are heading in. The wider ambit is better able to answer our deepest questions — even if we do not like those answers — and is effectively the best end-to-end explanation that this author is capable of presenting.

In order to set the scene, let us just preview some selected topics that will be covered in this book:

- Why do we experience time differently from the way it is described by physics?
- Why does time appear to have a preferred direction? Does the moment that we call '*now*' have any fundamental significance?
- What is the nature of consciousness? How different is the universe in the absence of conscious entities?
- Does aesthetics have any relevance in the absence of consciousness? How can we judge a theoretic description of the universe based upon its 'beauty'?
- What is the nature of free will? Is it incompatible with a deterministic universe?
- Is the universe fundamentally based upon probability? Is that the best description we can hope for?
- What is the nature of measurement, and how does that influence our perception of reality?
- Was there an origin to the universe? How can something appear from nothing?
- What is the relationship between physics and mathematics? Why does the universe appear to be governed by mathematical principles, and yet mathematics is incapable of describing experience?
- What is the origin of mathematics? Is it fundamental and pre-existing, or a construct of the conscious mind?

In order to address these topics, and to examine the interrelation between them, we will draw upon established theoretic works, such as *quantum theory* and *relativity* — hopefully yielding some genuine insights into their foundations — as well as philosophical works from a time when science still considered philosophical questions to be important. In particular, the interpretation of *quantum theory* presented in this book is rather different from the mainstream ones (there is no single accepted one), and the reasons for this will become evident as we work through the topics. More recent works are mentioned when there is either significant agreement or disagreement with the book's claims.

Many fields have their own set of technical terms, and we will strive to use their accepted terminology here. This may sound a little heavy going and formal, but the material should remain accessible to most people with an interest in either science or philosophy. A small number of new terms are necessary (see Glossary), though this is certainly not an attempt to disguise our unknowns with florid jargon or opaque symbolism.

1.1   Metaphysics

The term *philosophy* is derived from the Greek word *philosophia* (φιλοσοφία), meaning 'love of wisdom', and originally embraced a study of all things. It is more recently that *natural philosophy*, or the study of natural things, has been separately described as *science*, a term derived from the Latin word *scientia*, meaning 'knowledge'.

Philosophy now stands apart from science, and in order to understand the modern meaning it is helpful to consider the five main branches of philosophy[3]:

- *Metaphysics*: The study of reality beyond the reach of physics, including causality, God, the soul, and the afterlife. Also the study of all existent things (ontology) with an inventory of their nature and qualities (categories).
- *Epistemology*: The study of knowledge, including what it means to know something is true, and how knowledge is acquired.
- *Ethics*: The study of moral values, including right or wrong conduct, morality, and good and evil.
- *Aesthetics*: The study of art and beauty, including the nature of art, and whether beauty has value in our absence.
- *Logic*: The study of right reasoning. This is distinct from the mathematical field of formal logic, although they share similar goals.

Why must some questions be deemed scientific while others are deemed philosophical? Is there a precise distinction, and at what point does it occur? An examination of these branches will confirm that philosophical questions are anthropocentric, and explicitly relate to our relationship to the world around us and to each other. We will frequently employ the adjectives *subjective* and *objective* in the following chapters to distinguish perspectives on reality, and to help clarify the associated arguments, but these branches are more subjective than simply studying the world as we see it rather than the world as it would be without us; the topics stem mainly from the core of our experience, and have little or no correspondence in an objective reality devoid of conscious life.

The nature of these philosophical branches means that they are not part of the measurable world, and so they cannot be addressed objectively through either physics or mathematics. This accounts for much of the current separation of metaphysics from physics, and the reason that physicists generally find it hard to integrate such thinking into their research. In contrast, fundamental physics would consider itself to be objective and non-anthropocentric — largely by relying upon mathematics — but subjective thinking and assumptions are insidious ingredients that we may not even notice. Rather than making a case for these philosophical branches to be irrelevant, we need to see more clearly how they sit relative to physics, and so better understand the limits of our perception and attempts at explanation. The objective and subjective viewpoints are both important to us, and it would be disingenuous to dismiss the subjective as not fundamental when we knowingly find it hard to define the boundary. A partial truth with an incorrect or missing context is no truth at all.

We must venture into each of these branches — except ethics (which I assure you is not indicative of the author having no moral compass) — but particularly that of metaphysics. We are all aware of a body of questions — such as 'why are we here?', and 'who or what created the universe?' — that science is unable to answer, and which we defer to the branch of philosophy called metaphysics. We all harbour similar questions because we have an innate desire to know the *how*, *why*, and *when*. At the end of this search, we are forced to put a circle around the remaining unknowns, yet whether we write 'big bang', 'God', or something else in that circle then it never yields a complete and satisfactory answer as there cannot be a final answer that does not lead to further questions. We must here differentiate between an answer that constitutes an explanation and an answer that has a mathematical basis. The only possible end to this infinite regress is the latter, unpalatable as it may be, and that is where our search will take us.

1.2   Faith and Science

Faith in the literal sense — the strong belief in something or someone with little or no direct evidence to support it — and science are not opposites, but the interpretation of faith is an emotive topic that we must examine because it leads to a raft of ambiguous related terms associated with religion. We must clarify the terminology to be used here in case future arguments are laid open to misinterpretation.

For example, the search for explanation leads to some discord between so-called 'people of faith' and 'people of no faith', where the latter is an entirely misleading term that, through either ignorance or design, simply denigrates anyone who believes in something quite different, such as the applicability of mathematics to an understanding of the universe. The fact that mathematics so adequately describes the observable universe, and our faith that this is everywhere so, and will always be so, is a very important topic that will be treated in depth in Chapter 10 (Mathematics). In fact, physics is underpinned by several more-subtle aspects of faith that derive from our subjective experience, and one of the goals here will be to identify them and question whether they are trustworthy.

We must separate the notions of personal spirituality (the feeling of there being something more in a non-physical sense, but not necessarily a supernatural one) and theism (belief in the existence of one or more deities) from organised religion, which is the acceptance of some man-made dogma and adherence to its associated rituals and restrictions. As with all dogma, it is as often divisive as inclusive, and it risks leaving weaker minds open to some other agenda (cf. the Crusader cry "God wills it!", Latin: *Deus [id] vult*). Also, atheism is a disbelief in the existence of all deities — although ubiquitous in its application in relation to the single Abrahamic God of the modern era — and agnosticism is a term coined by English biologist and anthropologist Thomas H. Huxley in 1869 to represent the view that the existence of God is unknown or unknowable — although routinely used to describe people who are personally unsure.

With the advent of pandemics and global climate change, science has been accused of being politically motivated, and so has become distrusted, but this betrays a shallow appreciation of what science is. Most people are aware of the need to fact-check assertions — even though they rarely do — but fewer people are aware of the unfortunate fragmentation and polarisation of opinions (not just in science but also politics, religion, and other fields) caused by software algorithms selecting content for their social media based upon the simple goal of maximising their usage of it. With some modest background knowledge then it is possible to differentiate mere opinions from scientific knowledge or reasoning. What is the background and motivation of the person? Do their comments make sense? Is there a political or commercial motive? Science is not always sure, or correct, but scientific ideas should be justified with evidence or sound reasoning. Not all statements should be accepted (or rejected) on blind faith because the universe does not care about titles or uniforms, and certainly not about political or religious affiliations.

In these times of 'militant atheism', great communicators such as English evolutionary biologist Richard Dawkins may have left a prevailing impression that there is a war of ideologies when science does meet religion. Further, that scientific knowledge is held and dictated by a privileged few, and so must be mistrusted or denied as a means of answering our deepest questions. This is a sad misunderstanding of science that is probably held by many people to some extent. *Scientific knowledge* is the body of work that we believe to be true, or most likely to be true, or even the best that we have been able to come up with so far. This work is forever growing, and subject to change with our increased understanding. Nothing is provable in science — in contrast to mathematics — and so any of this knowledge may need reviewing in the light of new observations or measurements; it is not dictated by anyone (at least not in good science). The *scientific method* is the process by which we acquire such knowledge and assimilate it into a consistent knowledge hierarchy that describes the universe. It is evidence-based, and it relies upon objective observation and measurement. New theories are constrained by the work of the experimentalists: if the predictions differ from experimental results then the theory needs work, no matter who the theorist is. As an eminent scientist, Dawkins is fully aware of this distinction, and so when he asserts that evolution rather than 'intelligent design' is responsible for the array of life on our planet, then he is comparing a theory that is backed by a huge amount of non-conflicting evidence with a conjecture largely based on naïve intuition.

On our planetary scale, the question of 'intelligent design' versus emergent complexity is not a credible one — such is the weight of evidence and economy of explanation supporting the theory of evolution — but we will later take this argument to a cosmic scale where the situation is more complicated, and with some surprising loopholes. People with a sense of spirituality may take some solace in the fact that this will yield mysteries that cannot be questioned — an odd phraseology that will make more sense when we get there.

Science may be unable to answer metaphysical questions, but what the *scientific method* can do is identify fantasy: beliefs that do not fit observation or logic. Whether personal spirituality has any foundation will be debated forever, but it cannot be dictated.

1.3   Goals of Physics

Physics has two major goals: predictability and understanding,[4] which are less than distinct because they are sought hand-in-hand as part of the *scientific method*. We will justify this statement with an example, below, and then proceed to look at some history of the *scientific method* and our approaches to understanding.

Following repeated measurement and observation, consistent patterns can be represented by mathematical equations that allow us to make predictions from similar circumstances in the future. As part of a process known as *theory reductionism*, such equations might be generalised if underlying patterns and connections are subsequently noticed in their basis and form. A single equation that works in all known circumstances is much more powerful than having a selection that we have to pick from according to the situation. Understanding, though, is a quest for explanation that presupposes the notion of causality, or cause and effect: that every effect has an underlying cause that precedes it in time.

Consider a cannon launching a cannonball through the air. Measurements would show that the cannonball takes a consistent path for a given initial velocity and angle of trajectory, and that the shape of this path is a parabola, or an inverted catenary. Eventually, through a combination of empirical results and analysis, it would be found that the path can be represented by an equation of the form:

$$y = x \tan \theta - (g\,x^2)/(2\,v_0{}^2 \cos^2 \theta)$$

where
y = vertical position (m)
x = horizontal position (m)
v_0 = initial velocity (in cannon's direction, m/s)
g = acceleration due to gravity (9.80 m/s^2)
θ = angle of the initial velocity from the horizontal plane

This is a description of the static path and so only involves the x and y coordinates. A more complicated equation would represent the x and y positions as a function of time (t), and so would describe the evolution of the trajectory as we observe it.

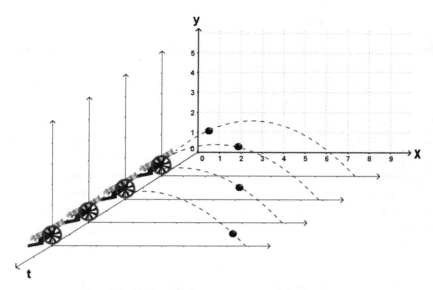

Fig. 1-1, Cannonball trajectory in a block universe.

But by themselves, these equations do not tell us why the cannonball left the cannon, and why it took that particular path. The aforementioned body of *scientific knowledge* would allow us to explain the scenario as follows. An amount of gunpowder, called the lift charge, is packed behind the projectile. When ignited, this burns very rapidly involving a complex set of reactions, and the force of the sudden 'explosion' of gaseous by-products ejects the projectile with a given initial velocity. Another force, that we call gravity, acts constantly upon the projectile in the downward direction, gradually slowing it until its vertical velocity is exhausted at the apex of the trajectory, at which point it causes the projectile to fall with increasing velocity back to the ground. All the time, the projectile's horizontal velocity is unchanged, if we ignore air resistance.

This type of explanation is entirely causal, and is bound to our subjective view of what happens around us; it is not part of those equations. Also, without the implication of causality then there can be no *explanation*. So, the equations describe the observed and measured behaviours, but it is associated theories that try to explain why and so provide us with our understanding.

Our *scientific knowledge*, then, is formed of theories, but how do they arise from the observation of predictability? We certainly learn about our environment through our sensory experience (*empiricism*) — as do many other species — but that type of knowledge is not the same as an understanding; to observe the Sun regularly passing through the sky every day is not the same as knowing why.

Until the middle of the twentieth century, the consensus (called *logical positivism*) was that only statements about the real world that were verifiable through direct observation could have any meaning, and that this did not include metaphysical statements because most could not be said to be either true or false. This stance began to fail because all such statements must eventually rely upon other knowledge that would involve unverifiable truths, and hence there could be no such thing as a pure language of observation. It was associated with another view (called *inductivism*) that a universal law could be established by the repeated confirmation of predictability between similar causes and effects, or between an assertion and repeated observations. Logical positivists had sought to verify theories through the use of induction. The difference between *laws* and *theory* will be discussed later, in §5.2.

This was all challenged by Austrian philosopher Sir Karl R. Popper in 1934 who substituted the idea of falsifiability in place of verification. Falsifiability is the capacity for a theory or assertion to be contradicted by evidence, in contrast to a reliance upon corroborating evidence. A much-quoted example is the assertion that 'all swans are white', which could never be verified without observing all swans (and we could never know whether 'all' had been satisfied), but it could be refuted by the mere observation of a single black swan. As a result, all understanding must be provisional, and theories can only be provisionally confirmed or conclusively refuted; nothing can be proved in science.

Although Popper's reasoning is not challenged here, we will not try to follow it directly. We will, instead, follow an independent line of reasoning that acknowledges the concept of a *block universe*, and this will entail looking at the very nature of measurement (§5.4) and questioning the fundamentality of causality. In other words, what does evidence really mean, and how independent is it of conscious minds?

1.4   The Block Universe

The three-dimensional picture in Fig. 1-1 is static; there is no movement of the cannonball, no flow of time, and no changing moment that we can label '*now*'. All instants in time are equally represented, and nothing is truly lost or gained. If this picture could be extrapolated to depict the whole universe across all time then we would call that a representation of a *block universe*.

The philosophy of a *block universe*, or *eternalism*,[5] can be traced back to a Greek philosopher called Parmenides of Elea from the late sixth or early fifth century BCE. The only work of his that survives (albeit fragmentary) is a poem, "On Nature", which describes two views of reality: 'the way of truth' (Greek: *aletheia*), which explains how all reality is timeless and uniform with change being impossible, and 'the way of opinion' (Greek: *doxa*), which explains the world of appearances, and how our sensory faculties lead to false conceptions. These views are eerily akin to the *objective reality* and *subjective reality* that will be presented in these chapters.

In the proem introducing the whole work, Parmenides describes his journey from the ordinary daytime world to a strange destination, outside our human paths, and carried in a whirling chariot to the temple of an unnamed goddess by whom the rest of the poem was spoken. This goddess resided where "Night and Day have their meeting place".[6] If you were to imagine that this must be above the Earth, and looking at the shadow of night cloaking part of the globe, then you would not be alone. Most texts do not treat this introduction as literal, though, as otherwise it would raise some very serious questions about the source of this truly staggering insight.

Many physicists agree that the concept of a timeless *block universe* must be true, but few fully embrace it in their theories. Some popular science books mention it, briefly, before resorting to more traditional interpretations of things. And the fact is that it is very hard to work with. How can it be reconciled with both *quantum theory* and what we see every day? How can concepts such as consciousness, causality, and time itself, emerge from a static unchanging universe?

This is the essence of the arguments to be presented in this book.

— 2 —

Objective Time

How does mathematics treat time? Is it really an adequate description of what we experience?

Mathematical physics is almost totally about the modelling of a system as it evolves through time. However, the reader may be surprised to know that there is absolutely no basis for our concept of '*now*': that point in time that separates past from future. It seems that there is no special preferred moment in time, and not a single equation embraces this concept, let alone explains what it is or why it is there.

Even more surprising is that mathematics does not represent that apparent flow from past to future. You may be thinking 'equations of motion' or 'derivatives with respect to time', but take a moment for a deeper look. As we have seen, the equation that represents a cannonball leaving a cannon and hitting the ground does not say that it left the cannon and hit the ground, or *vice versa*; it merely describes the shape of the trajectory, even if it includes the time variable. Putting this another way, there is no difference between the equation describing a trajectory and one describing a similar shape on a static graph. We associate the extra semantics with the equation, but the equation itself is both static and acausal.

We usually think of the universe as consisting of many objects in motion: moons around planets, planets around stars, stars around galaxies, etc. Everything appearing to be in constant motion relative to other things means that it is hard to imagine, and to accept, that this is illusory. If there were no conscious observers then the motion of a moon around a planet would be a type of static helix in space-time. Just glance again at Fig. 1-1 and try to imagine it as the reality in our absence.

In 1920, English physicist and mathematician Sir Arthur S. Eddington, who had contributed enormously to the understanding of Einstein's theories of relativity, commented, "In a perfectly determinate scheme the past and future may be regarded as lying mapped out—as much available to present exploration as the distant parts of space. Events do not happen; they are just there, and we come across them".[7] In the 1940s, German mathematician and theoretical physicist Hermann K. H. Weyl (pronounced 'vial', rhyming with 'mile') made known a similar view: "The objective world simply *is*, it does not *happen*. Only to the gaze of my consciousness, crawling upward along the life line of my body, does a section of this world come to life as a fleeting image in space which continuously changes in time".[8] Or, appropriating a line from William Faulkner, "The past is never dead. It's not even past".[9]

In a 'timeless' *block universe*, we have to abandon certain cherished or intuitive concepts: there can be no motion, no wave-like propagation, no *quantum fluctuations*, no oscillation, no creation or destruction, no death, nor any dynamical change at all. Our whole lives are a permanent part of the universe that might be imagined as lines — *world-lines*[10] — that run from one instant in time to another. To emphasise this point a different way, nothing moves forwards, or even backwards, in time. Everything has an extent across the time dimension from one instant to another. So, for example, if we detected that an electron-positron pair was created from a high-energy photon, and the positron subsequently annihilated a different electron, then the positron's world-line would extend from the position and instant of its supposed production to the position and instant of its supposed annihilation. All instants on that world-line would be equally real, and the positron could no longer be considered a mere particle moving through time.

But although time is considered the fourth dimension — the other three being the normal spatial ones, i.e. length, width, height — it is fundamentally different in a number of ways: we are free to move in space, but not in time; we have conservation laws that apply along the time dimension; and we have the subtle concept of 'persistence of form'. The fact that the laws of physics are the same at all instants in time (at least as far as we can know) leads to a continuity of all change, and by *Noether's theorem* to the law of conservation of energy.

Albert Einstein (technically pronounced 'ein-shtein', but English speakers rarely do) was well aware of the disparity between the objective and subjective natures of time. On learning of the death in 1955 of lifelong friend Michele A. Besso, whom he had known since his early days in the Bern patent office, he wrote his friend's family: "Now he has departed from this strange world a little ahead of me. That means nothing. People like us, who believe in physics, know that the distinction between past, present, and future is only a stubbornly persistent illusion".[11] Einstein died just over a month later, on 18 April 1955.

2.1   Persistence of Form

'Persistence of form' is quite different from any conservation law. It is taken for granted and yet it is a fundamental component of our experience. We recognise objects and people, not by their physical constituents but by their overall pattern, or form. For instance, it has been shown that all of our constituent atoms are replaced within a period of a few years,[12] and yet we retain unique identities. There is a well-known UK television sitcom episode in which a road sweeper has owned his broom for 20 years; it has had 17 new heads and 14 new handles but it is still *his broom*.[13] This is actually about *information* — a subject that we will visit again — rather than mass-energy. A broom is a broom, even if parts are repaired, but when all the component parts are replaced then does it have any connection with the original, other than the ownership implied in this particular case?

If 'persistence of form' is not about anything conserved, then what is it? The related philosophical concept of identity is surprisingly deep, despite the fact that we accept that without question too. However, since its arguments can be confusing, and littered with new terms and symbolic logic, then we will adopt a first-principles approach here, and begin by noting that identity is something that we, as conscious entities, assign. Despite all the philosophical debate, the claim here is that identity is part of our subjective reality, and is meaningless in a *block universe*.

Identity is defined as the relationship something has only to itself, which sounds rather shallow. It basically means that each thing is identical to itself (not much better, is it?), and this is known as the 'law of identity'. The 'identity of indiscernibles' (sometimes referred to as 'Leibniz's law', after a version by German mathematician and philosopher Gottfried Wilhelm Leibniz) is a principle that goes further by stating that no two objects can be identical (having all possible properties in common) if they are distinct, which makes a little more sense. We need to be careful, though, because we use words such as identical, same, or similar in everyday speech with more relaxed semantics. In order to avoid confusion between identity and mere appearance, we will use the term self-same for when two references are to the exact same entity rather than to two entities with identical properties or appearance.

Another reason for skipping much of the philosophical analysis is that it is largely based on the unrealistic premise of uniform, everlasting, and irreducible entities. If we start with a fundamental particle — say, an electron — then does it have an identity, given that it is fundamentally identical to all other free electrons in terms of its properties and behaviours? Measuring its location, or other properties, requires both an interaction with the environment (e.g. the measuring apparatus), and a space-time reference frame to make measurement possible (explained in §5.4). You might be thinking that an electron can be tagged via its spin, but that only means something — as does its position, momentum, etc. — when there is something else to compare it with. If a hydrogen atom loses its electron and then gains another then is it the same atom? This may sound a trivial question but we are trying to build up to the bigger picture. When that same hydrogen atom is in a molecule then — depending upon its symmetry — we may be able to identify its position relative to its neighbouring atoms.

A mountain, or a planet, is easily identifiable to us, and even if its constituents change over time (by gaining, losing, moving, or replacing them) then we would still reference it by the same identifying name(s). As with all macroscopic objects, we can identify distinct forms despite such changes to the constituents or their layout, and this is a phenomenon of scale that does not apply to molecules and below. But what makes a form distinct? If we consider a deck of cards being shuffled then there are fewer arrangements that appear distinct to us than the indistinct ones that we want to generate through that operation. We will look more deeply at card shuffling in Chapter 3, but the essential difference is that the distinct arrangements can be described by a relatively small number of relations between the cards — the fewer relations then the more distinct is the arrangement. For instance, they might be in numeric order, or all being of the same suit, or having the same face value. The overall form of a macroscopic object can be described by a set of relations that do not fundamentally change with respect to changes of the constituents because the huge number of them affords some redundancy in their individual significance. So, without the concept of structure (as opposed to amorphous states) then we cannot have distinctness of form.

We have already mentioned that a human form is identifiable even though its constituents will be regularly replaced, but what about clones? There are several films based on the premise that some person and a clone thereof are indistinguishable from each other. Notwithstanding the fact that a real clone would not have the same memories and personality, and would not display injuries or bodily changes occurring since birth (e.g. a tattoo), what would identity mean if they really were indistinguishable? Such scenarios occur in several science fiction stories, so let us just imagine one for the sake of argument: a transporter accident in *Star Trek*. Both persons would have the same notion of self, and neither would be aware of having a different history, but they would be distinct in that they occupy different space at any given time, and so would not be self-same. A variation of this scenario concerns two identical spheres in a space devoid of everything else. The forms would be identical, but they would be distinct relative to each other (even though left-right, etc., would have no independent meaning[14]), and so would not be self-same. NB: if distinctness of position is generalised to that of addressability then it provides the basis for stored information, and hence for memory, consciousness, and computing.

But we have not considered time in these paragraphs. If this transporter accident placed the duplicate persons in disjoint time periods (i.e. lives not overlapping) then in what way would that differ from self-same instances existing at different instants of time? The answer is their provenance, or history from their beginnings. Distinctness of provenance actually applies to everything that is in motion, and we implicitly link together their form as observed at different instants, beginning with the first observation. For instance, as we watch a bird in flight, its physical form is undergoing many changes, such as the movement of its wings, but if we are following that flight then we can attest to the distinctness of its provenance, and so infer that it is the self-same bird at the start and the end of the flight.

We have identified three types of distinctness here: form, position, and provenance. If two entities are the same within the scope of each type then we can say that they are self-same. For aggregate objects, form is about the overall pattern rather than the specific constituents. The 'persistence of form' that underpins our subjective reality, and which allows us to assign unique identities, is therefore a consequence of an inherent tendency of the universe to form structure, and of the continuity of all change over time.

Returning to that road sweeper's broom, it is not self-same if a significant portion of it is replaced with a similar one, such as a head or handle rather than a simple nail, and each such portion would have its own provenance.

Hence, the owner's belief that it is still his broom is correct, even though it is modified at each change. Consider, for instance, the situation if two road sweepers were to exchange the heads of their brooms with each other.

2.2   Special Relativity

Physicists can skip most of this section as it will be a crash course on *special relativity*. A more detailed mathematical tour of this may also be found in Appendix A.

The *principle of relativity* states that the laws of physics should be the same for all observers, or, putting it more accurately, in all frames of reference. This makes a lot of sense since if they were not the same then we should argue that our expression of those laws (i.e. the equations) is incorrect and not general enough.

The term 'observer' is ubiquitous in physics, but is generally taken to mean a position (or frame of reference) from which measurements may be made. It does not imply an actual person, or any other type of conscious entity, although subsequent chapters may qualify it as 'conscious observer' in order to make any distinction clearer.

Albert Einstein published two theories of relativity:

- The theory of *special relativity* (1905). This considered observers travelling at a constant speed in a straight line (including being at rest), and in the absence of a gravitational field. The technical term for these observers is 'inertial observers', or 'inertial frames of reference'.
- The theory of *general relativity* (1916). This generalised things to include 'non-inertial observers', or 'non-inertial frames of reference', such as ones accelerating or decelerating, rotating ones, and ones in a gravitational field. See Chapter 11 (Space-Time and Gravitation).

In 1864, Scottish physicist James Clerk Maxwell had devised a set of equations demonstrating that electricity, magnetism, and light were all manifestations of the same phenomenon: the electromagnetic field. But Maxwell's equations introduced a problem for the *principle of relativity*: they referenced the speed of light but there was no indication of what it was relative to. For these equations to be valid for all observers then the speed of light would have to be the same for all observers, no matter whether the light was travelling towards them or away from them. This was inadvertently confirmed in 1887 by American physicists Albert A. Michelson and Edward W. Morley while trying to demonstrate the existence of the *luminiferous aether* — a hypothetical medium through which light waves propagated — by measuring the differences in light speed in the direction of the Earth's motion and perpendicular to it. If there was no such *aether* then there was no absolute motion (with respect to that medium), and all motion must be relative to other objects. Unexpectedly, they found no differences in the speed of light in any direction.

In summary, Einstein's basic two precepts for *special relativity* were that the laws of physics must be the same for all inertial observers and that the speed of light was a universal constant of nature.

It is often said in non-scientific literature, and especially in fiction, that according to *special relativity*, as you get closer to the speed of light then you start to shrink (*Lorentz–FitzGerald contraction*), that time goes more s..l..o..w..l..y (*time dilation*), and that you get heavier (or at least that your mass increases). In fact, none of these are true statements; it is a matter of perspective rather than physical change, and two observers moving relative to each other would each measure similar differences from their neighbour. Consider, for instance, the fact that as an object moves more quickly relative to some observer, that observer will measure its relativistic mass to increase beyond its rest mass: that as measured when they are in the same frame of reference. Einstein showed that this increase is virtually identical to the classical kinetic energy (the energy of movement) divided by c^2, and this is where the famous equation $E = mc^2$ originated. The point to be made here, though, is that since all motion is relative then kinetic energy is also relative, and so is the increase of the relativistic mass.

Shortly after *special relativity* was published, German mathematician Hermann Minkowski reformulated the equations using a four-dimensional space-time notation, previously defined by French mathematician and physicist Henri Poincaré. In this 'four-dimensional space-time continuum' of (x, y, z, ict) — where c is the speed of light (short for *celerity*) and i is the square root of minus one — the equations took on a much simpler form, as did those of Maxwell following a similar reformulation. When we mention space-time in this book then we are talking about this mathematical framework of an orthogonal combination of space and objective time, and using this as a model for the *block universe*.

Two inertial observers who are travelling relative to each other can be depicted on a Minkowski diagram as frames of reference that are rotated relative to each other. The angle of separation is then related to their relative velocity by:

$$tan\ \alpha\ =\ x\ /\ ict\ =\ v\ /\ ic$$

This rotation of the frame of reference is relative, just as motion is relative — they are rotated relative to each other, and not to anything else — and so measurement effects recorded by either observer are entirely reciprocated by the other. When these observers measure the separation between two events then they will see different amounts of space-like and time-like measures, but the overall interval (i.e. distance in space-time) would be invariant.

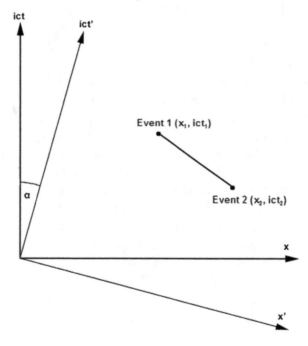

Fig. 2-1, Relative motion in Minkowski space-time.

This difference of perspective is generally known as *parallax error*, and we see it all the time in our everyday lives. Two people viewing a building from different positions would see different amounts of the short side and the long side.

Fig. 2-2, Parallax error resulting from different perspectives on a shared object.

So, in other words, the equations of *special relativity* are equivalent to *parallax error* in *Minkowski space-time*. Because all motion is relative, no two inertial observers can say that one of them is moving and not the other, and so the predicted effects of *special relativity* are completely reciprocated between them. They are the result of a different perspective of the observer, and not of a physical change in the frame being observed. You could say that the measurement anomalies are 'in the eye of the beholder'.

An important consequence of this theory is that there is no universal concept of simultaneity: whether two events appear to occur at the same time or depends upon the observer. Consider then the importance that we attach to the concept of '*now*'. Although we each are aware of this moment, it can have no objective significance in the light of this theory, and so it must have a subjective basis (i.e. a psychological origin).

Special relativity — especially when viewed in *Minkowski space-time* — is often considered to be a *block universe* model because of its four-dimensional geometrical approach, and the fact that it reduces the concept of motion to a simple reorientation of one frame of reference relative to another. Einstein never took this route and he continued to imagine objects in motion in both his theories and his thought experiments; such was the strength of physicality in his intuition. This means that it was only a 'block' in terms of the dimensionality constituting a single unchanging block, but in a true *block universe* you cannot have motion, or any dynamical change, because there would be nothing to meter it by. As we have already stressed, the content of such a universe would be entirely static

— 3 —

Entropy and Thermodynamics

A so-called law of physics that does not actually define
an arrow or asymmetry of time.

If the laws of physics are time-symmetric then why does a reversed video look wrong to us? Why do certain processes (e.g. a breaking object) appear to be irreversible but the laws of physics show no asymmetry in the dynamics? This issue is known as 'Loschmidt's paradox', after Austrian scientist Johann Josef Loschmidt, and it supposedly remains an unsolved problem.

Our apparent preferred time direction, or 'arrow of time', was attributed by Sir Arthur Eddington to entropy, and hence to the *second law of thermodynamics* (i.e. that entropy — often equated with *disorder* — cannot decrease in an *isolated system*[15]), but this is a misinterpretation of that law so let us start by refuting this myth.

Entropy is a contrived quantity, meaning that it is not observable and does not follow directly from the measurement of any other quantity. It has a number of interpretations that are convenient in different areas, including thermodynamics, information theory, and *quantum theory*, but it is the stochastic description due to Austrian physicist and philosopher Ludwig E. Boltzmann that we will examine here. By giving entropy a probabilistic interpretation, he showed that the *second law of thermodynamics* is a mathematical law and not really a law of physics. But if it is a mathematical law then how can it be linked to temporal asymmetry, or even to time at all?

The increase of entropy is a time-symmetric but irreversible phenomenon — terms that may appear to be contradictory: if it is time-symmetric then surely it must be reversible. Many people would use these terms interchangeably, and yet when we get to the chapter on *quantum mechanics* (especially §7.4) then we will see how the act of measurement there is believed to be an irreversible process that punctuates an otherwise symmetric evolution of the *wave function*. The problem is that irreversibility does not imply the presence of time, and it can describe algorithmic transitions too; conflating it with time leads to many cases of confusion.

A common analogy for explaining entropy in a probabilistic way is the shuffling of a deck of cards. There are 52! (52 factorial) different arrangements of a full pack — about 8×10^{67}, or roughly the number of atoms estimated to be in our Milky Way galaxy — and so the probability of all the card suits finishing in numeric order is basically impossible. Thus we expect any initial ordering to be lost during the shuffle. The consensus is that this improbability accounts for a reversed video being unrealistic, and hence that our experience is a consequence of this law.

It is impractical to consider the micro-mechanics of the shuffle operation and so we resort to a probabilistic analysis, but if those mechanics are time-symmetric then the same probabilities apply in the reverse time direction. The probability of any one arrangement transitioning to another one is independent of the actual arrangements, and independent of the time direction. The difference in the shuffle illustration is that it starts with a specific arrangement but does not end with one, and that makes it irreversible.

If S is the set of possible arrangements (or states) $\{a_1, a_2, ... \; a_n\}$ then $a_j \gg \varepsilon a.\, a \in S$ (some specific arrangement transitioning to any member of S)[16] is a symbolic representation of the shuffle, but the inverse $\varepsilon a.\, a \in S \gg a_j$ represents an impossibly unlikely change. Note however that $a_i \lll\ggg a_j$ (any specific arrangement transitioning to any other one) is symmetric, and the difference in the previous relation is that one term is unconstrained, leading to a probabilistic asymmetry.

Since time-asymmetric and being irreversible are often confused, let us distinguish them as simply as possible. Mathematical physics deals with *T-symmetry*, which amounts to flipping the sign of the 't' variable in its equations, and showing that they still describe observable sequences, but this can be hard to relate to if there is no objective flow of time. Temporal asymmetry is about specific observable states, and the fact that $a(t_1) \lll\ggg a(t_2)$ may not hold true. We must be careful here not to suggest that t_1 is before or after t_2 — however tempting it may be — since that would presuppose some absolute direction of progression (more on this in Chapter 8). Irreversibility is about algorithmic transitions[17]: ones where the step-to-step sequencing is unrelated to time. Separating these terms will be important as we re-examine some basic concepts of physics and philosophy within a *block universe*.

Reasons we will later consider for irreversibility include improbability (as with entropy, here) and information loss (see Chapter 9). In fact both of these are related to information, but not specifically to quantum information, or even to information theory in general. We are using the term here to refer to structural correlations between two things (i.e. information about something else), and will frequently qualify it with *semantic* to differentiate the content from the representation. It is a concept based upon the distinctness around us, and the usage of that distinctness to represent things, or to record things.

In the case of the deck of cards, we would recognise the suits being in numeric order, or reverse numeric order, or like numbers placed together, and many other combinations. When we try to randomise the deck then we want to move from a recognisable arrangement to an unrecognisable one, and there are many more of the latter. But the probability of any specific arrangement transitioning to any other specific one is identical. We will try to avoid the subjective terms *ordered* or *disordered* because they are hard to pin down, and they are actually not that relevant.

But let us take a deeper look at the mathematics of Boltzmann's work. He was looking at the dynamics of gas molecules and showing how the truly stupendous number of different molecular arrangements and transitions gives rise to macroscopic properties that can be described using just a few variables, such as pressure, volume, and temperature. To simplify the analysis, he considered uniform idealised particles (could be atoms or molecules) in a rarefied distribution (i.e. so that collisions rather than forces would be the main factor). In order to do this, he used a *phase space* representation, which is an abstract mathematical space used to depict the dynamics of mechanical systems. This space has six dimensions for each independent component (which would be each individual molecule in the gas case), representing its position (three dimensions) and momentum (three dimensions): the microstates. The volume of this mathematical space is therefore stupendous as it is given by the size of each of the six dimensions, for every single molecule, all multiplied together. If the space is partitioned according to all the unobservable microstates (positions and momenta) that share the same common observable (and distinct) macrostate, then the largest of these, by far, is the one representing *thermodynamic equilibrium*, where there is no net macroscopic flow of mass or energy. Assuming that the molecules are in random chaotic motion then they will virtually all become distributed in that partition since it is always incredibly close to the total volume of the *phase space*. Boltzmann's entropy is given by $S = k \log_e W$, where W is the relative size of the partition and k is *Boltzmann's constant* (1.380649×10^{-23} J/K), and so *thermodynamic equilibrium* corresponds to the highest value for the entropy, and all other configurations will trend to that equilibrium state, and so to maximum entropy.

But despite all the fancy mathematics, this is just the same stochastic description as with the playing cards. If you introduce a hot gas (molecules having higher momenta) into a colder one then they will mix evenly, or if you introduce a different gas altogether then they will mix evenly, or if you introduce a gas into a vacuum then it will spread evenly. If we think of the gas as undergoing a constant shuffle then the individual microstates of the molecules are equivalent to the card positions in the deck, the initial set of microstates to some initial card arrangement prior to the shuffle, and *thermodynamic equilibrium* to the final randomised card deck. The reason that the gases do not unmix is simply due to the colossal odds against it, and the mixing would happen in either direction of time as it is not a temporal issue; it is the result of protracted 'shuffling' spread over repeated steps rather than instants in time.

Note that identity is involved in both of these scenarios as it allows us to associate elements of distinctness with the different arrangements. In the case of the playing cards, if we were looking at their reverse (which we will assume to be identical) then the ordering is irrelevant, but if we look at their faces and isolate each of them then distinctness is irrelevant. In the case of the gas, the molecules may be identical but in place of a simple sequencing they have relative properties (position and momentum) that can be measured, and it is from the distribution of these relative properties that we observe elements of distinctness.

The question we should be asking, though, is why things are not already in equilibrium; why do some regions of low entropy exist at all? James Maxwell devised a thought experiment, known as 'Maxwell's demon', where an imaginary demon watches the molecules as they pass some connection between two separate chambers of a closed vessel, and it sorts them according to their speed (and hence their momenta). In effect, it could achieve a separation of hot from cold in violation of the *second law of thermodynamics*. The modern consensus is that energy has to be expended in order to perform such sorting, whether by an imaginary demon or by some real-life nano-gadget, which would therefore imply an increase in entropy elsewhere — note the implied connection between entropy and energy. If this were not so then the resulting difference between hot and cold could be used to do work for free, via a heat engine. It is therefore claimed that the demon would have to be included in the measured scenario, and that the total entropy in that bigger picture would still increase, i.e. that the demon would contribute a greater amount of entropy than it could ever reduce in the gas.

NB: It may be tempting to ponder on the influence of free will in the case of this imaginary demon, but do not hold your breath; we will address this subject in §6.4.

Yet energy is not entropy. If the demon had performed the molecular sorting on some apparently random principle then the result would be neither distinct nor ordered, but the same amount of energy would be expended. In reality, the demon would require energy to make any type of selection, whether it imposed some distinctness or not. We all know this because it applies to almost everything we do in life: we can create 'order' in our world but change — all change — requires energy. In §5.2 and §5.5, we will explain how energy is really just the capacity for such change. What makes this thought experiment so interesting, and probably accounting for the continued debate on the subject, is the implication that some separation of entropy could occur locally.

Although the second law is of mathematical rather than physical origin, it is taken as inviolate, and this leads to some confusing scenarios. For instance, when considering what preceded (using the direction of our subjective time) some state of low entropy (e.g. all the gas sucked into one of those two chambers) then we would expect it to be even lower because of the belief that we must always observe it increasing. However, applying the same mathematics in the other direction of time would suggest it must increase in that direction too because the laws of physics are time-symmetric, and any probabilistic phenomenon surrounding them must be time-independent. But then returning to our subjective time again, the probability of a significant low-entropy state having suddenly appeared from a high-entropy one is colossal, and so these two views are at odds.

What we observe is a 'causal asymmetry', but this is not a consequence of the *second law of thermodynamics*. The second law is based upon the statistics of systems composed of huge numbers of components in random and chaotic motion, motion that is essentially symmetrical. The individual atoms and molecules affect each other over time through collisions, transferring small quantities of energy in each instance, in contrast to, say, the transfers of energy when igniting an inflammable gas. When in *thermodynamic equilibrium*, the behaviour of the gas would appear time-symmetric, and it is only when some agent has caused the state of the system to be in non-equilibrium that we detect a transition in a particular direction of time. As already stated, these transitions have a statistical nature, and would happen in either direction of time, except for the fact that our causal agent (e.g. the experimenter) is external to the *isolated system* and so not addressed by the mathematics.

We could take a step back and consider a bigger *isolated system* in order to address the specific causal agent, but this would involve an 'infinite regress' in order to include the cause of the cause, etc. Although we will examine our subjective experience of causation in §4.1, it will not be until §8.2 that we look at the fundamental nature of causation. The laws of physics are deemed to be time-symmetric, but they admit 'cohesive influences'. This term is deliberately loose because it includes the fundamental forces, mechanical devices, and even conscious entities like us. These all have the capacity to reduce entropy in some local region through physical processes that we deem to be causal (e.g. the experimenter using a pump to get the gas into just one chamber), albeit at the expense of some energy. For instance, if the atoms or molecules in our gaseous example started to form bonds then their entropy would decrease since their degrees of freedom would be less due to the bonded states no longer having independent motions within them.

It requires energy for us to construct, say, a building, but it also requires energy for us to destroy it. In other words, it takes energy for us to make any deliberate change; it is not an issue of order versus chaos. In reality, both the constructed and destructed states are just alternative macroscopic states of the building. It can be argued that the constructed state is different because it is more regular, and possessed of some structure and symmetry, but there are many possible states that would fit that same description. Only a relatively tiny proportion of those regular states would be identifiable to us as a functional building, despite the other regular states having an element of distinctness (just like the unshuffled card decks mentioned above). The essential point here is that the second law is about the loss of usable energy, energy that can effect changes of position or velocity, and not about any tendency to disorder. For some reason, our universe is not in a state of *thermodynamic equilibrium*, and so such change is possible, but that capability to effect change gradually diminishes in any *isolated system*. We will pick this thread up again in Chapter 8 when we look for the real 'arrow of time', and we will look at the meaning of energy in a *block universe* in §5.5. In the meantime, it is worth noting that this confusion between the energy gradient, which is an asymmetric physical property, and statistical evolution, which is a time-independent mathematical phenomenon, has plagued physics for almost 100 years.

So is entropy a reasonable measure of a system? If we consider a single object (particle, molecule, or bigger) in free motion in empty space then we cannot assign a meaningful value for its entropy since its position, velocity, and kinetic energy are all relative to some undefined frame of reference. If we have two or more of them then we can only define these quantities relative to their average position. This may sound arbitrary since entropy is not a physical quantity, but if it is to form part of our description of the universe then it must transform from one frame to another without affecting that description. In other words, the laws of physics should be the same for all observers. Unfortunately, the way entropy, temperature, and pressure should transform from one frame to another is still debated in the subject of *relativistic thermodynamics*.[18]

When we look at macroscopic objects — objects with definite form and measurable properties, as opposed to more-amorphous distributions of indeterminate entities with 'hidden variables' — then the interpretation of entropy is not as straightforward. Because the measurable properties of the aggregate objects (e.g. our cannonball from §1.3) are more relevant to us than the 'hidden variables' of the now constrained individual molecules then we resort to some laws of motion rather than to statistics (e.g. Newton's or Einstein's). How, then, can we interpret entropy on a cosmic scale? If you believe in the so-called 'big bang' model of the initial universe then there is an argument for it having had very low entropy (because the *phase space* description would be smaller) and that the entropy has increased thereafter, along with the expansion of the universe. Because the second law is widely believed to be inviolate then such an entropy gradient causes problems for those models that also include a collapse of the universe (the inverse of the observed expansion) at some different time. We will consider these models of the universe in Chapter 11 (Space-Time and Gravitation).

There are a number of points that can be distilled from this chapter. The *second law of thermodynamics* is about the tendency of a system to even out its usable energy (i.e. approaching *thermodynamic equilibrium*) and nothing to do with order or disorder. Although temporal asymmetry is a physical issue, irreversibility is an algorithmic issue, which means that it cannot constitute an 'arrow of time'. Given that entropy is not an observable quantity, and is not strictly defined in all circumstances, then it puts limitations upon its usefulness for describing the universe. If irreversibility is not related to time then it is virtually meaningless in the context of physical processes, and especially so in the context of a *block universe* where there is no flow to reverse. Finally, it takes usable energy to create structures and configurations with recognisable elements of distinctness, but as the energy differentials diminish then the predominant influence is the irreversible changes in those configurations, thus leading to a loss of that distinctness. This is where the association with order and disorder stems from.

NB: we have used the term algorithmic to describe both the card shuffling and the chaotic mixing of idealised gases. Although the Glossary contains a very general definition — one that embraces this usage, and which does not presuppose either a mathematical or computer application of it — it does not convey the importance of the concept in this book. It lies at the very heart of our cognition and assimilation of change, and hence of all things subjective.

— 4 —

Subjective Time

*How does time appear to us? What are the essential
details that support our notion of reality?*

This term is being used to embrace the different way that we perceive past
and future (we remember the past, but not the future), the apparent passage
of time, and the moment that we call '*now*' that separates past from future.

The past and the future are sometimes defined relative to an observation, or
a measurement, but inanimate apparatus do neither of these. The observation
must therefore be that of a conscious entity, and this means that '*now*' must be
a subjective notion that we appear to share with other conscious entities (within
the constraints of *special relativity*). As they say: 'there's no time like the present'.

American theoretical physicist Steven Weinberg remarked that "Duration
in time is the only thing we can measure (however imperfectly) by thought
alone, with no input from our senses ...".[19] This is an important observation
because it makes a strong connection between subjective time and our thought
processes, and hence with our consciousness.

We saw in Chapter 2 that the equations of physics do not describe motion
as we perceive it, and that mathematics is incapable of describing our general
experience of any dynamical change. What is missing is a special temporal
reference point that shifts monotonically in one direction of time. Physics
does not have this, but we do and we call it '*now*'. In other words, if there
were no conscious entities in the universe then there could be no subjective
time, and so there would be no flow of time, no distinction between past and
future, and no concept of '*now*'. But where does that perception of flow come
from? Do all conscious entities experience the flow at the same rate?

We perceive the passage of time as a type of motion, but a physicist cannot
answer the question 'how fast does time pass?' The question is lacking any physical
meaning, and to respond with 'one second per second' would not be a useful
answer.[20] In effect, there is no objective measurement of the swiftness of time's

apparent flow. We all know of sayings such as 'a watched kettle never boils' or 'time flies when you're having fun', which respectively indicate an apparent slowing or quickening of that flow depending upon the circumstances, but there is a little confusion over their interpretation stemming from the difference between experience and recall. What is happening is that we are marking time according to the changes associated with the intervening events, or rather micro-events; if nothing much is happening then we have less marking and a feeling that something is taking longer. However, when we later recall those periods then we have more recorded events in the second case, giving us more resolution and hence the apparent ability to expand small periods of time. This results in the impression that the recall can be slowed down as in a slow-motion replay. Again, this observation supports a strong connection between time and the conscious mind.

In either case, though, the perceived march of time is relentless, and we still sense this in the absence of observable external changes; even in the absence of all normal sensory input. If submersed in a sensory deprivation chamber then it has been shown that we would find it harder to gauge the passage of time, and to generally perceive that a longer period had elapsed. This is important because it confirms that two phenomena are present: that we sense a passing of time in all (conscious) circumstances, but also that we mark, or measure, the passage in terms of environmental changes (both internal and external to us). The accepted explanation for the former is that the passage of time is real, and so applicable to everything, but we postulated that subjective time arises from an innate temporal sense. This is present at least from birth, and maybe even before, in all conscious entities.

English theoretical physicist Stephen W. Hawking suggested that we remember the past and not the future because that is the direction of increasing entropy, and because that would be a requirement of all recording devices.[21] We have already shown that entropy alone does not define an 'arrow of time', but we are also considering the case of a timeless *block universe* and so it must be true that an inanimate recording device is not only unaware of any passage of time but that it does not even record events sequentially.

You may be taken aback by this. Surely the recording would start when you press one button, and stop when you press another. However, in a *block universe* the recording of all events would happen between those points *together* — we are being careful here not to say 'at the same time' — and as a static correlation between the intervening events and the recording medium. In order to visualise this, you may have to return to the cannon diagram in Fig. 1-1 and imagine that it is being filmed. In a *block universe*, each frame of the film would be correlated with a particular scene in the progression of the cannonball, as though all the scenes had been impressed together onto some associative medium. It is only when we play back such a recording that we can note anything sequential, but then that is simply because of our subjective time — a concept we possess but not the recording device. In fact, this applies to any measuring apparatus, and we will frequently note that measurements and observations are something that conscious entities perform, not inanimate equipment.

A physicist reading this might argue that we can see the movement of fundamental particles in, say, a cloud chamber, and hence that it is incorrect to say that a particle is a world-line — or, more accurately, that whatever the true nature of a particle is, it can be represented by a static world-line. A cloud chamber consists of a supersaturated vapour, and when a charged particle goes through the vapour then it leaves a trail of ions (losing a bit of energy as it goes) and the ionisation causes condensation of the vapour and so leaves a visible trail. That physicist might argue that the length of such a trail grows during successive observations, and so clearly demonstrates that the particle's path is dynamic. Admittedly, it is hard to adopt the viewpoint of some super-observer capable of observing the universe as a block (i.e. of space and objective time), but if you can then you would see the fallacy of this argument.

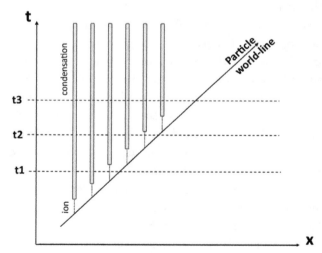

Fig. 4-1, Cloud chamber in a block universe.

This diagram shows that successive instants on the particle's world-line are associated with the generation of an ion, and each of these ions has a world-line of its own that is associated with a more permanent condensation in its vicinity. An observation at $t2$ would show a longer span of condensation than an observation at $t1$, and longer again at $t3$, but there is no movement; all the condensation points are statically correlated with the world-line of the particle.

There is a common quotation that "Time is what keeps everything from happening at once".[22] Some physicists actually believe that time does not exist at all, and that it is simply an independent variable by which we describe the relations between other quantities. But the fact that we cannot see or touch time is no different from the situation with space. We accept that space is defined by the separation of objects, and similarly that time is defined by the separation of events. Our way of thinking differently about time stems from the fact that we employ time as a measure for almost everything in our subjective experience. For instance, we measure how things have progressed as a function time, we organise our everyday lives by time divisions of a day, and we plan our futures according to time periods. Interestingly, though, the transitions of electrons between the two hyperfine ground states of caesium-133 atoms are used to create a standard measure of time, and atomic clocks are built on that standard. This is one converse of time as an independent variable.

Closely related to this viewpoint is the one that time is merely a measure of change. This makes some sense if we are talking about dynamical change, which is an experiential aspect of our subjective reality. If we look at the objective reality, though, then all dynamical change is replaced by a static pattern of change in its 'fabric'. In other words, both levels of reality demonstrate a variation of form, position, etc., over time, but in our subjective reality we happen to experience it as a dynamical flow. For reasons that we will try and determine in later chapters, our conscious awareness of time is actually a differential one that recognises changes between moments of time, and so it acts as a meter by which change is noticed rather than an actual measure of change. There is a well-known optical illusion where continually flipping the colours in a static image gives a very convincing impression of movement, despite the subjects of the image being entirely stationary.

But what about our shared reality? If we each have our own subjective time then how can we have a shared subjective reality? Well, the subjective time of different conscious observers will be marked by the same events, i.e. points in the space-time of the single *block universe*. And what about simultaneity? Does *special relativity* not show that this concept depends upon the observer, and if so then how can we share a consistent reality? Among the events that are truly shared between those conscious observers — that is, ones separated from them by time-like, or even light-like, intervals (in contrast to those separated by more than light speed) — then it is easy to show that event ordering is not affected by *special relativity*. The transformations between its frames of reference involve a term called the *Lorentz factor*, or $1/\sqrt{1 - v^2/c^2}$. Its value ranges from zero (when the relative velocity is zero, $v=0$) to infinity (when $v=c$), but it is never negative. Hence, in the *special relativity* phenomenon known as *time dilation*, two observers may measure the temporal separation between such events differently, but the magnitude of the difference cannot change sign. Hence if $t_A > t_B$ and $t_B > t_C$ then $t_A > t_C$, and these relations are preserved under a transformation. Cutting to the chase, the apparent chain of causality is preserved, and our subjective realities are then consistent with each other.

So, what if someone is temporarily unconscious, or even dead, for a short period of time? The same argument is valid: the broken span of consciousness is correlated with a broken span of subjective time, and the first '*now*' moment after the break corresponds with the events at that instant in objective time. In other words, our cognition resumes at the point they reawake. The following illustration shows consciousness as a world-line because it is, essentially, one-dimensional; it can identify directly with time but not with space, meaning that (perceptions and recollections aside) it has a sequential nature but no seat anywhere in space. The diagram places this world-line in the context of space-time events that feed our consciousness, but the spatial position is that of the physical brain rather than consciousness (see §6.3 for a more explicit account).

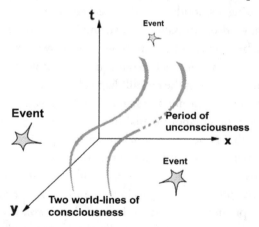

Fig. 4-2, World-lines of consciousness in a block universe.

Why is it not possible to be aware of two independent streams of subjective time? Would there not be some evolutionary advantage to this? No, it is not really possible since this type of question presumes that our awareness of time and our consciousness — yes, they are connected — are progressive phenomena that are somehow ticking along in synchronisation with those events. In a *block universe*, each '*now*' moment is correlated with a particular instant in objective time, and consciousness arises through the successive differences along a set of such '*now*' moments. But there is no principal or objectively singled-out '*now*'; they are equally extant and our consciousness involves the full total of them. Since consciousness and subjective time are intimately related then independent streams would require independent conscious minds. We will look at this subject again when we consider the mind in Chapter 6.

What we have not explained here is why subjective time appears to progress in a particular direction, something that we will come back to in Chapter 8.

4.1   Causality

Let us take the concept of subjective time a step further. If the passage of time is an illusion then so is causality: the view that every effect has a corresponding cause that precedes it in time. An instance of causation cannot occur in a static unchanging reality, and if we recall past events (i.e. in the absence of our '*now*' moment) then they will simply reflect the state of things at each instant of time, and demonstrating a smooth transition between them. It is through our direct experience that we deem causality to exist, and if we try to forget this experiential knowledge (as best we can) then we might just as well be looking at successive frames on a filmstrip. Going back to our cannon example (Fig. 1-1) then the path of the cannonball is part of the overall shape of things in that *block universe*, and there is neither movement nor any suggestion that it was fired from the cannon.

Physics is very much about explaining or modelling in terms of cause and effect, and yet this is no more inherent in its equations than is the passage of time. Our memory is a differential one that records change — movement and transitions — and our conscious mind recognises patterns and infers causation, sometimes incorrectly as in the cases of *apophenia* and superstition. It is hardly surprising then that we believe the *determinism* and causality of personal experience to be fundamentally significant, and so we attach those semantics to the equations in the same way as we do with the dynamical ones.

It is important to note the difference between *determinism* and causality as it will be an issue in future chapters. A good general definition of *determinism* is that "... in the case of everything that exists, there are antecedent conditions, known or unknown, which, because they are given, mean that things could not be other than they are".[23] This actually embraces forms of *determinism* that are causal and ones that are mathematical.

To illustrate the difference, consider some local measurements of the arc of some colossal circle in a hypothetical universe. From those measurements, we would know the structure of the rest of the circle, not because it is determined causally, but because it is determined mathematically through the interpretation of those measurements in the knowledge that the whole is a circle. In many ways, the difference between *causal determinism* and *mathematical determinism* is similar to the difference between dynamical change that we experience and a static change that can be described mathematically. Had sufficient measurements been taken then we would know that it was a circle in our illustration rather than an ellipse, but we would have no way of knowing whether other instances might be ellipses rather than circles, and whether we were looking at a special case of something more general. This is a good analogy for the deterministic pattern that we will later propose for the underlying objective reality, and the importance of mathematics in probing that pattern.

Gottfried Leibniz is widely credited with the maxim "There is nothing without a reason" (Latin: *Nihil est sine ratione*), but this is a misquote as it is derived from a truncated form of what he originally wrote. His original Latin phrase was "*Nihil est sine ratione cur potius sit quam non sit*" which would be translated more accurately as "There is nothing without a reason why it is so and not otherwise", and this is usually interpreted as "There is nothing without a sufficient reason".[24] More-informative explanations of his 'principle of sufficient reason' are given as "... the great principle, ... which teaches that *nothing happens without a sufficient reason* ; that is to say, that nothing happens without its being possible ... to give a reason sufficient to determine why it is so and not otherwise"[25] and "... sufficient reason, by virtue of which we consider that no fact can be real or existent, no statement true, unless there be a sufficient reason why it is so and not otherwise, although most often these reasons cannot be known to us".[26]

The observations concerning the subjective nature of a flowing time — that the flow is not objectively measurable and is intimately related to our thought processes — categorise it as a quale: an element of subjective experience, but what about causal relations? We deem these to occur in the direction of our subjective time, with each cause preceding its associated effect, but if the flow of time exists only within our mind then so must causality. There must be some direct connection between the cause and the effect, but it is surprisingly hard to define them as distinct phenomena, or to differentiate causation from correlation (§8.2). Whatever the nature of that direct connection, it must be something that we experience on a regular basis (i.e. that we always observe the correspondence in the same order at different times and places), leading to us inferring a fundamental rule that governs all things in our experience.

It is easier to understand these statements if we consider the levels of disconnection between the mind and the objective reality. The latter is most distant from the mind, and not directly accessible to us. What we do access, through observation and measurement, constitutes our subjective reality. The processes within the mind, including thought and emotion, are not part of the measurable world, but are just as real in a non-physical way.

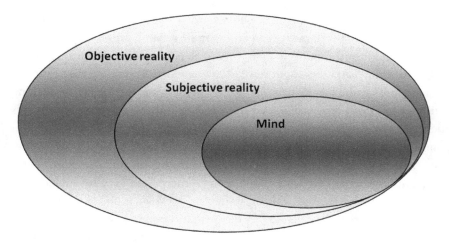

Fig. 4-3, Levels of reality.

During the eighteenth century, there was a well-known difference of opinion between Scottish philosopher David Hume and German philosopher Immanuel Kant over the nature of causality.

Hume held that we never actually observe causality, only the repeated conjunction of two events. In other words, it is an illusion resulting from the observation that one event repeatedly follows another in close proximity, or when mediated by some agent through which causation could be communicated. He declared.

> Thus we remember to have seen that species of object we call flame, and to have felt that species of sensation we call heat. We likewise call to mind their constant conjunction in all past instances. Without any farther ceremony, we call the one cause and the other effect, and infer the existence of the one from that of the other. In all those instances, from which we learn the conjunction of particular causes and effects, both the causes and effects have been perceiv'd by the senses, and are remember'd.[27]
>
> We have no other notion of cause and effect, but that of certain objects, which have been always conjoin'd together, and which in all past instances have been found inseparable. We cannot penetrate into the reason of the conjunction. We only observe the thing itself, and always find that from the constant conjunction the objects acquire an union in the imagination. When the impression of one becomes present to us, we immediately form an idea of its usual attendant; and consequently we may establish this as one part of the definition of an opinion or belief, that 'tis an idea related to or associated with a present impression.[28]

Hume was spot on in terms of causality being an illusion, and his words largely agree with our position here that causality is an assessment of a pattern observed in our subjective reality, but note that this could equally stand as a description of all scientific investigation. We will come back to the relationship between science and causality in §8.2.

Kant and Hume both agreed that the perceived ordering of things alone was not really enough to infer a causal relationship, although we do learn such relationships through repeated experience, including through scientific observation. But what Kant did was to turn the argument around such that the perceived ordering must be the result of some objective ordering, i.e. causality. He stated:

> In our case, therefore, we shall have to derive the subjective succession in our apprehension [perception] from the objective succession of the phenomena, because otherwise the former would be entirely undetermined, and unable to distinguish one phenomenon from another.[29]

In other words, Kant argued that we can distinguish between events (something happening at a particular time and place) from non-events (static situations or, using Hume's language, ideas rather than impressions), and that we cannot change the perceived order of events but we can of non-events. We might perceive event B following event A, but within our mind we can summon them in any order. Hence, our perceptions must be underpinned by the fundamental ordering that we term causality.

Kant was correct in that there must be an objective ordering, but incorrect in that it was causality. There is no specific ordering for the case of two events in the objective reality, based upon the laws of physics being time-symmetric. But to our perceptions — in our subjective reality — then their order is according to our subjective time, and causal relation are inferred from repeatable correlations in that same temporal direction. Causation is a phenomenal description rather than a specific physical process. This is a roundabout way of saying that the identification of causation and the perception of temporal flow (and hence consciousness itself) are dependent upon some other underlying process or mechanism.

At the end of Chapter 3, we briefly noted the importance of algorithmic sequencing (in its most general interpretation) for our cognition of change. We will later posit that the *block universe* exhibits a mathematically determinate pattern of change, but this alone could not support conscious awareness. For that, we must have some way of relating parts of the pattern to other parts, whether retrospective or predictive, and this is what we call causality. It constitutes the rules by which our algorithmic assessment of change works; we do not simply note each moment in isolation of prior ones and with no expectation for the future. There is a well-known maxim that you cannot unknow something, meaning that once some sequence of events has been assimilated into our knowledge, where it is compounded by change upon change, then it is not possible to remove it. Those causal rules allow us to assimilate change as a directed network of dependencies, but that directedness is a consequence of our consciousness and not of a physical arrow of time

But what of *retrocausality*: the notion that things in the future can affect things in the present? Although this has been explored within *quantum mechanics*, it has also been argued against by people such as British-American philosopher Max Black in 1956.[30] The reasoning of his 'bilking argument' was that if an effect was to precede its cause then it should be possible to intercede after the effect and prevent the cause, thus creating a contradiction. Implicit in this argument is the belief that our subjective time is real, and hence that our experience of things evolving in a particular order is fundamental. Furthermore, the argument requires that the efficacy of any *retrocausality* could occur in a direction entirely independent of our perceptions. The argument does lead to a contradiction, but it is based upon an incorrect view of both time and causality.

Not only are we arguing that subjective time cannot exist in a *block universe*, we are also arguing that causality is illusory and so is inappropriate within any aspect of fundamental physics (including *quantum mechanics*). The past and future are connected in an acausal, mathematically deterministic way, and this will underpin our interpretation of *superdeterminism*, to be discussed in §7.6.

4.2   Chance and Choice

Motion, change, and causality are not the only phenomena that are inherently tied to our subjective time. So are our concepts of chance — the notion that things may happen in one of several ways, and by implication the concept of probability as a measure of this — and choice — the notion that we can consciously select one of several possibilities, leading then to the notion of free will.

You may be wondering how many aspects of our subjective reality are illusory, and whether there will be anything left in the objective reality, but this process is very important. We cannot grasp the nature of the objective reality if our perspective is rooted in all things subjective, nor can we expect to understand why mathematics is so useful at that level. We have already noted that mathematics is incapable of fully describing change (including motion) or causality as we perceive them, but the same is also true of chance and choice.

In a *block universe*, both the past and the future co-exist, and there is no fundamental difference between the two, other than our perception of them. For reasons yet to be uncovered, we perceive a single past but no specific future. We therefore believe — quite dogmatically in most cases — that we can influence the future because it has not yet happened. But there are no real alternatives; every scenario has a unique outcome, which already exists in the *block universe*.

When we apply probability to outcomes that we have not yet experienced then we are really looking at the possible outcomes that are consistent with a description of the state at a prior moment, and with our knowledge of the way things have behaved in similar circumstances. In other words, probability is really a measure of the density of those possibilities if they could all be laid out in a *block universe*. The mathematics of probability is entirely consistent with this view, and yet it is incapable of describing chance as we perceive it. This interpretation of the mathematics may feel quite alien because our subjective reality is so dependent upon alternative outcomes and our assessments of their relative likelihoods. We will examine the use of probability in *quantum mechanics* in §7.6, and look more deeply at the nature of probability in §10.3.

If there are no real alternatives in a *block universe* then there are no real examples of choice either. We are part of the *block universe* and so our perceived choices must also be illusory. It is not the case that we are somehow separate, and that we have some special capability that transcends *determinism*. One way of looking at this is that all the choices we have already made today cannot now be undone, but neither could they have been changed yesterday. Lack of knowledge of what they would be is not the same as them not existing or not being defined.

Choice is the result of a conscious agency taking advantage of chance, and an apparently indeterminate future, through the process of mental causation (i.e. free will). All of our choices are born of knowledge and experience from prior moments (there are never any inputs from future moments) and our apparent ability to instigate a physical effect from a mental cause. In the absence of consciousness, then, there are zero choices in the universe; they exist only in conscious minds. We will expand upon the true nature of free will in §6.4.

There is a well-known concept in the mathematics of set theory called the 'axiom of choice', and it illustrates this gap between mathematics and choice. It is not at all difficult to define; in fact its purported importance is hard to convey simply because it seems so obvious. Given a collection of mutually disjoint (i.e. no common elements), non-empty sets then it is possible to form a new set containing just one element from each of those member sets (called a *transversal*). The controversial axiom was formulated by German mathematician Ernst Zermelo in 1904 in order to prove something known as the 'well-ordering theorem'.

A well-ordered set is one where every subset has a first member (e.g. a minimum value). If we consider numbers expressed in their natural order, the set of positive integers is well-ordered, but not the set of general integers as there is no minimum: one member could be arbitrarily negative. Neither is the set of non-negative real numbers because the subset above some fixed number (e.g. 1) has no minimum: there could be an infinite number of values infinitesimally close to that number (e.g. 1.1, 1.0001, etc). This is not to say that the same sets cannot be ordered in some other, non-natural fashion. Zermelo proved that a set was well-ordered if it was possible to select some 'special' element from any non-empty subset of it.

The controversial issue is that the axiom states that it is always possible to form a set by choosing an element from each member set of any infinite collection, but without specifying any constructive algorithm (or 'choice function') to achieve that selection, and this raises the question of what constitutes a choice. That the choice is represented by a procedural algorithm rather than a mathematically declarative construction is not so much of an issue as the fact that it is a placeholder, and presumes that such a selection is always possible. For a set of simple numbers, where we can apply arithmetic and comparators, then we can construct a rule that uniquely specifies a selection, but that is not always the case. The entities within the sets require some comparable property upon which the choice algorithm can operate

English mathematician and philosopher Bertrand A. W. Russell explained this as "To choose one sock from each of infinitely many pairs of socks requires the Axiom of Choice, but for shoes the Axiom is not needed",[31] meaning that shoes have a left or right property, but socks are indistinguishable. When we have such a rule then it implicitly constructs the resultant set, but the axiom is representing an arbitrary choice by a 'choice function', and so is incorporating a real-life phenomenon into mathematical logic by way of that hypothetical function — in real-life, we can always make an arbitrary selection that would appear to have no specific criterion.

Employing such a function with an infinite collection implies a one-by-one selection and so would require an infinite number of steps. Criticisms of the axiom often speak of it requiring an infinite amount of time, but that is confusing real-life steps with mathematical, or algorithmic, steps. Algorithmic steps are necessarily sequential because they are procedural, and involve decisions (i.e. selection of a subsequent step) based on the current state. Choice is more general than algorithmic selection as it includes conscious selection based upon a whim rather than a determinate criterion, and so mathematics has no way of modelling the fundamental nature of choice.

4.3   Time Travel

Digressing slightly — is time travel possible? We need to address this question since many readers may believe that it will be possible, one day, or they may have been misled into thinking that mathematical physics says that it is possible.

There are countless science fiction stories that get mired in 'temporal anomalies' and seeming contradictions associated with time travel. What happens if I go back and change something, such as killing an ancestor? One very simple argument against time travel is that no one from the future has ever been known to have visited us. Hence, by implication, no one in the future — ever — will invent a time machine or find some magic 'portal' back to us here.

An amusing bit of graffiti once observed on a wall in Ireland sums this up nicely: "What do we want? Time travel! When do we want it? That's irrelevant". As you might imagine, these problems result from an erroneous view of time. If you like, these anomalies and contradictions are nature's way of telling you that you have it all wrong.

There are more scientific arguments against the possibility of time travel: dematerialising from one time, and re-materialising at another, would violate the conservations laws for mass-energy and momentum. These laws are fundamental to our understanding of the universe, and nothing has been observed to violate them so far. It would also violate the principle of causality; causality may be an illusion, but everything we know about the universe seems to support that illusion.

Notwithstanding the fact that the surface of the Earth is rotating around its centre at about 1000 mph, the Earth is orbiting the Sun at about 67,000 mph, and the Sun is orbiting the Galaxy at about 490,000 mph,[32] meaning you would re-materialise in a very cold void and die a horrible death in outer space, there is another theoretical possibility: an *Einstein–Rosen bridge*, or 'wormhole' (a term coined by American theoretical physicist John A. Wheeler in 1957). This is merely a hypothetical structure that results from one solution of Einstein's equations for *general relativity*. No one has ever observed one, and there are no observations that would benefit from a 'wormhole' explanation. Explained as simply as possible, it would constitute a tunnel linking two points otherwise separated in space-time. Imagine the surface of a sphere (a hypothetical two-dimensional universe) that is distorted such that a depression at one point is connected to a depression at a distant point; that connection would then constitute a shortcut from one point in this space to another.

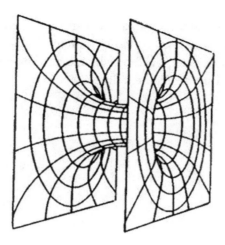

Fig. 4-4, A wormhole pinching two space-time locations.

However, this would require space-time to be a pliable manifold that can be bent or distorted, and we will come back to this in Chapter 11 (Space-Time and Gravitation).

Within a *block universe*, the original question has no meaning; time is not moving, and we are not moving through time. Rather than being of mere spatial extent, we (or at least the forms that we are identified by) also have a temporal extent, and so we occupy some region of space and time for the whole period that we are deemed to exist. The only thing that appears to be moving is the '*now*' moment of our consciousness, but that is an illusion.

This is not the same as travelling in time since the state of the *block universe* at a particular instant is immutable, and whatever entities (including people) and events existed, or will exist, are indelibly imprinted on that instant of time. Sometimes when a *block universe* is discussed, arguments are presented in which someone travelling to the past cannot change events because they are immutable, yet this is a flawed view of such a universe; the real issue is that there is no option to travel at all. It is not possible to introduce other entities, or to change events associated with that instant, because there is no dynamical change, no real movement, and no causation.

So why do things appear to move? Why do things appear to change from one moment to another? We will later explain that our total consciousness is composed of a series of informationally linked '*now*' moments, each of which is related to our external environment at that instant. So, even if it were possible to bridge from one space-time location to another, our consciousness and memory would be determined by whether information can be linked in the required way, and in the required direction.

— 5 —

Objective Reality

How would the universe appear if there were no conscious entities within it?

We have used the adjective *subjective* to refer to time as observed or interpreted by conscious entities, and *objective* to refer to the underlying unobserved nature of the time. But time is the backbone of our reality and so we must extend the usage of these adjectives to differentiate the associated perspectives on reality.

We perceive a reality that includes motion, dynamical change, causality, and even consciousness, but what is the nature of the objective reality: the universe in the absence of any conscious viewpoint? What form would it have, and would it be meaningful to us? The answer would not only be 'no', but to a surprising extent 'no'. If we could imagine the universe in our absence — as some type of super-observer — then we would not see planetary motions, galactic rotations, chemical processes, nuclear processes, propagating waves, or anything that is dynamical; everything would be static, as in the *block-universe* picture of the cannon (Fig. 1-1). Change would still be present, but only as a mathematically describable pattern along the temporal dimension. The absence of all things dynamical means that there cannot be any change as we experience it, nor any genuine alternatives.

Some readers may want to pause for a deep breath here so that they can re-read this. Rather than having a universe of entities — animate and inanimate — that move, change their form, or undergo creation and destruction, then we have a universe that is a static block that encompasses all things, all their apparent motions, and all their forms, whether past or future, because there is no longer any difference. For us, it means that none of our lives or our creations — no works of science, art, or literature — are ever lost, but it also means that there is no future other than the one that lies ahead of us.

Whether we can infer the nature of the 'fabric' of the objective reality depends upon what we have access to — what we can observe or measure

47

— and the nature of both measurement and knowledge. We will later posit that this 'fabric' (whatever it is) is static, continuous, and deterministic in a mathematical sense (see DPC in §10.3), but we may never be able to comprehend its true nature. When we look at the nature of measurement (§5.4) then we will see how important our concepts of space and time are when we deem to make measurements, and because of this key fact then we will begin with the assumption that the 'fabric' is dimensional, and hence constitutes a four-dimensional *block universe*. It may be that this dimensionality is an emergent phenomenon (§11.5), rather than being a fundamental property, but this is an unattractive proposition since it would make the task of fundamental physics so much more difficult.

We noted that the mathematics of *special relativity* is considered a *block universe* model, but can this model describe the objective reality or is it too simplistic? More importantly, what is the relationship between our subjective reality and that objective reality? We assume that through observation and inference that we can deduce the fundamental nature of the universe, and that this fundamental nature will include those same elements ubiquitous and essential to our perceptions, but to what extent is the objective reality knowable? In the worst case, that 'fabric' may be out of our reach, and not directly related to measurable quantities such as energy or momentum. It should not be viewed as physical since that is an attribute of our subjective reality, and it might only be addressable in mathematical fashion.

In 1927, English scientist John B. S. Haldane summed up this detachment rather nicely as follows:

> Now, my own suspicion is that the universe is not only queerer than we suppose, but queerer than we *can* suppose. I have read and heard many attempts at a systematic account of it, from materialism and theosophy to the Christian system or that of Kant, and I have always felt that they were much too simple. I suspect that there are more things in heaven and earth than are dreamed of, or can be dreamed of, in any philosophy.[33]

You may be wondering what we are talking about with the objective reality. Surely, at the subatomic level, our reality consists of uncountable numbers of fundamental particles, all whizzing around and interactive with each other. Furthermore, these would be doing exactly the same whether we were trying to detect them or not. Well, that is not quite true! Despite being able to detect these particles individually, and even observe their ion trails in a cloud chamber, we have never seen one. If we were not observing them then there would be no way to prove that they traverse some path over time, or whether they would appear more as the static world-lines, with no concept of '*now*' and nothing to distinguish any past from future.

We can calculate the size of a proton (actually the 'rms charge radius') to be in the range of 0.84–0.87×10^{-15} m by using scattering data, but particles such as the proton and neutron are not really fundamental — they are composed of quarks (pronounced 'quorks') — and so have internal structure. Electrons and photons are fundamental and yet most people think of them as quite different, despite both giving similar interference effects (Chapter 7). On a diagram, photon paths are invariably drawn as wavy lines whereas electron paths are drawn as straight lines, so what is the real difference?

Electrons have a mass whereas photons do not, but we should not interpret this as meaning that a particle with mass is somehow solid and tangible, and occupies space — this is similar to the view, still taught in some schools, that atoms have spherical objects called protons and neutrons bound in the nucleus, and smaller objects called electron orbiting the nucleus like a small solar system. Inertial mass is effectively a measure of inertia — the resistance of something to being accelerated or deviated from its natural path — and a force is defined as something that changes the path or velocity of an object; hence $F = m\,a$. Concepts such as mass, inertia, force, and even energy, have obvious interpretations at the macroscopic scale, but those interpretation becomes vaguer at the subatomic scale. We infer the presence of a force if we observe a change in an object's path, but does that really mean there is something real, that we call a force, that is making that change? Certainly not if we have abandoned causality as nothing more than an illusion.

Einstein's *general relativity* described gravity not as a force but as a change in the geometry of space-time, and hence that the non-linear paths of particles in a gravitational field (including those of massless photons, which experiments showed were bent by massive stars) were simply modified natural paths. The point being made so far in this section is that we carry our macroscopic concepts and bookkeeping down to subatomic levels as a consequence of *reductionism*, and we make them work with the introduction of fundamental forces, but we have no direct experience of reality at that level. By describing the objective reality as having a 'fabric' then we are forcing a split from our subjective notions, and so starting with an empty slate that does not include causally related quantities such as momentum and force.

These considerations are quite like asking whether a falling tree makes any noise if there is no one in the forest to hear it. But if we know that the falling tree creates disturbances in the air, and that we understand how an ear can detect these and pass signals to the brain, and how a conscious entity can interpret the signals as noise, then that question is answerable. Hence, there is hope ... maybe!

But we are slightly perplexed as to why mathematics (a product of the mind) so adequately describes the evolution of observed phenomena, often to the point of confusing the two and missing the fact that mathematics does not actually capture our experience of that evolution. Motion, and changes of motion, have an experiential aspect that no mathematical equation or graph embraces, and so we are forced to decide whether mathematics or our experience is the true pointer.

We will, on occasion, use the familiar terms 'material world', 'physical world', and 'measurable world', so this is a good place to introduce them. They are often used interchangeably, but we need to distinguish them here in order to give some precision to future arguments:

- *Material world*: This includes all things tangible or composed of matter.
- *Physical world*: This includes the material world, plus the properties of material objects (e.g. momentum), and the forces that may affect them.
- *Measurable world*: This comprises all things that we can observe or measure, and it therefore plays a pivotal role in our subjective reality since it is our (imperfect) window onto the objective reality. It includes the physical world, plus space-time which, as will be explained in a moment, is fundamental to the act of measurement. Space-time is only implicit in the first two terms, but included explicitly here as it is directly measurable itself.

We can now return to our separation of realities in Fig. 4-3 to add these 'worlds' as follows:

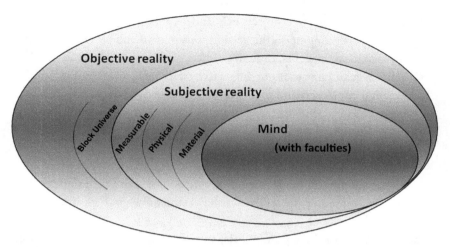

Fig. 5-1, Levels of reality including our 'worlds' terminology.

5.1   Transcendental Idealism

During the so-called 'age of enlightenment' of the eighteenth century, a number of differing theories were presented on the reality, or otherwise, of space and time, objects, and the relations between objects. In particular, on whether these existed independently of an observer, whether the perception of them was directly related to an objective reality, and even whether there was evidence of God.

All of them postulated some initial constraint that would appear to describe a universal order, and from which they could build a model of reality, albeit a subjective one. The level of subjective belief about the nature of reality is particularly evident in the number of different philosophical standpoints. Just a few of the more common ones would include the following:

- *Rationalism* maintains that the criteria of truth come from intellectual reasoning rather than from the senses. Because the objective reality has a logical structure then certain rational principles and truths exist in mathematics and logic, and these can be grasped by the mind without sensory input.
- *Empiricism* maintains that knowledge comes primarily from sensory experience. As such, this is a core principle of evidence-based experimentation and the *scientific method*, even when measurement equipment is being observed by the experimenter. But see notes in §1.3.

- *Realism* maintains that objects exist independently of our subjective reality. Depending upon the version, this may include material objects, mathematical concepts, causality, time, consciousness, and the mind.
- *Idealism* maintains that our subjective reality is fundamentally a mental construct, and that it is not possible to understand any mind-independent thing. In asserting the importance of consciousness, some versions are believed to deny the existence of an objective reality.
- *Materialism* maintains that matter is the fundamental component of nature, and that all things, including consciousness and the mind's faculties, are simply the result of material structures and their interactions.

There are many of these standpoints, and every one of them has variations applying some further adjective to the base name, e.g. *objective idealism, naïve realism, interactionist dualism,* and *transcendental idealism.* We need to be aware of their main differences, but nature does not care about our terms, and there is nothing to be gained by pinning our hat to any one of these ahead of some deeper thought.

During this period, many great names associated with science, philosophy, and mathematics strived to explain the world around them, and so become independent of church-enforced dogma. Indeed, the distinction between these fields was much finer than it is today, and all were considered important in this endeavour. Many of these viewpoints drew from much earlier works such as Aristotle's *hylomorphism,* and so it is worth summarising some of his terms and concepts as they were employed in those later viewpoints; plus they can be hard to relate those same terms and concepts to things that we know and believe now.

Hylomorphism is simply the theory that the essence of everything that exists is a compound of 'matter' and 'form'. 'Matter' cannot be created or destroyed, but it can take on different 'forms', and it can be studied according to those 'forms'. A 'substance' (ousia, Greek: οὐσία) is a fundamental entity of reality — usually an object or a thing — that is distinct from its properties. Hence, a *thing-in-itself* (see later) is a 'substance' considered separately from its phenomenal properties (if that is at all possible). A 'substance' may be a 'secondary substance' (i.e. classifications, also called 'universals', such as a cat), or a 'primary substance' (i.e. an instance of a secondary, such as the cat called Felix). 'Substance' properties may be essential (without which it would not be the same 'substance') or non-essential (which may change while retaining identification as that 'substance'); these usually being described as substantial or accidental, respectively.

'Substances' can be composed of other 'substances', and they may be classified according to monist, dualist, or pluralist varieties depending upon how many exist, so *monism* asserts that some set of existing things can be explained in terms of a single 'substance'. 'Categories' enumerate all the possible things that can be the subject or the predicate of a proposition. In addition to 'substance', there are a number of abstract 'categories' such as 'quantity', 'having', and 'doing'. A 'primary substance' can be the subject of a proposition, but only 'secondary substances' and the other 'categories' can be predicated. Hence, cat is predicated of (said of) Felix. A 'primary substance' is usually equated to a particular compound of 'matter' and 'form', but although 'matter' alone can be a subject of predication, it is not considered a 'substance'. According to Aristotle, a 'substance' must be both separable (having independent existence) and have an identity, but if 'matter' is separable from 'substance' then it has no identity, and if it has identity then it is not separable. Finally, if one 'substance' is made of another then they share the same 'matter', but when it cannot be disassembled into other 'substance' then it is considered to have only 'prime matter' (i.e. 'matter' with no 'substantial form').

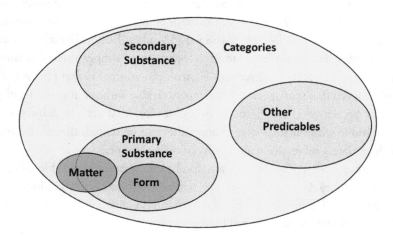

Fig. 5-2, Aristotle's metaphysics.

Aristotle clearly put a lot of thought into his ontology, but it seems both dated and simplistic in the light of modern knowledge.

French philosopher, mathematician, and scientist René Descartes (1596–1650) laid some important foundations for scientific discovery. His Cartesian geometry had a strong influence on perceptions of space and time, including those of the young Newton, but he also made a break from Church doctrine by taking the stance of 'certainty' (what can we be certain of, and determine through our own reasoning?) rather than 'truth' (as understood, at that time, to come from God, or rather Church dogma) and so set the scene for *rationalism*. This did not stop some of the later philosophers using their deductive powers to try and prove the existence of God.

English mathematician and physicist Sir Isaac Newton (1642–1727) believed that space and time are absolute, and entities in their own right, existing independently of conscious entities. The view of Gottfried Leibniz (1646–1716), later described as *relationalism*, was that space and time can only be described in terms of the relations (positional and causal) between objects. We cannot conceive of objects outside of space and time, and although we can imagine space and time devoid of objects it cannot exist in reality because there would be no observer and nothing to observe. The theory of *special relativity* later showed that space-time and motion were all relative, and so echoed the views of Leibniz, but *general relativity* then gave space-time substance (external to objects) that could be described geometrically. English philosopher and Anglican clergyman Samuel Clark (1675–1729) believed that space and time, eternity, and immensity, are not substances but the attributes of a self-existent being (i.e. God). Irish philosopher and clergyman George Berkeley (1685–1753, a.k.a. Bishop Berkeley) believed in a *subjective idealism* where familiar objects were simply mental constructs that would not exist if not perceived. Scottish philosopher David Hume (1711–1776) believed that spatial extension is inconceivable without intervening objects that can be sensed through touch or sight; also, that temporal intervals are inconceivable without successive changes that can be sensed, thereby beginning to differentiate a subjective reality from an objective one.

Immanuel Kant (1724–1804) was critical of these earlier views. He coined the term *thing-in-itself* (German: *Ding an sich*) to describe objects as they are, independent of observation.[34] He then argued that space, time, and causation are mere sensibilities of *things-in-themselves*, but that their fundamental nature is unknowable.

> These objects are not presentations of things as they are in themselves,
> and as the pure understanding would cognise them, but they are
> sensuous intuitions, i.e., phenomena, the possibility of which rests

on the relations of certain unknown *things in themselves* to something else, namely, to our sensibility.[35]

In fact, when we regard the objects of sense, as is correct, as mere appearances, we thereby at the same time confess that a thing in itself lies at their foundation, although we do not know it, as it is constituted in itself, but only its appearance, that is, the manner in which our senses are affected by this unknown something.[36]

But Kant also used other terms to distinguish something that exists independently of our senses or perception (*noumenon*) from something that is manifested to us, or experienced through our senses (*phenomenon*). His usage of *noumenon* and *thing-in-itself* are sometimes taken as synonymous, despite being used together, but a comparison of the detail in several of his references reveals a subtle difference.

One might feel inclined to think that the concept of *Phenomena*, as limited by the transcendental aesthetic, suggested by itself the objective reality of the *Noumena*, and justified a division of objects into phenomena and noumena, and consequently of the world into a *sensible* and *intelligible* world ... [37]

Hence arises the concept of a noumenon, which however is not positive, nor a definite knowledge of anything, but which implies only the thinking of something, without taking any account of the form of sensuous intuition. But in order that a noumenon may signify a real object that can be distinguished from all phenomena, it is not enough that I should free my thought of all conditions of sensuous intuition, but I must besides have some reason for admitting another kind of intuition besides the sensuous, in which such an object can be given; ... [38]

... the concept of a noumenon, that is of a thing which can never be thought as an object of the senses, but only as a thing by itself (by the pure understanding), ... [39]

Now I ask, whence can the understanding take these synthetical propositions, as the concepts are to apply, not to some possible experience, but to things by themselves (noumena)? [40]

... seems to us nevertheless a mode in which the object by itself exists (noumenon), ... [41]

... not therefore as a phenomenon, nor as a thing by itself (noumenon) ... [42]

The confusion is understandable because his text links the terms together in several places and different ways; however, where he used *noumenon* there was a suggestion that this was the mental conception, or understanding, of the *thing-in-itself* rather than the actual fundamentally unknowable *thing-in-itself*. In other words, that it was not simply the case that there were things-in-themselves within the objective reality and the phenomenal experience of them within our subjective realities, but that we had an innate conception of things beyond our direct experience.

He reasoned that although the *thing-in-itself* is unknowable except through our senses, yielding the phenomenon, we had a mental version of the object (the *noumenon*) that was distinct from the phenomenon, and that we were empowered with a capacity to assimilate sensory input into these forms. In other words, that our experience is structured by certain preconceived notions, that we all share, which he termed categories (original German: *categorie*); and so our subjective reality is not formed from sensory input alone, but is moulded from those sensory inputs in accordance with these notions. He distinguished his view, called *transcendental idealism*, from the accepted views of *realism* and *idealism*.

His *categories* are pure concepts of the understanding that characterise the appearance of objects before they have been experienced, and he defined the following twelve (in four groups of three exclusive cases):[43]

- quantity
  - unity
  - plurality
  - totality

- quality
  - reality
  - negation
  - limitation

- relation
  - inherence and subsistence (substance and accident)
  - causality and dependence (cause and effect)
  - community (reciprocity)

- modality
  - possibility
  - existence
  - necessity

Although these apply universally to all objects that may be cognised, they originate from our understanding of the objects rather than from some intrinsic properties of the objective reality. It is interesting to note that they can all be embraced by mathematical frameworks, in contrast to our perceptions.

For instance, Kant believed that our perception of space and time was directed by preconceived notions of expanse and containment of objects.

> Space is not an empirical concept which has been derived from external experience. For in order that certain sensations should be referred to something outside myself, i.e. to something in a different part of space from that where I am; again, in order that I may be able to represent them (vorstellen) as side by side, that is, not only as different, but as in different places, the representation (Vorstellung) of space must already be there. Therefore the representation of space cannot be borrowed through experience from relations of external phenomena, but, on the contrary, this external experience becomes possible only by means of the representation of space.[44]

This seems a rather weak and ambiguous proposal, and in 1770 he had already changed his view from the relational one of Leibniz to an absolute one, using arguments of 'incongruent counterparts',[45] so was this yet another change? This later argument also involved an invocation of 'incongruent counterparts', or what we would commonly know as mirror images.

> Those who are unable to free themselves from the notion, that space and time are real qualities (Beschaffenheiten) appertaining to the things in themselves, may exercise their wits on the following paradoxes, and when they have in vain attempted their solution, may suppose, being freed from their prejudices at least for a few moments, that perhaps the degradation of space and time to the position of mere forms of our sensible intuition, may have some foundation.[46]

He then went on to give a number of examples, the first being that of two spherical triangles — triangles drawn on the surface of a sphere — that share a common base on the arc of the equator. He claimed that they were 'internally' identical — meaning identical sides and angles — and yet they were different in that one could not be placed over the other; this revealing itself only by means of the "external relation in space".

He followed this with a real mirror-image case: that of a hand and its reflection. When specified independently, there would no difference at all, and yet spatially they were different, with one being a right hand and the other being a left hand. In reality, a mirror is not inverting left-to-right, or even top-to-bottom, but front-to-back. He was arguing, though, that a description of an 'incongruent counterpart' could only be determinate through a directional framework (for up/down and left/right) provided by a spatial intuition, and hence that space was an intuition based upon the relations of certain unknown things-in-themselves to our sensibility.

Kant's argument stemmed from a metaphysical stance based upon objects of his perception pre-existing, and criticised mathematical explanations (such as by German philosopher Christian Wolff) because they always began with a definition. So the fact that we can intuit such differences must mean that we have an innate capability for spatial awareness. But Kant seemed to be making far too much of our conventional designations for these orientations and geometrical congruence. Left/right and up/down only mean something in relation to something else, and a hand in complete isolation from anything else cannot be said to be either a left or a right. Yet handedness occurs in nature, independently of our senses, intuitions, and even our existence. Our intuition of these counterparts is formed from the assimilation of sensory inputs from a reality that exhibits such symmetry, and that symmetry itself is mathematically addressable.

Molecules can have mirror images, called *stereoscopic isomers*, or just stereoisomers. In the case of the glucose molecule, D-glucose (also known as dextrose) occurs widely in nature, but the isomer L-glucose does not. These are mirror images of each other, and have identical chemical properties, but they are not metabolised the same way: the body can tell the difference because of the shape of the molecule, and the fact that it does not fit, structurally, with other molecules. The shape and handedness of biological molecules plays a very important role in our inner workings.

Mathematically, the different orientations of a figure, or object, are related by a *symmetry group* of transformations that preserve its structure, and a *full symmetry group* includes the transformation of reflection (or inversion about an axis). Neither of the orientations can be defined in isolation, nor given absolute designations; these attributes are always relative ones, as are our geometric coordinate systems.

Thus, mathematics addresses the phenomenon of handedness. It occurs in nature independently of our direct observation, and so presumably in the objective reality too. This is to be expected if the objective reality is fully susceptible to mathematical description. Graphical relationships and geometric figures can all be described pictorially, but also by symbolic means with no loss. In §10.2 we will make the case that these fields of mathematics are constructed so as to suit our internal world-view: the notion of extent or expanse as fashioned into our subjective reality from sensory input. That we resort to pictorial representations in these fields is then a straightforward and natural step owing to the rationale for their creation.

So, we are claiming that Kant's reasoning was partly the wrong way around, and that our subjective reality is the result of assimilating sensory input with no preconceived notions, or categories. A newborn has no concept of space, and it takes time for them to become fully aware of their surroundings through sight, touch, hearing, and even smell. Any conscious entity will have some spatial awareness if it has sufficient sensory apparatus, and those with greater sensory acuity will have better awareness.

But let us consider another argument: since all of the animal kingdom possessing this sufficient apparatus has spatial awareness, then was Kant saying that we are all endowed with the same innate mechanism to intuit space around us? Would it not be simpler, and so more likely, that the commonality is in the world around us rather than in our perception of it? In other words, that his noumena emerge rather than being predefined.

Underpinning all this is the premise that a space-time continuum separating objects and events exists in the objective reality, although the perception of them in our subjective reality will not be quite the same. Kant's distinction between these phenomena and the noumena existing solely within our mind is more insightful (despite being slightly vague), and reflects the divisions in Fig. 5-1. The different way that we intuit space and time, despite their mathematical similarity, is crucially related to the emergence of consciousness (§6.3).

5.2   Laws of Physics

When we talk about the so-called laws of physics, or laws of science, they are not some constraint placed upon nature, or upon reality, but only an attempt to describe observed behaviours. They do not explain why or how such behaviours occur; this is where scientific theories come into play — mostly employing mathematics as a tool. Going back to the goals that we identified in §1.3, natural law (or laws of nature) is what happens (independently of us), scientific law (including the laws of physics) is our description of those phenomena (the goal of predictability), and scientific theory is our explanation of them (the goal of understanding).[47]

But mathematics is distinct from the reality, and it may describe further unobserved behaviours. Ideally, these will be predictions that can be confirmed later, and yet they might also be red herrings resulting from the mathematics being too naïve, or just plain wrong. It is a matter of faith amongst physicists that mathematics is a valid tool for describing, and to some extent even understanding, the universe, but we must not lose sight of the fact that it is not the reality itself.

In 2005, Australian scientist John D. Norton devised a thought experiment ('Norton's dome') supposedly demonstrating that Newtonian mechanics allowed "uncaused events". With an idealised particle sitting atop a smooth frictionless dome, there were two classes of solution to its evolution: one where it stayed there, and one where it could spontaneously slide down the surface of the dome with no apparent trigger and no ability to assign a probability to the occurrence. The point of the exercise was to present a simple violation of *causal determinism* in Newton's laws of motion. But our laws of physics do not dictate what physical systems must do; they are our attempt to describe their observed progress and so make them predictable. His thought experiment was a mathematical model of an unrealistic scenario. The crux of the problem was the unconstrained singularity at the apex of the dome. It was not a real situation involving two contiguous material surfaces, and so there was absolutely no reason why the particle had to stay put, thus admitting mathematical solutions where it did not.

An interesting variation on this dome is the 'Mexican hat potential' of British theoretical physicist Jeffrey Goldstone. If you imagine the dome surrounded by a potential trough then the initial condition (ball on top of the dome) is symmetric with respect to rotations, while the ball having fallen into the trough is asymmetric. It is interesting because it is claimed to be an example of 'spontaneous symmetry breaking' — a concept deemed to be crucial in the explanation of the differences between our fundamental forces — despite both the initial condition and the spontaneous event not being physically realistic.

But in a *block universe*, where we have no motion and no causality, then what is our mathematics doing? The continuity of all change means that we can identify patterns in our successive measurements, and so the laws of physics are essentially modelling the 'shape of change' within those observed patterns — something that mathematics is ideally suited to — but the equations themselves are static and acausal. This is because the underlying objective reality (which is not directly observable) has a static pattern, and the applicability of mathematics arises from the nature of that pattern.

Let us illustrate this claim with a trivially simple hypothetical universe: one that contains a single measurable quantity (y) that appears to oscillate along the time dimension. Hence $y = b \sin(a\, t)$, where a and b are constants.

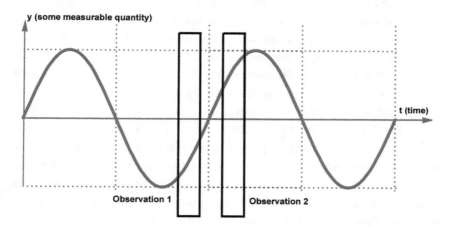

Fig. 5-3, Laws of physics for a simple 1+1 dimensional space.

Repeated measurements would demonstrate a pattern in that quantity, and hence a predictability. In order to explain this variation, we might infer a causal relation between successive measurements, such that each reading can be related to previous readings. This is an important consideration since it demonstrates that although causality implies an underlying *determinism*, *determinism* does not imply or require any causality; there are other types of *determinism*, and this one is based upon a pattern that can be described mathematically.

We might further infer the presence of some background potential causing the variation, one which similarly oscillates but with a different phase, i.e. $V = d \cos(c\,t)$. We might then observe that the quantity $y^2 + V^2$ is invariant and so constituting a conservation law. We might decide to introduce an extra dimension and reinterpret the oscillation as a rotation in the two spatial dimensions, and hence as a helix in a three-dimensional *block universe*.

So does this example wave really propagate or oscillate, or is it merely a static sine wave? The latter would be true here, and we are using terms such as pattern, or 'shape of change', to represent the fact that quantities in the objective reality simply have a static variation across time. Underpinning our perceived subjective reality is the observation that these variations are finite, continuous, and non-random.

This is all very schematic, and not intended to be realistic. The goal is to clarify the claim that the laws of physics that we seek are simply describing patterns of change observed in our subjective reality, and that the mathematical forms we use to describe those patterns are arrived at through causally-based theories.

But fundamental physics, being closer to the static acausal objective reality, is far more reliant upon mathematics since it deals with quantities outside of our direct observation. We should not be using causality as a guide to deriving the associated mathematical forms at that level, so what should we be using? We still need a guide since those forms will not be unique, and by themselves they cannot convey any fundamental understanding of that reality. Introducing abstractions or other variables may simplify the mathematics, or make the interpretation more 'beautiful' (discussed later in §6.2), but we have no way of ascertaining whether they are significant beyond the mathematics. One very powerful tool used in fundamental physics is the concept of symmetry, and symmetry groups. A symmetry is a property that remains unchanged under some transformation, and when exhibited by equations then they often take on a simplified form that can be said to be more general. Imposing requirements of symmetry in a physical theory can be viewed as removing redundant degrees of freedom, and so pinning down its mathematics in this way.

For a more realistic illustration of the interpretation of observables, let us switch to a quantitative property that we can measure: energy. Energy comes in many forms: kinetic, potential, thermal, chemical, radiant, nuclear, etc., but we cannot point to it; it is not some substance that we can directly observe. We define it as the capacity to do work, which in turn is (at least in the classical sense) the application of a force over some distance or displacement. For instance, if some weight is dropped to the ground then the work done by gravity acting over that distance is deemed to convert the potential energy held by virtue of its original height into the kinetic energy of its motion. In other words, work is effectively the transference of energy from one form to another. A looser but more accessible definition of energy is the capacity to effect change in a physical system — which basically means changes of position, velocity, or state — and the concepts of energy and work are merely a form of mathematical bookkeeping for the observed changes.

This is important for the discussion of the 'fabric' of the objective reality. Despite having divested of notions involving dynamical change, we still have no idea what the relation is between the quantities that we believe can be measured and whatever the objective reality consists of. Our laws of physics must be backed by some deterministic pattern of change in that 'fabric', but we may never be sure of what that is. We are suggesting that it is dimensional when we speak of the *block universe*, and the reasons for this are that (a) it gives us an obvious source for our perceived space and time, and (b) it gives some hope that our acts of measurement — which depend upon space and time (§5.4) — have some relevance beyond our subjective reality.

5.3 Existence

Leibniz, in the same work that described his 'principle of sufficient reason', posed the question "Why is there something rather than nothing? For nothing is simpler and easier than something".[48] The question is clearly rhetorical since if there were nothing then we could not pose the question, but it is also profound. It is the basis of probably the biggest questions of all — why are we here? — but any attempt at an answer must be fundamentally different in a *block universe*. Not only is the question unanswerable, but we cannot formulate any question that could yield an answer that could be construed as a meaningful explanation.

As usual, terminology could be a problem here as the term existence has two meanings in this context: the fact or state of having reality, or (rather recursively) all that exists.

Existence — capitalised from here on to emphasise a meaning of all space, all time, and everything that appears to persist or act within their bounds (i.e. the ultimate proper noun) — is a unitary concept: there is no absence of Existence (because we would not be here thinking about it), there is no partial Existence, no inverse, no complement, and no alternatives. It is just there! We must not be tempted to say 'Existence is there for all time' since time is part of Existence rather than the other way around. The term 'universe', without the *block* adjective, is different as it is usually a reference to a spatial extent, and all its contents, with the implicit assumption that they all progresses through time. In other words, if a universe is a time-dependent spatial container then a *block universe* is a space-time container. So if the *block universe* is a proposed container, or framework, in the objective reality, then we must adjust the notion of Existence to include emergent concepts such as our mind and our subjective reality. The fact that the mind exists is not really open to question — at least not in the same way that we might question its composition or mechanism — but the objective reality only embraces that which would still exist in the absence of conscious minds, and so Existence is effectively the contents of Fig. 5-1 in its entirety.

The concept of causality creates a serious philosophical conundrum known as 'first cause', or the 'cosmological argument'. If every effect has a prior cause, which in turn has a cause of its own, then we have an 'infinite regress': a chain of causation that either extends through an eternity of past, or originates from some single special-case event that somehow sidesteps causal issues. Depending upon your background then you may have been told that this is either God or the singularity informally known as the 'big bang'. This does not stop us asking questions such as 'who created the creator?', or 'what came before the big bang?', but proponents of both views would argue that such questions are meaningless — albeit for quite different reasons. As a result, neither case is entirely satisfactory because it can be argued to be incomplete.

The previous chapters on time have attempted to change our concept of time from the 'flat earth' dynamical view to the more geometrical view associated with *eternalism*, and in doing this they have meant the loss of concepts such as movement, dynamical change, and causality. This removes all questions of 'first cause', but at some cost: we cannot, then, ask any meaningful metaphysical question about the objective reality. All the fundamental questions we would like to ask will involve a *how*, *why*, or *when*, but these all presume the fundamentality of our subjective reality. It means that we cannot ask anything about a supposed creation: asking 'when?' is meaningless since time is part of Existence and not some external meter by which we can chart its origin; asking 'how?' would presume that causality existed outside of space-time; and asking 'why?' would presume a rationale, which in turn would require the concepts of conscious choice, intelligence, and causality.

Since Existence, as described here, is the existence of all space, all time, and everything within them, then it must preclude the concept of multiple existences — or multiple realities, as typified in science fiction — since if there were some connection between them (causal or otherwise) then they would, by definition, be part of the same Existence. And if there were no connection then we would never know about the others, and to all intents and purposes they would not be there. It is worth pondering on that for a moment since it is not an arbitrary statement.

There are a couple of popular invocations of this multiplicity that have some credibility at the moment. One ('multiverse') involves the concept of an infinite variety of universes, each with different laws of physics, or at least with different fundamental constants, primarily to explain why we appear to live in a universe ideally suited to life. This view is also used to get over the fact that the fundamental constants of nature are not predicted by our theories, and so must be taken as given. We will consider the associated *anthropic principle* in Chapter 12 (Conclusions).

The other invocation is known as the 'many-worlds interpretation' (MWI) of *quantum mechanics*. It was originally proposed by American physicist Hugh Everett in 1957 in order to remove the concept of probability that plagues *quantum mechanics*. It treats all possible alternate outcomes as real and representing distinct universes. At each event where different outcomes are possible, it claims that they all occur and so reality is effectively forking at all such events. In other words, everything that could have happened or may happen is represented by a distinct 'world', and every event is a branching point. We will deal with these probabilities in *quantum mechanics* using a different scheme in §7.6.

Note that the MWI 'worlds' must be causally linked whereas the plain 'multiverses' are causally disjoint. However, in the model of *eternal inflation* (or 'chaotic inflation'), causally linked bubble-like worlds are forever appearing, and undergoing exponential inflation, due to random events of unknown cause or mechanism.

Unfortunately, 'multiverses' and MWI must involve an infinite number of realities in order to encompass the required variations of all possible parameters.

Although we will later posit that infinity has no physical application, at the very least these ideas encumber physics with complexity instead of simplicity. They are also untestable, and so not falsifiable, as all outcomes are equally possible, somehow, somewhere.

The (usually science fiction) notion that we are in some type of computer simulation, as in the *Matrix* films, falls into this same category as it replaces a manageable number of unknowns with a multitude of further questions and arbitrary inventions. Theories normally try to explain observations with the simplest of schemes, and with the minimum number of independent notions. Introducing an infinite number of degrees of freedom can be used to explain anything, but none of these ideas are falsifiable, meaning that we can never disprove them. Remember that in physics we can only disprove stuff, not prove anything beyond doubt, and so that route is a fundamental requirement. In effect, these ideas are either mathematical devices that simply tie off our loose ends, or an avoidance of the fundamentally unknowable (more on this in Chapter 12).

But let us return to the description of Existence, as presented above, since we need to emphasise how hard it is to grasp the repercussions. Information, as the term is being used here, is a representation of something (physical or otherwise) that relies upon the inherent distinctness and addressability of some recording medium. This could be digital data, analogue recordings, our memory, symbols on a written page, or even spoken words, but the semantic nature of that information is only evident to a conscious observer of it, and it can only be described as knowledge when it relates to a context familiar to that observer. The *block universe* embraces objective time as a static component, but the notion of consciousness is tied to a flowing subjective time, and so consciousness (as we know it) cannot exist outside of the *block universe*. Moreover, this means that all things — including semantic information and knowledge — are part of Existence, and so to ask any question of what else there might be is necessarily without meaning.

The static nature of the *block universe* has eliminated virtually all bases for our metaphysical questions. Not only can there be no creation event, or destruction event, there can be no conscious agency exhibiting what we know of as rationale or free will because that would require our flowing subjective time to be a fundamental component outside of the *block universe*. If we found evidence of extra dimensions (which we have not) then we would argue that they are part of this *block universe* rather than some container for multiple four-dimensional universes because the difference would be unknowable. Whatever reality means at that level, we are incapable of asking meaningful questions about it, and we have to take our accessible part of it (Fig. 5-1) as given.

Since Existence is a unitary concept, this can be extrapolated to define the binary concept of 'is' and 'is not'. We will argue in §10.2 that this binary concept forms the basis of Boolean logic and hence of our mathematical apparatus. In the final part of our Conclusions (chapter 12), we will consider the issue of what it means for something to exist, given that the concept of being *real* depends upon the scale between objective and subjective, by looking at Existence as a 4+(1) dimensional concept.

5.4   Nature of Measurement

We take the process of measurement for granted as it not only underpins all of science but also our everyday lives. We expect to be able to make reproducible measurements and observations that would be agreed upon by another observer. By including the term 'observation' then we have implicitly extended the process to include other species, or other conscious entities, and this is important because our subjective realities largely coincide. We will exclude inanimate measuring apparatus because, as explained earlier, they merely exhibit a static correlation between observed events and some recording medium; it is our later subjective interpretation of that medium that is the real measurement.

Observation and measurement differ in a qualitative versus quantitative way, but are not fundamentally different. They provide the link between the objective reality and our subjective realities, but to what extent? We can only measure real-valued quantities, whereas mathematical physics suggests that the objective reality requires *complex numbers* and other mathematical structures in order to model it successfully. We supplement our measurements with probabilities to cater for instances where we have insufficient information to yield a fully deterministic outcome, but probabilities have no place in a *block universe*. So we have some fundamental questions: what does measurement really mean in a *block universe*, and do our results represent fundamental properties of the objective reality?

By way of analogy, if we were looking at dynamical silhouettes on a screen then we could make measurements of their shape, size, and movement, but to what extent would those measurements relate to the hidden entities making those silhouettes? We will come back to this subject when we discuss the quantum reality in Chapter 7.

This is a particularly deep philosophical subject because it requires us to divest of almost everything from our world of experience in order to understand it. Obviously, all measurement must eventually involve our sensory inputs, but we must note the difference between a numerically based measurement and an empirical estimate. We might gauge the sound of something to be louder than something else, but that is entirely subjective (based directly on a stimulation of the senses) rather than a measured value of something external to us.

We can broadly categorise our measurements as follows:

- *Countable*: This is arguably the most difficult of the categories to appreciate, and yet the most basic. Countability requires items (objects or events) to be distinct in space-time. For example, we can count physical objects (whether they are similar or not) if they have distinct locations, and we can count events if they occur at distinct times (§2.1).[49] It is tempting to say that this also applies to the mind since we can count by marking time, or imagine a number of items in the same image, but we will cover that in Chapter 6. The difficult aspect of this category is in accepting that counting is not a fundamental process. In §10.2, we will explain how our *natural numbers* (0, 1, 2, 3, ...) are defined symbolically, and that our application of these notions effectively classifies a system according to its elements of distinctness. In other words, we are now stripping this right back to look at the essence of what we are doing in the absence of our conscious intervention. Note also the difference between a calculated count and a measured count: we can roughly calculate the number of atoms in an object, but we do not count them directly.
- *Comparative*: This is where we measure by direct comparison with something of the same type. Maybe surprisingly, this only really applies to extents in space and time, where we use some form of measuring rod or clock to gauge similar extents elsewhere. By implication, this also includes motion since that is just an extent in space-time (i.e. x-by-t rather than just x-by-y), but it does not include, say, masses.

- *Causal:* This is the largest of the categories, and includes all situations where we infer the value of some notional quantity by measuring the effects, or resulting artefacts, of an associated causation. For instance, if two balls collide then we can relate the mass of one to the mass of the other by measuring how they bounce off each other. We would not be directly comparing their masses, but we would be applying our laws of physics to model what we deem to be the causation. Consider the motion of a mass in a gravitational field, or the motion of a charged particle in an electric field; by measuring the resultant path then we can infer the quantity of mass or charge. When we weigh something, we are actually measuring the force of gravitational attraction on a mass (by looking at some change in a spring, or position of a balance) but since the force is the same for all objects of the same mass (at the same altitude) then we simplify things by using the same units: we use the units of mass (kg) as a measure of that weight force.

Of these categories, only the first two are direct, and they both relate to aspects of space and time. The causal category requires our laws of physics to relate notional quantities (usually one at a time as there will be dependencies, such as an acceleration depending upon both the mass and applied force) to some extent of space-time (e.g. to a movement, displacement, or duration).

This is a subtle point, but consider an object's mass; we can point to the object and say that we have measured its mass to be m, but we cannot point to the mass itself. Quantities such as mass, force, energy, etc., are not directly accessible to us in the manner that space and time are. We infer their existence because we can correlate their presence with consistent observations. But what about, say, the brightness of some light source, or the loudness of some sound source, or the temperature of a surface? Well, we have already noted that our empirical assessment of these is based upon direct stimulation of the senses, and so is entirely subjective. In order to obtain an objective numerical assessment then we would need a mechanism to create a change that is directly observable in space-time.

Again, we emphasise that the apparatus itself (e.g. a thermometer) does not actually make a measurement, just as the recording devices mentioned in Chapter 4 do not record sequentially. In a *block universe*, that aspect of space-time (e.g. the rising of the mercury level) is statically correlated over a period of time with some so-called causation (e.g. the state of the atoms and molecules in the object under test influencing those in the bulb of the thermometer). It is only when a conscious entity, such as ourselves, interprets that correlation that the 'measurement', or numerical assessment, is made.

But what about when we measure probability? Well, we do not actually measure probability; we calculate it. We may measure different outcomes from some repeatable event, but the relative frequency of the outcomes is not a physical quantity that can be truly measured. This will be examined in more depth in §10.3.

The role of consciousness in this process should not be taken the wrong way — it does not change the system being observed. However, that assessment that we term measurement is part of a conscious awareness, and that means that a system must come into contact with such entities, and hence with the macroscopic world, for measurement to be meaningful. So are we really saying that no measurement apparatus actually makes a 'measurement' in a *block universe*? Yes, the movement of the dials or needles, the displacements of fluids, the generation of electrical impulses, or the reaction of detector screens, are all protracted 'events' that are statically correlated with what we deem to be a cause. There is no objective movement or dynamical change.

Even if we had some computer, or robot, taking a particular reading and recording it on a piece of paper for us, it is no different; it is not until we assimilate that value in the context of our apparatus that it constitutes a measurement of something that occurred (or existed) at a particular instant. We can look at this a different way to appreciate the circularity involved: our laws of physics involve relations between measurable quantities, and our measurement operation is utilising those laws to interpret a predictable correlation between some cause and an effect. And our interpretation, and general thought processes, are similarly correlated with the *block universe* (Chapters 6 and 9), which is a roundabout way of saying that measurement is specific to our subjective reality, and has no meaning in the absence of conscious entities.

At the subatomic level, virtually all distinctness vanishes, and the idea that we can directly count or observe individual elementary particles is wrong. We need them eventually to interact with the macroscopic environment, such as the measuring apparatus or a cloud chamber, at which point we can then measure properties through the knock-on effects within space-time (see Fig. 4-1). But we have no way of knowing whether those measured properties are fundamental, or merely the only ones available to us in our subjective realities. Worse still, we are not sure how relevant space and time are at that level. Although we are assuming, here, that the objective reality is dimensional (i.e. a *block universe*), and we will examine the consequences for *quantum mechanics* in §7.6, it may be the case that space and time are emergent rather than fundamental (§11.5).

Assuming the objective reality to be just a deterministic pattern (meaning that the time evolution could be modelled precisely from an arbitrary point) of possibly complex-valued data, then the real-valued properties that we are capable of measuring may just be scratching at its surface and not describing real states. Furthermore, when looking at measurement within our subjective reality, it has been shown that there is a limit to the predictability of complex 'chaotic' systems (e.g. the weather) when based upon a finite number of property measurements, no matter how accurate they are.[50] Complexity and 'hidden variables' are both reasons why we resort to probabilities in real life, and we will revisit the 'hidden variables' concept in §7.5. When those real values are predictable within the bounds of some probability distribution then they achieve one of the two goals of physics identified in §1.3, but by themselves they do not afford any deeper understanding (the second goal).

Mathematically, these 'observables' are represented in *quantum mechanics* by something called *Hermitian operators* because they have the property that their *eigenvalues* are real. By itself, though, this does not explain why they should be real-valued when quantum states (which are what those operators act on) should be complex-valued. For reasons that are uncertain, the direct measurements that we make of changes and differences within space-time are real-valued, and this must then dictate that our inferred 'causal' measurements are also real-valued. An interesting point is that real-valued quantities are comparable in a linear sense (i.e. they can be ordered on a one-dimensional scale) whereas complex-valued quantities cannot. This must be related to our perceptions of space and time, but the fundamental nature of the relation is unclear.

The case being made in this section is primarily that the only quantities that are directly measurable are extents in space-time, and that countability is a classification of distinctness within a space-time frame. All other quantities are derived from the observation and measurement of changes within space-time (e.g. durations, displacements, and changes of position or velocity) combined with our bookkeeping that endeavours to make a predictable pattern from those observations.

5.5   Mass-energy

Understanding the nature of measurement is subtly important because we are often led astray by our mathematics, and into forgetting what we have measured and what we have inferred from the mathematics.

Classical mechanics described the behaviour of dynamical systems in terms of equations of motion involving mass, energy, momentum, and forces. These were later improved upon using variational principles with an attribute known as 'action' (see also §7.3), called the *principle of least action* (more accurately called the *principle of stationary action*), showing that the equations of motion simply describe the paths for which this 'action' is a minimum. *Noether's theorem* (§8) states that smooth symmetries in our laws of physics (actually, in the *Lagrangian* used to calculate the 'action') naturally lead to quantities that are conserved, such as energy and momentum, but it does not mandate these notions itself; they were already employed in the derivation of 'action'.

So let us just consider energy for a moment because the majority of people probably think of it as some type of 'substance' that flows from one place to another, rather than just some bookkeeping that helps explain observed movement. Kinetic energy (the energy of movement) depends upon the relative speed of two objects, and so it is not an absolute property of either one of them (see *special relativity* in §2.2), but — surprise, surprise — neither is potential energy. It is only possible to calculate potential energy in connection with two relative locations; it does not make sense to say that it is some absolute property possessed by an object, or that it is somehow stored up by it.

Mathematically, its calculation requires integration between two points, which also yields an arbitrary constant of integration. For instance, the (Newtonian) gravitational potential energy for two masses, separated by a distance r, is given by $-GMm/r + constant$, and the constant can be chosen arbitrarily to fix a zero value at some preferred location. In everyday life, the zero value would be at the Earth's surface, but for large-scale problems then it is fixed at infinity so that there is no potential energy for two objects separated by an infinite distance. This makes sense, but it then yields a negative value for potential energies at finite distances. Everything works, mathematically speaking, but it does emphasise that the potential energy is not really a physical 'stuff' possessed by an object.

So what is potential energy? We are so used to the classical teaching that we rarely ask whether it is a fiction or a representation of something real. It is often described as a form of energy held by virtue of the proximity of one object relative to another, which could be on a macroscopic level, such as something held above the ground, or on a much smaller scale, such as the molecules of a material under stress. Specific examples include gravitational, chemical, electrostatic, elastic, and nuclear.

This definition is all well and good if one object 'knows' of its neighbours. In fact, with one exception, these examples are all about forces, and the energy required to resist the natural tendency under the action of some force. Removing that resistance allows the natural paths to be taken, with some of the potential energy being replaced by kinetic energy. The exception occurs in thermodynamics: the tendency for things to even out (i.e. the *second law of thermodynamics*) is effectively a potential that could be used to do work, as when heat flows from one place to a colder place, and is referred to as an 'entropic force'. But, as explained in Chapter 3, this is quite different in not being related to the fundamental forces, or even to physical processes at all, as it is a consequence of mathematics alone.

Note that in Newtonian mechanics, the calculation of the gravitational potential energy yields an infinite value when the separation of the objects goes to zero. The equation clearly breaks down, but it is still possible to calculate the intrinsic potential energy associated with a single spherical mass of radius R and uniform density by dividing the problem into infinitesimal shells and integrating over them, yielding $-3GM^2/5R$. This is possible because the innermost shell (at $R = 0$) has no mass.

The notion that a single mass may have a negative potential energy is important because it is taken to imply a small mass deficit due to the famous $E = mc^2$. It must be remembered, though, that two attracting objects are gaining kinetic energy at the expense of their potential energy, and so the total of the two is mostly the same. That is, until they collide, at which point their kinetic energy is changed to some internal energy, such as heat, or radiated away resulting in a genuine deficit. The energy required to disassemble that pair of objects, or all the shells of that single spherical mass, away to an infinite separation is termed the *binding energy*.

The subject of potential energy gets a little tricky in the field of *general relativity*. Einstein's equations have a representation of energy and momentum on one side (and including internal potential energies, such as stress), and a representation of space-time geometry on the other side (§11.1), but the gravitational potential energy is there by virtue of relative positions and so is implied by the geometry term. Furthermore, that energy (negative as it may be) is equivalent to mass and so must be considered as part of the total mass contribution of the system. Not only does this make those equations horribly complicated and non-linear, it also makes it hard to interpret the law of conservation of energy in *general relativity*.

We will consider the subject of energy in a *block universe* in a moment, but it is worth noting one further point here. It has been suggested that the total gravitational potential energy of a mass by virtue of the rest of the universe may balance its rest energy, $m_0 c^2$, and hence that the total energy in the universe amounts to zero. This was noted by German theoretical and mathematical physicist Ernst Pascual Jordan in the 1940s, and then by American theoretical physicist Richard P. Feynman in the 1960s,[51] but it was American physicist Edward P. Tryon who, in the 1970s, proposed that the whole universe could have sprung originally from a *quantum fluctuation* without violating the conservation of energy,[52] thereby setting the scene for later theories of *cosmic inflation*.

So we are basically saying here that all measured quantities are related, in some way, to spatial and/or temporal displacements, and even that countability is the result of entities being distinct in space-time. By implication, the fact that all measurable quantities are real-valued must be related to our ability to measure differences in space and time, which are similarly real-valued. Without any violation of *Noether's theorem*, energy — the driving factor in all change — can be viewed as the capacity to effect a relative change of movement or position. But there is no real movement in a *block universe* and so both kinetic and potential energies must be determined by the relative orientation of two world-lines and the nature of the fundamental forces of nature. For instance, two world-lines inclined relative to each other would be deemed to have a corresponding symmetrical kinetic energy relative to each other, and when the inclination is non-linear then we introduce the concept of force to account for it.

Yet what about when we convert mass into energy? Well, this is a misconception of Einstein's equation, which merely indicates an equivalence between mass and energy, and not that they are the same 'stuff' in different forms. Einstein was initially a little vague on this subject. Having demonstrated that the increase in kinetic energy of a moving object is equivalent to an increased mass, in 1905 he wrote "The mass of a body is a measure of its energy-content …",[53] but in 1907 he wrote "The principle of relativity, in combination with Maxwell's equations, leads to the conclusion that the inertia of a body increases or decreases with its energy content in a completely determined way".[54] The more enlightened interpretation is of energy affecting the inertia of an object, and hence that the inertial mass of an object is measured to be greater when moving relative to an observer, and in proportion to its increased kinetic energy (see Appendix A).

Interestingly, if we assume the earlier conjecture, that the rest energy of an object is equivalent to its total potential energy with respect to the rest of the universe, and that this energy increases the inertia, then the rest mass of the object might then be attributed to the contents of the rest of the universe, as per 'Mach's principle' (§11.5).

Whatever the true nature of energy, it is a conserved quantity; unlike mass which is simply a measure of the inertia of an object (the law of conservation of mass only really applies in classical mechanics). But a common view is still that mass is solid, and hence tangible, and that some small part of it is converted to energy in, say, nuclear processes. The solidity in this view is actually of matter rather than mass: a conglomerate of particles, atoms, and molecules that, because of structure resulting from forces between these units, occupies volume, and is resistant to something else composed of matter (such as ourselves) occupying the same volume.[55]

So, considering the two main types of energy, kinetic energy is associated with motion, and is related to the relative orientation of world-lines in a *block universe*, while potential energy is associated position, and is related to the proximity of non-linear world-lines (i.e. ones we deem to be in the presence of a fundamental force). Since both are relative then energy cannot be some absolute property, or substance, that flows around, but our bookkeeping shows very accurately that it is a conserved quantity. Having suggested, above, that energy is the driving factor in all observed change, then in a *block universe* it must be related to the static change of the world-lines (viewed as a pattern) relative to the time dimension (i.e. to changes of their direction or curvature) rather than to any capacity or potential for change as there would be no dynamical change.

But what about photons or electromagnetic waves? Well, there is another type of 'motion' associated with particles that demonstrate wave-like characteristics, and Fig. 7-4 will later depict this as a helical rotation in a complex plane, giving rise to an associated frequency and phase (both of which are also relative), and hence an energy.

A more accurate definition of energy in a *block universe* would therefore be a measure of the static change, and not the source of any dynamical change.

— 6 —

The Mind

How are our thoughts, perceptions, and even emotions,
relevant to a description or interpretation of reality?

In this empirical analysis of brain and mind, we will try and avoid making the arguments specific to human beings. Notwithstanding the possibility of there being conscious species elsewhere in the universe, we certainly have other such species here. We are not as different from those other species as some people might like to believe, and the obvious differences are more a matter of degree of development than of fundamentally different faculties.

It would be a wasteful exercise to ponder, for instance, in the face of clear evidence, whether we really share capabilities of qualia, emotion, and spatio-temporal awareness. We have the capability of language and problem-solving, but then so do some other species, albeit not in written or symbolic form. Even artistic creativeness may be demonstrated in the complexity of birdsong.[56] The specific case of abstract thought is difficult to define. It may be taken as the abstraction process where we generalise things according to type rather than to specific instances, or the abstract representation of concrete concepts, or even thought that is completely disassociated from the objects and perceptions of our subjective reality; but we have no reason to suppose that a fundamental difference in make-up prevents other species from attaining the same.

The mind, as distinct from the physical brain, is a set of *cognitive faculties* usually deemed to include at least memory, imagination, reasoning, sensory perception, emotion, and induction. These are functional elements, derived from an empirical study of *cognition*: the process of gathering knowledge and understanding through thought, experience, and the senses. Although local areas of the physical brain seem to be more specialised in the support of different faculties, the faculties themselves cannot be associated with precise or unique areas of the brain. This is an important point that we will expand upon later.

The relevance of the faculties to the physical world, and hence to physics, is still debated because of their ethereal non-material nature. It is staggering to think that their very existence has been debated because they have no direct physical manifestation, implying that anything in the mind is just imaginary and unreal, or possibly even that anything which is not a direct consequence of matter and forces is tantamount to being supernatural. Note that the common word *immaterial*, which is distinct from non-material, is synonymous with irrelevance, unimportance, and being of no consequence.

Possibly the most common viewpoint is that of *methodological reductionism*: the belief that everything in the universe can be understood by taking it apart and studying its components. Although a complex system might exhibit emergent behaviours, they would accordingly be dependent upon the properties and behaviours of those components. With this viewpoint, the mind is simply a consequence of neural signals and pathways, and it can be fully understood in terms of those physical components — plus substantial amounts of hand waving, smoke, and mirrors. The problem is that a non-physical phenomenon can only be deconstructed into other non-physical parts; there is no way to go from non-physical to physical, and so to suggest that taking apart the brain somehow explains the mind is a huge presumption, and not a direct application of *reductionism*. We will argue that the mind not only exists, and has non-physical structure (the faculties), but that it plays a critical role in our relationship with the universe. As we shall see, the cognitive faculties and mental states can have physical consequences, and so to ignore them would yield a very skewed and naïve understanding.

Consciousness is sometimes equated with the mind itself, and sometimes considered to be another cognitive faculty, but there is no accepted definition of what it is, and no agreed explanation for how it arises. Consciousness is really an overall state of mind — different from being unconscious, delirious, or dreaming — that is considered to be alert, aware, and active. In what follows, we will often refer to the conscious mind, acknowledging that consciousness is a phenomenon exhibited by the mind in its normal active state.

The dictionary defines a phenomenon (as used in this context) as a fact or situation that is observed to exist or happen, and more specifically in a philosophical context as an object of our perception. But a more generally accepted definition in the world of philosophy would be an object of our conscious experience, and this small difference is noted here since we are aware of non-physical aspects of our reality (e.g. emotions) without them being directly observable. Accepting this generalisation avoids potential ambiguity over the nature of observation or perception, and this is important when analysing certain well-known philosophical arguments against *physicalism* that involve 'phenomenal knowledge' or 'phenomenal concepts'.

The knowledge argument claims that we can learn of "non-physical truths", such experiencing colours for the first time, and these cannot be deduced from "physical truths" such as a detailed knowledge about colours; hence physicalism must be false. The conceivability argument is similar but involving novel objects of our conception, such as "zombies", for which we have no evidence but they are "metaphysically possible"; hence physicalism must be false. Neither argument is supported here because they conflate things that we are attempting to differentiate, and *vice versa*. For instance, all knowledge is subjective, and it is either based on inferences from our collective experience (phenomenal) or entirely of mental creation. It can be argued, therefore, that "physical concepts/knowledge" do not exist.[57]

We will explain in this chapter that our conscious sensations, such as colour or touch, truly exist, but as products of the mind. Through our combined sensations then we intuit a structured environment. We can imagine examples of that environment that we have not encountered, and fanciful variations that we can never encounter, but both cases truly exist as products of the mind. We have no way of learning of our environment through any other source, and so to suggest that there are distinct "physical truths" that have some direct connection with the real world is creating a false category. To differentiate between our experience of light from an object as colours and our experience of its other properties — including a spatial extent resistant to pressure, a tactile shape and texture, and a surface temperature — is just wrong. In other words, there is no "epistemic gap" between factual knowledge of the physical and non-physical. There is an argument that such an "epistemic gap" could lead to a "metaphysical gap" that separates the physical reality from the phenomenal reality,[58] and although this is closer to our argument, we do not mandate that same dependency.

Our stance, here, is that there are different types of reality: the underlying objective reality (to which we have no direct access), the mental states and its creations, and our perceived subjective reality (Fig. 5-1). We can conceive all manner of things — including gods, ghosts, and honest politicians — but our subjective reality is a special case: an image of our environment, based upon our sensory input, including a spatio-temporal structure and the rules by which it appears to evolve. Note that we have equated the physical world with a part of our subjective reality rather than the objective reality, and this makes a comparison with these arguments difficult. Also, the arguments are almost entirely anthropocentric and make little attempt at an end-to-end description or a generalisation to other conscious entities. It is not that they are totally incorrect, but in a fashion somewhat typical of philosophical arguments, they craft and refine their ontologies while rarely providing the necessary scientific connection.

The view that everything is physical, and that there is nothing beyond the physical, is known (unsurprisingly) as *physicalism*. The term *materialism* is usually taken as synonymous with this, though given our distinction between the physical world and the material world (Fig. 5-1) it means that we are interpreting them differently here. In the field of consciousness, these contrast with another view, *functionalism*, where these faculties are simply defined by their functional roles and relations to other faculties. But this slightly linear view is not unlike that of software programming, where the functionality of a program can be deconstructed into the interactions of individual elements of the programming language, or even to instructions in some machine code. A more enlightened view, known as *emergent materialism*, asserts that the conscious mind is a product of the material brain, and it cannot exist without this material basis, but it emerges through the collective interactions of the whole rather than its discrete physical parts. In other words, that it is an irreducible existent phenomenon that cannot be studied solely through the physical structure of the brain.

We have to ask ourselves, here, why something that is tangible, or can be correlated with the state of some measurement apparatus, is any more 'real' than something that cannot? The physical world is identified with an aspect of our subjective reality in Fig. 5-1, and although this might appear closer to the objective reality than the mind, this does not mean that it is, itself, fundamental. More importantly, it cannot, alone, form a complete and coherent description of our subjective reality and requires a consideration of such non-physical phenomena. The view that everything that is real is made of 'stuff' (i.e. *physicalism*) stems from our perception of real-world tangibles, and yet we must not forget that we have many scientifically-accepted intangible and non-material precedents such as space-time (Chapter 11), energy (§5.5), entropy (Chapter 3), and semantic information. Even though some of these are of mathematical origin, we have little difficulty in accepting them as real. All the arguments for *physicalism* presume that our physical world is fundamental, and that there is little (if any) difference between our subjective reality and the objective reality.

Emergent properties or behaviours arise through the collective interactions of the parts in a greater or more complex whole, and the recognition of such incommensurable layering is important in many fields, including physics. If you are not familiar with the notion of emergent properties or behaviours then a good example to consider is *society*: the collective interactions of a population. It is a level of reality that cannot be reduced to the specific mechanical, chemical, or biological processes on which it relies, or even to the specific mental states of the individual people, and yet it exists. To some, this is the only reality; not that of nature, the planets and stars, the universe, or anything else that is independent of us and that will hopefully outlive us, but only their day-to-day existence.

Maybe an easier example to visualise — specifically an emergent behaviour — is the flight of a large flock (say thousands) of birds. As a group, they can exhibit incredible formation patterns of swooping, twirling, twisting, folding, and unfolding, yet no single bird is the leader, those patterns are not in the mind of any bird, and no solo bird would fly in the same way; the behaviour emerges from complex interactions between them.

In the case of the mind, we are saying that its faculties and the way they work together cannot be analysed in terms of the underlying physical and chemical processes. Putting it another way, if you could devise a microscope that could see the individual atoms and molecules in the brain then you still would not see consciousness. Or, putting it less clinically, you could dissect a body all you like, but you would never find the *person*.

Let us provide a little more detail on the subject of emergence as it is so important to our argument. It might be described as a large-scale object exhibiting measurable properties or observable behaviours that are not evident in its small-scale constituents. A commonly cited definition is that by American economist Jeffrey A. Goldstein in 1999: "Emergence ... refers to the arising of novel and coherent structures, patterns, and properties during the process of self-organization in complex systems".[59] For our purposes, we will consider emergent properties (e.g. temperature), behaviours (e.g. weather systems), and structures (e.g. crystals). These are all considered examples of 'weak emergence': emergent phenomena that can, theoretically, be simulated using a computer, but which cannot be derived through reductionist analysis. These phenomena would all disappear well before we could probe down to the atomic or molecular level, and yet we can understand how they arise. In this form of emergence, the interconnected components retain their independence, and any causal influence of the emergent phenomenon can be attributed to the collective properties of its many components. 'Strong emergence' is a more holistic outcome where the whole may be considered more than the parts, and where any causal influence cannot be reduced to those component properties. It is said that such emergence cannot, therefore, be simulated, but this would be a hard (and not especially relevant) claim to support.

The difference is that the phenomena of 'weak emergence' are manifest in the physical world, thus allowing that reductionist connection to be made, whereas those of 'strong emergence' are non-physical. Neither a conscious thought nor an emotional feeling can be described in physical terms, and yet they exist in our subjective reality.

'Strong emergence' is a controversial subject because its irreducible causal influences would seem to come from nowhere. As American philosopher Mark A. Bedau put it: "Although strong emergence is logically possible, it is uncomfortably like magic. How does an irreducible but supervenient downward causal power arise, since by definition it cannot be due to the aggregation of the micro-level potentialities? Such causal powers would be quite unlike anything within our scientific ken."[60] Well, the case to be made here is that the conscious mind is an emergent causally linked entity, with both it and its constituent properties and behaviours being non-physical, and hence beyond direct measurement or observation. We must hasten to add that this is not a supernatural stance, but simply a way of thinking when the unique fundamentality of the physical world has been abandoned, and everything (physical or non-physical) is considered to be variations in the pattern of the objective reality.

Drawing analogies between the brain and our current generation of computers is entirely unhelpful in understanding the mind or the brain. They cannot be pictured as a CPU (central processing unit) connected to passive modules such as memory or device interfaces by some interconnecting bus, but we will revisit this criticism in §9.1.

Before we attempt to understand the structure of the mind and the nature of consciousness, let us first differentiate consciousness from sentience: the capacity to feel, perceive, or experience subjectively; or the capacity to feel as distinct from to think. An inherent part of feeling is the concept of qualia, which we have deduced to include subjective time, but we have also suggested that consciousness and subjective time are strongly tied together. So does this mean that all sentient life (here or elsewhere) is necessarily conscious? Not all sets of qualia are guaranteed to rely upon a subjective time, thus there may be cases of sentience that do not qualify as conscious. In order to leave this possibility open, we will focus upon the specific term consciousness rather than sentience in this chapter.

6.1   Qualia and Emotions

Qualia (singular: quale, pronounced 'qualee') are instances of subjective conscious sensation. These are qualities or properties as perceived or experienced by a person, or really by any conscious mind, which include the interpretations of sensory input, such as colour, sound, or sensation. They tend to be ignored by physics because they are not part of the measurable world, yet they obviously play an important part in our understanding of reality.

Before we substantiate this, let us pose a straightforward question: 'how would you describe the colour red to someone who has been blind since birth?' You cannot describe it as the colour of fire, or of anger, as they presuppose that we have a common frame of reference. Even when describing it to another sighted person, we would have no way of knowing that we perceive red in the same way as them (even if neither is colour-blind), and to ponder whether 'they might see red as green' would be completely missing the point: there is no way of relating the perceptions of one person to another.

At the physical level, we may all see the same wavelengths of light, or hear the same wavelengths of sound, but it is the mind's interpretation of those inputs that we cannot compare; it is in the mind that colour and music exist as distinct from light or sound, and not quite in the eye or ear of the beholder. This is important because what we remember is this assimilation of the sensory inputs, not the inputs themselves. For instance, when we recall the taste of a particular food, or something unpleasant such as an injury, then the recollection is never quite the same as the original experience, and rarely triggers the same response in our system. So the mind must be structured to remember and manipulate only those digested forms of the sensory inputs: the qualia.

With mental images, whether dynamic (as in sequences of events) or static (as in an object or scene), again the recollection is never quite the same as the original experience. Even with a very good memory, the recollection (also known as the mind's eye) is not only less faithful but 'feels different'. Many of us are guilty of assuming that our memories of such imagery are not unlike those of an analogue camera or video recorder, and this is reinforced by science fiction films suggesting that electronics can tap into those memories to reconstruct images, both before and after someone's death. High-functioning *eidetic memory* has been observed in some children, but a genuine 'photographic memory' is held to be a myth. It is unclear quite how we assimilate visual images into our memory, though it seems better attuned to recognition of shapes and events — or, more specifically, to the incremental differences over small spans of space or time — than to internal image reconstruction.

Note, for instance, that even when confronted with a static image, we have limited capacity to take it all in at once. We typically scrutinise each section and assimilate the changes between it and its neighbouring sections. We can recall all those details but we never really conjure up some photographic equivalent of what we saw.

As another example of a quale, consider our subjective time. Objective time is just another dimension of the *block universe*, but our subjective experience is of a flowing time with a focus that we call '*now*'. We do not experience each moment in isolation, we do not experience moments in the reverse order, and we do not experience them as a block. Somehow, our sensory data is processed instant-by-instant, rather than as a solid block of instants, and we will refer to this as our temporal sense. This, in turn, allows us to become aware of differences, or changes, from one moment to the next. Although we can recall different sequences of events (e.g. eating a meal, or driving down a road) in any order we like, we still recall the moments of each sequence in the order that we experienced them; they are still recalled sequentially and in that the same order. What is particularly interesting is that there is no specific '*now*' moment in our recollections of events. What we remember is clearly digested from our experience, but the recollection of those memories is not faithful to that experience.

Not only does this conundrum of being unable to measure or compare internalised states apply to qualia, it applies to emotions such as anger, elation, arousal, sadness, amusement, embarrassment, sympathy, boredom, confusion, interest, and pride. Although we can distinguish broad categories of emotion, we cannot directly compare them as they exist only within each mind. In fact, there is a very close relationship between qualia and emotions such that no strict differentiation is available, although a working distinction is that qualia are directly related to sensory inputs.

Australian philosopher and cognitive scientist David J. Chalmers is well-known for differentiating the "easy" problems of consciousness — the cognitive aspects — from the one "hard" problem — that of phenomenal experience.[61] Basically, why do we feel things at all? Although Chalmers tries to avoid the specific term qualia, he does refer to both sensation and emotion, concepts sometimes collectively described elsewhere as qualia. Our differentiation of qualia from emotions is important because emotions appear to be more a form of subjective assessment — of qualia, recollections, or mental states — than of instances of direct sensation. We will therefore continue by using the term emotion in the more general context of subjective qualitative assessment, such that even expressing a personal preference may be considered an emotion rather than a logical selection. In other words, we are endowed with the capability for various situations — ranging from some simple combination of colours to a complex sequence of events in our lives, or even a thought — to trigger an emotional response. This capability offers many categories of response, as mentioned above, as well as different intensities (we can feel elation, pain, sadness, etc., to different degrees), and their usage as a form of subjective assessment offers an explanation for why we have emotions at all.

Our environments are hugely complex, not just with physical elements but with emergent non-physical ones too (e.g. society), and so no rational analysis of a situation, or any unambiguous decision of what to do next, can be made from the senses alone. There is therefore an evolutionary advantage to any species that has a different form of assessment: a subjective one that does not have to be logical, or even contribute directly to its personal survival. It is a natural step from there to argue that the development of the emotional faculty is an evolutionary step in all conscious species. Some assessments may be cases of simple association, such as feeling acutely uncomfortable when hearing the whine of a dentist drill, but the majority will be more complex because of the structure of our environment. Decisions based upon pure logic may be useless in our day-to-day lives, but even problem-solving in fields such as mathematics and physics may involve a creativity that cannot be reconciled with logical deduction.

So can we experience more than one emotion at the same time? The emotional faculty is probably responsible for a single amorphous state with many more variations than we have labels for, but it is certainly possible that we may attach multiple labels to any given state.

Perhaps a more noteworthy factor is that the advantage perceived by an entity (which could simply be a desire) is not quantifiable, and is not part of the measurable world. A scientist may try to quantify the advantages of different animal behaviours according to access to food and water, or procreation, but they are associated with more basal instincts. Does a cheetah in the jungle think 'There is a 30% chance I can kill something at this late hour, but a 72% chance I'll be ravenous by tomorrow morning otherwise. Oh, and I also need to impregnate as many females as I can in order to preserve my DNA'? Of course not! Its mental goals and the consequences of its behaviour are not the same thing.

We clearly have different categories of emotion, though our day-to-day terminology is less than helpful in identifying them. Take, for instance, pain: the uncomfortable (or even distressing) feeling associated with physical damage, or at least with intense physical stimulus. Although ubiquitous in sentient beings, we rarely try to differentiate the physical sensation from our assessment of it being painful, possibly because they are more closely tied than other emotional assessments of qualia. But not all physical sensations are considered painful, some that should not be painful may be so (*allodynia*), and some pain might not be associated with a specific physical cause. In fact, it is even possible to feel pain from a non-existent limb ('phantom pain'). In making a case for the sensation and the feeling being separate, note that our anaesthetics block the actual sensation (leaving an area feeling numb) rather than our assessment of it as pain. This may suggest that the condition known as *congenital analgesia*, where someone is completely insensitive to pain but still experiences sensation, is related to an impairment of the emotional faculty rather than to some abnormality of the greater nervous system. In support of this, doctors recently discovered a genetic abnormality in a 71-year-old woman, Jo Cameron, who not only was insensitive to pain but did not feel stress, anxiety, panic, or depression.[62]

There are other feelings of acute discomfort that we describe as pain, such as bereavement, even though they are quite distinct as assessments since they relate to mental states rather than to qualia. The antonym of pain is mostly given as pleasure, but as a feeling this is hugely subjective — in stark contrast to pain — as we not all find the same things pleasurable. An antonym of pleasure might be displeasure, but as a feeling this is more related to annoyance or disapproval. The point of this is that our terms are less precise than our emotional categories.

Perhaps one of the most overloaded terms is love, and so with some temerity we will attempt to dispassionately dissect its usage into different classes. Philosophical theories of love introduce many categories that are claimed to be distinct (cf. 'colour wheel theory of love'). We can all think of specific instances of the word's usage, but many of these might be better considered subdivisions. There is no limit to the number of terms that we can invent so we will start with the following broad classes:

- *Appreciation*: This class is where the term is applied to an appreciation of objects or other aspects of our environment, including food, places, art, music, activities, physical appearance, etc. This usage, which forms a matched pair with hate, is effectively a more intense version of like (and dislike).
- *Bonding*: This class is where the term describes an affinity, attachment, or affection for other conscious entities (even beyond their lifetime). There are several subdivisions possible:
  - *Pets and other animals*: It is easy to forget that this class is not specific to human interaction. We are including this entry to describe human-animal interaction on the understanding that later subdivisions will generically relate to other sentient species.
  - *Groups*: From tribal groups to countrymen, this class is for social groups associated by origin, interest, or necessity.
  - *Close Friends*: This class is for what is sometimes termed 'platonic love' (named after Plato).
  - *Family*: 'familial love' (or storge) includes the love between parent-child, siblings, and more.
  - *Spouse*: The 'romantic love' associated with a spouse (using the modern generalisation of that term) is deliberately separated from other 'familial love' as it is strongly associated with 'sexual love'.
- *Spiritual*: This class, sometimes known as 'divine love', or agape, includes instances related to gods, churches, and all things religious. It does not easily fit into the other classes and so we will leave it on its own to avoid distracting from the main argument.

On the face of it, the first two classes have a clear connection with assessment; the first allowing us to make decisions regarding our environment (what is good/bad, nice/horrible, useful/useless, wanted/not-wanted, etc.), and the second to make decisions about other conscious entities (originally for mutual benefit, survival, procreation, and so on). The combined emotions of affection ('romantic love'), sexual desire, and sexual ecstasy between couples ensure the continuation of the associated species — how could we possibly make such decisions upon purely logical or practical grounds? That the higher species require two parties is partly to ensure a mix of genes (for evolution), partly because that is how we are structured physically and genetically, and partly because requiring any higher quorum would be fraught with difficulty (except in certain areas of LA, allegedly).

This raw breakdown of the emotion of love may sound rather flat and lacklustre, and it can be retrofitted to almost any sentient species. If our own perception of it feels more intense then it may be because we are capable of appreciating more abstract concepts (the first class) and there is a greater desire for bonding between minds (the second class). It is almost as though a consequence of our minds getting increasingly distanced from our subjective reality, as a result of a greater intelligence, is that we have a greater need to reach out and evade the inevitable insularity. We will pick this up again in the next section.

We have probably digressed more than usual in this section, but the goal was to propound the view that qualia are associated with direct sensory perception, whereas emotions are a form of subjective assessment that can be applied to qualia, recollections, or our mental states as induced by more complex events. Emotions may also be activated unconsciously, leading to moods that appear to have no basis. Finally, our memory is capable of recording the qualia — but not the raw sensory inputs themselves — and also the emotions, both of which can be recalled when wanted or when necessary.

6.2   Aesthetics and Art

Let us take a moment to look at the notions of aesthetics, beauty, and art. At the heart of associated philosophical debate are questions such as 'is beauty in the eye of the beholder?', 'is beauty perceived similarly by all?', and 'does beauty exist in the absence of conscious entities?' We are here discussing beauty as an abstract assessment, in contrast to animal attraction, which is largely about perceived potency.

We can quantify symmetry, harmony, economy of form, and contrasting forms, but that is not the same as perceiving something as beautiful. Those quantifiable properties have significance external to our minds, but no aesthetic assessment can exist in the absence of individual conscious minds. So what is art, and does it have a purpose?

Although we have no way of directly communicating qualia or emotions between minds, we use the reverse process of their invocation to create a common frame of reference, and there is a valid argument for equating this with *art*. When we want to communicate a feeling or mood then we can create something in the physical world — including arrangement of shapes and colours, mixtures of notes and rhythms, and organisations of words — that is imbued with the essence of our emotions. In an idealised world, where art is not produced simply for kudos or financial gain, and is not judged simply upon academic criteria, then we might expect another person to demonstrate a sympathetic reaction to it within the same category of emotions.

In fact, this is the essence of any communication, whether written, verbal, or non-verbal. Words and symbols can communicate many things to another person, but a mere facial gesture communicates something too. The essence of comedy is as deep as it is broad, but the ultimate goal is a particular case that really makes this point: what is the point of being funny without an audience?

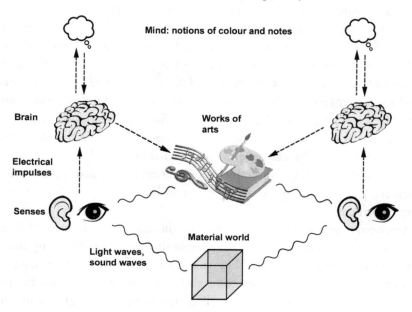

Fig. 6-1, Relating qualia and emotions between two minds.

This diagram illustrates that two brains may receive electrical impulses from the senses after receiving light or sound of the exact same frequencies, but how those minds assimilate them is not comparable. However, each person might cause something to be produced in the physical world designed to invoke the same category of emotions in another observer.

What about true-to-life sculptors and super-realist painters? This genre is much more about the skill of being able to generate a realistic article or image, and the choice of subject will be important, but there is still a compositional aspect that will involve an expression of those internal feelings. The harmony and balance in a photographer's choice of the conjunction of different forms and colours, the specific lighting, and the perspective, constitute a personal contribution over and above the actual subject matter.

And what about abstract or non-representational art, where the components would have no specific relation to real-world objects? Now this is especially interesting since the juxtaposition of different shapes, colours, and textures on a canvas is still capable of inducing an emotional response in the observer. There is a strong parallel here with musical forms that have no words, or even real-world sounds, and it suggests that we do have some innate aesthetic sense that plays a part in the general communication of emotions between us.

Again, these are important for our overall picture because they are a fundamental part of our perceptions, and so affect our subjective reality. In fact, theories in the field of fundamental physics are often judged upon a sense of beauty, and this is controversial (cf. *Lost in Math: How Beauty Leads Physics Astray* by German theoretical physicist Sabine Hossenfelder) as beauty is a subjective assessment that cannot be defined or quantified. There are arguments that this particular sense of beauty equates to some elegance of the equations (although that can depend upon the mathematical framework being applied), to the economy and simplicity of their concepts (usually achieved by introducing abstractions with that goal in mind), or to their derivation from simple postulates.

American theoretical physicist and mathematician Frank A. Wilczek (pronounced 'will-check') recently suggested that this sense of beauty might work the other way, and that "Humans do better in life if they have an accurate model of nature, if their concepts fit the way things actually behave. So evolution rewards that kind of feeling that being correct gives you, and that's the sense of beauty".[63]

6.3   Consciousness

The first problem in discussing *consciousness* is that there is no accepted definition of what it is. We all intuitively know what it is, but defining it is a much harder task. Without a definition then we have no starting point for explaining how it might emerge from the structure of the mind or brain. And so attempting to explain it within the context of a *block universe* might seem a step too far, but it is necessary in order to understand our subjective reality and so complete the picture.

Because of its mysterious and rather nebulous nature, some explanations tend to be rather fanciful, including those that employ supernatural elements, or even 'quantum mysticism'. It has frequently been equated with an awareness of one's inner self, yet although we are capable of introverted contemplation this does not occupy our full time and so is not a prerequisite for a functioning consciousness. It would also raise questions as to the balance of consciousness and self-awareness in other species. Other species also experience consciousness, and share many of the same mental faculties as ourselves, including memory, emotion, planning, and free will. Some species are certainly aware of themselves, and understand that a reflection is of themselves rather than another, but we cannot tell whether they are aware of their own thoughts. Maybe the biggest differentiator that we can demonstrate is our capacity for rational thought (logic, mathematics, etc.) and creativity (both abstract and practical).

An interesting point is that possession of consciousness cannot be a simple yes/no. Having pointed out that other species experience consciousness, we must accept that some primitive forms do not, though where is the cut-off point? It is likely that this is a grey-scale, with more primitive species sharing fewer of our faculties, or having them to a less sophisticated degree. There is a huge range of variation between an amoeba and a human, and although it is patently clear that many of the higher mammals share our mental states, emotions, and qualia (whatever some scientists might say), we may never know whether the less expressive species even have something that can be described as a mind. A simple fly is aware of heat, light, water, and chemical signals, but of thoughts? A fly trapped inside a window will move around looking for an exit. These movements may not be logical, but neither are they a direct reaction to any external stimuli; something else directs them.

What we can do, however, is to look at variations of consciousness in our own species. We already exhibit variations between having full control of our mind (*compos mentis*) and being fully unconscious. As you would expect, we have many terms for the various states that do not have precise definitions — either medically or legally — so let us start with some of the obvious ones.

- *Conscious*: Aware of the passing of time, and able to make reasonable assessments of circumstances and planning for eventualities.
- *Unconscious*: Unaware of the passing of time.
- *Comatose*: Deep state of unconsciousness from which a person cannot be awakened.
- *Dreaming*: Faculties such as memory and world-view operating without explicit control or volition, and unrelated to sensory inputs.
- *Delirious*: State of acute confusion brought about through chemical, structural, or operational changes in the brain.
- *Drunk*: Temporary intoxication through alcohol causing poor judgment as well as reduced sensory and motor capacity.
- *Dementia*: Gradual and long-term degradation in faculties such as memory and reasoning. Examples include Alzheimer's disease and vascular dementia.
- *Insanity*: Broad range of abnormal and irrational behaviours, usually associated with mental illness. Accepted as a legal defence, but so is 'settled insanity' (damage through long-term substance abuse) in some US states (and originally in England too).
- *Congenital idiocy*: Showing reduced capacity for intelligence, understanding, and reason, from birth.

Even if we ignore mental disorders, which cover a huge range including hallucinations, delusions, mood, social and relationship issues, cognition, attention and concentration, phobias, etc., and altered states, then we still have differences that are deemed to be statistically normal and more socially acceptable. These might include our different capacities for numeracy, literacy, artistic appreciation and expression, music, structural or practical application, etc. Their association with the subject of consciousness will be rare, but the point to be made here is that our consciousness is built upon our faculties with their respective differences. We function to different degrees in different aspects of our lives, and so it is inevitable that we will develop differently and adapt to our environment differently. It is well known that brain surgery is not just capable of impairment or damage to our facilities but also of profound changes to the personality of the subject. Putting things another way: we are all dissimilar, and the phenomenon of consciousness cannot be defined from a purely experiential standpoint.

If we wind back our own lives then we can appreciate that consciousness emerges over time. No one could make a case for a fertilised egg having a conscious mind, but somewhere between there and a being young child (where we can recognise aspects of consciousness in its interactions) it will have appeared gradually. We cannot, then, ask at what point it appears, but rather consider the stages of its evolution. To ask whether a newborn has a mind, let alone a conscious mind, is pointless as the question presumes that our terms are both precise and fundamental. Nature involves continuous changes over time, and so our arbitrary definition of, say, consciousness will only apply over some limited span.

For instance, a person may be living, but so would be their individual cells. If, then, a person's brain activity has ceased but the body is on life-support then what does life mean? Is death to do with cessation of breathing, heartbeat, brain activity, or the mind? We are not going to attempt to answer this because it would entail highly subjective arguments based upon terms that we (not nature) have defined. However, we will leapfrog this to try and unravel the nature of consciousness as exhibited by adults in the more developed species for it is not only important to the reality of our experience but to reality as embraced by scientific study. We have no strict definition to base this on, but it does involve identifiable traits that are shared by those species.

It is interesting to note that our perception of others is primarily of their body, but the perception of ourselves is primarily of our mind. We know that others have a mind and that we have a body, but our own consciousness is centred in the mind rather than any specific physical location. This means that objective study of the mind is difficult: introvert analysis would be entirely subjective, and there is no objective evidence to be analysed for the minds of others, except physical consequences, but these do not have a direct correspondence with physical stimuli. In essence, it is very hard to deconstruct consciousness because it is not only an emergent phenomenon but also inaccessible to us as an external phenomenon that can be directly observed or measured; we can only observe it through the faculties of our own mind.

We have already described consciousness as a world-line (Fig. 4-2), akin to a particle world-line, and used this to help us visualise it in a *block universe*; but the point about the mind having no physical location is important though likely to be misunderstood. We often assume that our mind, and hence consciousness, is centred in the brain, mainly because we think of them together and because we know that the mind cannot exist without the physical brain. But as a non-physical entity, the mind is one-dimensional: it has an extent through time but not through space. If you were in a sensory deprivation chamber, your consciousness would be fully functional but you would be unaware of any specific physical location in relation to your body or your environment. Not only would you not know where your physical body was, such an experience would emphasise that the mind has no spatial dimensions of its own and does not occupy space.

The objects of our environment are located in a three-dimensional space that we have modelled from sensory inputs. This space is defined by the separation of those objects, including from ourselves, meaning that there is no such thing as absolute positions. This is quite different from our perception of time, which is the crux of our consciousness. We perceive the conjunction of those objects as undergoing changes from one moment to another, but we cannot perceive time as any sort of external expanse; we internalise it. In other words, although time and space may be very similar in the objective reality, and treated orthogonally in mathematical physics (see Appendix A), they are perceived very differently in our subjective reality. This view is quite close to those of Immanuel Kant: "... we represent to ourselves objects as external, or outside ourselves, and all of these in space" [64] and "Time is a necessary representation on which all intuitions depend". [65]

René Descartes introduced the dictum "I think, therefore I am" (French: *je pense, donc je suis*) in his *Discourse on the Method* (1637), but a more accurate translation might be "I am thinking, therefore I exist". The famous Latin form of this (*cogito, ergo sum*) appeared some seven years later. [66] This proposition was criticised by other philosophers regarding the nature of both 'I' and 'thinking', and because it presupposed that an 'I' existed that knew what 'thinking' was. Descartes was not suggesting that 'I' existed as a material entity but rather as a thinking entity; one even capable of pondering over its own existence. Clearly, there is some circularity as a logical proposition, but as an atomic statement then it makes more sense since it implies that thought and a conscious self — it made no statement about other selves — are an intrinsic unit. But what was meant by 'thinking'? Despite our best efforts, our modern computers do not really think, and have certainly not attained any level of consciousness, but we will revisit this subject in Chapter 9.

Descartes also believed that reality was divided into two domains: the realm of extension (Latin: *res extensa*, or 'extended substance'), which plays host to our corporeal being, and the realm of thought (Latin: *res cogitans*, or 'thinking substance'), which plays host to our consciousness.[67] While this view, now called *Cartesian dualism*, did not explain what consciousness was, it did separate the conscious mind from material things, and so was in contrast to the restricted view of *physicalism*. This mind-body distinction is now widely accepted in some form or other, but his concept was more ethereal than the modern view — that consciousness is an *emergent phenomenon* — and presumed that the two were independent and could be separated. He did, however, note that certain sensations were irreducible and could not be ascribed to either one of those 'substances' alone.

> But we also experience within ourselves certain other things *which must not be referred either to the mind alone or to the body alone.* These arise ... from the close and intimate union of our mind with the body. This list includes, first, appetites like hunger and thirst; secondly, the emotions or passions of the mind which do not consist of thought alone, such as the emotions of anger, joy, sadness and love; and finally, all the sensations, such as those of pain, pleasure, light, colours, sounds, smells, tastes, heat, hardness and the other tactile qualities.[68]

Cartesian dualism suffered a strong criticism at the hands of English philosopher Gilbert Ryle in the 1940s. This was based upon what he called a 'category mistake': attempting to assign a quality or action to something that can only be assigned to things of a different category.

> Now the dogma of the Ghost in the Machine does just this [make a category mistake]. It maintains that there exist both bodies and minds; that there occur physical processes and mental processes; that there are mechanical causes of corporeal movements and mental causes of corporeal movements.[69]

He argued that it is wrong to treat the mind as something made of non-material substance because assertions made in relation to substance are not meaningful for a mere set of dispositions, and so confirmed that he viewed the mind purely in functional terms. However, he was guilty of errors of his own by implying that physical processes and mental processes were both directly responsible for the same corporeal movement rather than part of a chain, by presuming that causality was a unique and fundamental correlation, and that — as evidenced by his unfortunate use of the word 'ghost' — he could not comprehend the realism of anything non-physical.

The mind and brain are different things, but — unlike *Cartesian dualism* — are not separable, which can be expressed as the mind being supervenient[70] on the brain. A non-physical precedent that we mentioned above was semantic information. This is also non-physical, it supervenes on a physical medium, the semantics cannot be reduced to the components of that medium, and it is real only within our subjective reality. To try and liken the conscious mind to some ghostly or ethereal influence (especially in a disparaging way) does not help the argument identifying it as an emergent non-physical entity that plays a crucial part in the only reality to which we have direct access. In §6.5, we will look at how arguments involving causality, and potential conflicts over multiple causes, are ill-founded.

In order to define consciousness, we need to dissect what it entails, and what properties we associate with the notion. Each instant of consciousness corresponds to the moment we call '*now*'. In fact, these instants must define '*now*' since it has no other basis than in a conscious mind. As we have already explained, '*now*' has no representation in any of our laws of physics, and none of the associated equations make any reference to it. Fig. 4-2 illustrated the consciousness of two entities in a manner similar to one-dimensional world-lines. The state of those world-lines would clearly be related to events in the external environment, but this is not the same as there being any real temporal flow. In a *block universe*, every one of the '*now*' moments is extant, but this would seem to present an obstacle to acceptance for most people. How can all of our conscious instants exist together, and with no particular one being singled out?

Well, given that we have identified all motion as an illusion then it is not that big a step to think of a progressing consciousness as anything but an illusion. All your conscious instants of yesterday, tomorrow, and more, are equally real, but they are linked in one direction only: any given instant is only aware of conscious instances from one temporal direction, which we call the past. Consciousness, then, is just the total of all our '*now*' moments, streamed in a particular temporal direction, but streamed in what way, and why in that particular direction?

This reasoning reinforces the conclusion in Chapter 4 that subjective time, with its distinct past/future separated by '*now*', and its apparent flow, is a property of the conscious mind. But it also affords the mechanisms of consciousness itself, including reasoning, planning, imagination, etc. This might be restated as a *temporal anthropic principle* (TAP): **consciousness and subjective time cannot exist without each other; they are bound as part of the same phenomenon**.

An understanding of this apparent arrow is not obvious, and there is much room for confusion. There must be some asymmetry in the universe that allows us to remember the past and not the future, and hence to infer a sense of causality, but that will have to wait until Chapter 8.

Let us examine the main human *cognitive faculties* for which we can cite evidence. The actual division of responsibilities may well be finer grained than this but it will suffice to give us an understanding of consciousness. Note that we are not identifying consciousness as a specific faculty, but as the cooperation of all these component faculties together.

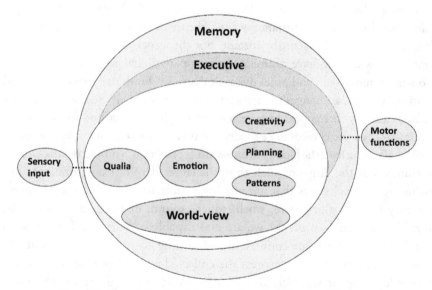

Fig. 6-2, Cognitive faculties associated with consciousness.

The lower-level faculties are normally under the control of an **executive** faculty, responsible for their coordinated access during acts of deliberation and volition. It is not always in control, as in dreams, and they each have some degree of autonomy to which the executive is responsive (e.g. an emotional change). This *unconscious activity* within the mind is different from the state of unconsciousness, and it is also different from the usage of the term by Austrian neurologist and psychoanalyst Sigmund Freud. He had proposed a *subconscious mind* that was inaccessible to consciousness, but then later adopted the term unconscious in preference to subconscious. When in control, the executive may be considered single-threaded as you cannot have two independent trains of thought at the same time, and you cannot recall different things from your memory at precisely the same time.[71] More instances of this limitation are cited in §9.1. The question of whether we actually think in our dreams will undoubtedly arise, but the images and events of those dreams are not consciously summoned, and our apparent actions within them can be considered reactive rather than wilful. In the diagram, for simplicity, we have the executive controlling motor functions, such as movement, which admittedly ignores instances of autonomic function and reflex actions.

Our sensory inputs (including the temporal sense) are assimilated in the mind as **qualia**, such as a particular wavelength of light being perceived as the colour red. In the specific instance of time, the temporal sense allows our sensory data to be processed instant-by-instant, but the associated quale — subjective time — is where we have assimilated the apparent changes from moment to moment as movement and other dynamical activity. From the predictability and continuity of these changes (as assessed by the conscious mind), we infer rules such as causality that appear to govern observed phenomena, and from these we intuit that there are choices to be made, and that we can steer our '*now*' moment.

We have described the faculty of **emotion** as providing a subjective assessment of things, but the range of such things is larger than our environment, and including internal states that are not susceptible to quantitative assessment. We may assess a given taste, smell, touch, sound, or image as pleasurable, horrible, or even painful, yet we are also capable of assessing a place, such as a house or an area of countryside, according to different aspects at the same time. How could we express the collected appreciation of some scenic beauty logically, or scientifically? We could not! We might resort to words, and especially poetry, or even music, but the fact is that these assessments are neither logical nor objective. We might feel content or happy with friends or family, or feel intense grief at the loss of a companion, or feel upset at hearing someone's words. This faculty forms an essential part of our analysis of past events, our planning of future events, and even our problem-solving.

Many scientists and mathematicians may assess some aspect of their (or other's) work as beautiful, but people of a more artistic persuasion may find that hard to comprehend, usually because they overlook the fact that it is a subjective assessment of something rather than an inherent property of the subject. All emotional assessments are complex, with many variations possible, but a fundamental question is whether the assessment of a physical theory can have any objective significance. Why should we expect the underlying patterns of the universe — the ones for which we devise theories to explain — to be in any way beautiful to us: a mere part of that total pattern?

An example of the complexity not conveyed by this diagram is 'blindsight', where someone has blindness in a good eye due to brain damage (i.e. cortically blind) rather than to eye damage. Their brain still receives sensory input from the eye but they do not perceive any image, meaning that those inputs are not being assimilated as qualia. The sensory inputs can still be used to guide their movement as the person is aware of objects and their relative speeds but unable to see or recognise them. Those same inputs may still be assimilated by other faculties such as the world-view.

The **world-view** faculty is associated with an internal model not just of the structure of our environment, but the rules by which it evolves. This is the faculty for which Kant claimed that we must have some pre-programmed notion since birth: "... representation of space must already be there" (see note 44). We suggested in §5.1 that the mere fact we share the same spatial awareness as many animal species must mean that the commonality is environmental rather than being pre-programmed within us all. This must also include the different way that we perceive time from space, the notion of dynamical change, and the apparent rules governing such change. But there is another facet to this: the fact that the world-view faculty can vary all aspects of that internal model in fanciful creation. In other words, the world-view is capable of much more than simply modelling our own environment, and can imagine people and places that we have never seen, and fantasy worlds that look nothing like ours or have different laws of physics (e.g. magic). There is no doubt that this is by way of extension since it follows from first modelling the perceived environment, and so the argument is that it would be capable of modelling many different environments had they been real.

The **patterns** faculty represents our ability to spot patterns and generally to recognise the form of objects, even as they undergo gradual change. It is not always accurate, and we may think we see something when it is not really there (*pareidolia*), or we may think we see a pattern in the sequence of events around us when none exists (*apophenia*, or even superstitious associations), but it also allows us to model our environment. The patterns we infer from our digested sensory inputs (qualia) allow us to intuit space, time, objects, and correlations between their apparent changes. It is also responsible for our recognition of words (verbal or written) and symbols, and hence underpins our communication, representation of knowledge, and mathematical or logical deduction. Without this faculty, we would not be able to give identity to people, places, and things; we would not be able to construct a three-dimensional model of our environment and allocate locations within it for external objects; we would not be able to track associated changes from one moment to the next, while preserving those identities; and we would not be able to infer any laws of nature.

It may be argued that other sentient species are more aware of patterns in their physical environment than we are — we having been distracted by the complexities of our social environment. As an example of another species using its pattern recognition to become aware of forces, consider a dog sitting in the back of a car and watching the road ahead. You can observe the dog shifting his weight in anticipation of the effects of going around a bend, and so preparing to compensate for the centrifugal force.

The **planning** faculty is responsible for reasoning how to achieve specific goals, but implicit in this is the notion of counterfactual choices: that we are capable of taking one of several lines of action, and so able to manipulate the path of our '*now*' moment. Underpinning this is the observation that things in our environment apparently have a dependency upon prior circumstances, which we term causality. This leads us to believe that we have free will, and that our choices come from our mind, with no direct antecedent causes.

The **creativity** faculty is employed not only for artistic conceptions, but also for practical creations (e.g. in engineering), planning, and problem-solving. It is loosely defined in general, but we will equate it here with the creation of novel ideas or approaches, or of products (physical or conceptual) that are expressive or useful. The term innovation is sometimes reserved for the implementation of an idea, but this distinction adds no real value here.

Backing all of this is our **memory**, an incredibly flexible faculty that has no correspondence with current computer memories. It can store and recollect images, sounds, sensations, emotions, spatial organisations, events, mental creations, language and symbols, strategies, and even our previous thoughts.

Our ability to recollect images (including dynamic events) is known as imagination, which is clearly confusing given the common usage of that term. In order to avoid this, the field of psychology uses 'creative imagination' to refer to that aspect of creativity that allows us to concoct mental images of people, places, and objects that are different from items of our experience. It also uses 'reproductive imagination' (yes, that makes me smile, too) to refer to recollected imagery. The fact that these two cases are so closely related, allowing us to modify our recollections or to imagine variant outcomes, illustrates that the empirical faculties in Fig. 6-2 are much more interconnected and cooperative in real life.

The executive faculty seems to need inputs when operating, and it is hard for us to adopt a state where this is not true (e.g. a deep meditative one). If we are in a state of deliberation and deep thought, or some other introverted contemplation, then we are less aware of our surroundings and might easily miss something. Conversely, if there are many external stimuli, such as in a dangerous situation or at a great party, then we would be drawn out of any introverted state. It is almost as though the executive cannot concurrently handle both to the same level, but there is more to this. During extended periods in a sensory deprivation chamber, we can develop several mood issues as well as hallucinations and strange thoughts. Hallucinations are also a symptom of the 'Ganzfeld effect', where a subject is presented with unstructured 'white noise'. There is a view that these result from the brain misidentifying inputs, but in the former case there is no actual 'experience', and this is therefore likely to be true in the latter case as well. If the deprivation of recognisable external stimuli forces the mind into an introverted state, then how long can it function in that state before it runs out of steam and has to invent substitutes?

6.4   Free Will

Free will, or the ability to act without imposed constraint and not subject to fate, is something we value highly, often letting it elevate our supposed importance within the universe. Being able to choose an action at our own discretion is widely believed to conflict with the *determinism* that appears to control all other things — a view described as *incompatibilism*. *Determinism* is generally a belief that all events are determined completely by previous circumstances, and so is largely equated with a belief in causality, but in §4.1 we distinguished these and argued that causality is an illusion.

Surprisingly, free will is still debated as an unexplained phenomenon, with some serious people even suggesting a spiritual connection that somehow transcends the reductionist physicality of their experience. A simple inductive proof of *determinism* is that all our free choices of today will tomorrow be set in stone, and so looking back through history reveals that there were never any free choices; we were always constrained by something.

Kant presented arguments for and against the concept of free will as follows:

[Thesis]

Causality, according to the laws of nature, is not the only causality from which all the phenomena of the world can be deduced. In order to account for these phenomena it is necessary also to admit another causality, that of freedom ... through which something takes place, without its cause being further determined according to necessary laws by a preceding cause ...[72]

[Antithesis]

There is no freedom, but everything in the world takes place entirely according to the laws of nature ... Transcendental freedom is therefore opposed to the law of causality, and represents such a connection of successive states of effective causes, that no unity of experience is possible with it. It is therefore an empty fiction of the mind, and not to be met with in any experience.[73]

His thesis was based upon the premise that mankind is somehow separate from, or above, the laws of nature, including the apparent chain of cause and effect. Hence, free will ("transcendental freedom") must be a separate type of causality that lies outside of those laws. His antithesis proposed the converse view that everything is part of nature, and so free will — which would be incompatible with the laws of nature — must be an illusion.

But why should this topic be so controversial? Well, if our actions are determined, as appears to be the case with everything else in the universe, then how can we appear to do things of our own volition? Conversely, if our actions are undetermined then they would be random, which they clearly are not. The flaw in this logic is the implication that determined means 'by external factors', thereby separating ourselves from everything else.

Behaviourism is a systematic approach to understanding the behaviour of animals, including humans, which assumes all behaviours are simply responses to certain stimuli in the environment, and so can be conditioned by modifying the environment (e.g. through reward and punishment, or pain and pleasure). *Methodological behaviourism* considers that only external behaviours can be objectively observed, and so internal thoughts and feelings are irrelevant. In the 1970s, American psychologist Burrhus F. Skinner (usually referred to as simply B. F. Skinner) pioneered *radical behaviourism*, which treated those internal processes as further behaviours that had to be considered.

The reason that this is important here is because it demonstrates a fallacy in behaviourist thinking: the cognitive faculties also have consequences, both physical (on the person or the environment) and on further mental states, and those consequences may be stimuli to subsequent behaviours of that individual, or of others. In other words, the chain of cause and effect — illusion that it may be — involves both physical and mental causes, and each cause may lead to multiple effects of either a physical or mental nature.

One way to envisage this is to think of the mind as part a parallel incorporeal layer that interacts with the physical brain during normal causal relations. The following schematic depicts causal influences between brains and other elements of the material world (via the senses and motor functions), and with the emergent conscious minds interacting directly only with the associated brain, and not with other minds (no telepathy) or with material elements (no telekinesis).

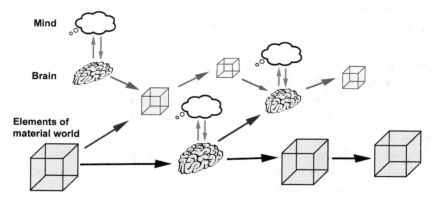

Fig. 6-3, Involvement of the mind in the causality of the physical world.

The diagram represents a physical layer consisting of brains and inanimate elements of the material world, and an incorporeal layer displayed above it consisting of minds. The reality within which we deem cause and effect to occur is then an extended environment where the minds play a crucial part, both as causer and affected. In other words, the appearance of free will is not at odds with normal causality or *determinism*, and only our self-deception makes it appear otherwise.

Having established that causality must be illusory in a *block universe*, we will soon show (§6.5) that it is neither unique nor confined to the physical world, and this allows us to adopt a different path: that the perceived phenomenon of free will is just a form of causality by a different name, and so is entirely compatible with it, despite neither being part of the objective reality.

A commonly perceived issue is that free will appears to have no antecedent causes, or at least an incomplete set of them. For instance, we may decide upon a particular action based upon current circumstances, but we may also decide to take some action for no apparent reason at all. This perception is wrong, though, and the missing causes are a combination of historical ones (basically prior experience and learning) and our internal state resulting from them. It is not that different from a simple alarm clock ringing with no apparent external cause; it would have been previously wound up and a time set, plus there would be internal machinations leading to the alarm going off that were dependent upon those prior events.

This view presented here is only partially covered by the position known as *epiphenomenalism*, where the mind is considered causally dependent upon the biochemical and mechanical events of the brain and body, but that the converse is an illusion as nothing can be dependent upon the mind. This position is far too restrictive, and would appear to go against evidence in plain sight. The difference in our view is that the mind (which, although incorporeal, is irreducible to corporeal elements) is another part of the illusory chain of cause and effect, and can influence things (as with free will) as well as be influenced by things. This view is usually described as *interactionist dualism*, though we do not use that term here since it may imply that the mind and brain are more independent than we are claiming; we are explicitly saying that the mind only has a causal interface with its associated brain, but also that the nature of the causality is not physical.

Scientists reading this will almost invariably leap on the suggestion that there can be anything that is real and yet non-physical, or that there can be any re-interpretation of causality, but let us just add some clarity ready for the arguments to follow. It is undoubtably true that change occurs, and that energy is effectively a measure of that change — although ubiquitously viewed as the source of such change. As the nature of a change is predictable (for similar circumstances, achieved by similar paths) then we describe it as causation and infer that it is fundamental, but it is not a physical process in itself, and identification of a so-called cause is largely a matter of convenience that depends upon the complexity and scale of the change (§8.2). When looking at the same scenarios in a *block universe* then all we have is patterns of change, and patterns can embrace other patterns (i.e. they are neither unique nor fundamental). For instance, when looking at the execution of a computer program, we can consider an assignment operation, as expressed in a programming language, to have modified the value of a variable, or that the execution of a low-level MOV instruction modified the associated memory address, or that a write operation in the computer's memory transferred the bits from the MDR register to the address specified by the MAR register — none are strictly true in a *block universe*. In other words, the 'principle of sufficient reason' is part of the illusion.

6.5   Birth of Subjectivity

Let us just recap the assertions and deductions so far made in relation to our perceptions and our subjective reality so that we can see how they might emerge in a *block universe*.

Our subjective time originates from the fact that our sensory data is processed instant-by-instant — something we have described as an innate temporal sense — thus allowing us to become aware of the differences from each experienced moment to moment. These differences, combined with the fact that we only record events from one side of the '*now*' moment, leads to all dynamical aspects of experience. We have not yet identified a mechanism that explains why we experience these moments in a particular direction, but we will revisit the 'arrow of time' in Chapter 8. As a result of it, we only directly experience the '*now*' moment, and since this appears to progress in a given direction then it separates a known past from an unknown future, and so is fundamental to the overall experience of subjective time. This, in turn, constitutes a quale, as with other instances of sensation.

Through a combination of senses that include sight, hearing, and touch, we intuit a physical environment around us. We notice that this environment changes gradually and deterministically, rather than abruptly or randomly. Objects within this environment — including other living things — have a form that our pattern recognition can identify, despite their physical shape and make-up varying over time. This 'persistence of form', and the distribution of these objects within the environment, afford us a sense of distinctness, and hence the concept of identity.

Our world-view embraces the nature of the environment, including the three-dimensional spatial structure, the presence of tangible objects, and the separation of events by durations of time. It also includes rules that apparently describe the movements of objects relative to each other (forces, momenta, etc.), the transformations of object states (e.g. the melting of ice), and the correlations between events at different times.

Having a set of rules that describe the transitions or evolution of a system, whether it is the environment or some system of symbols (as in mathematics, logic, programming, or even written words), allows our creativity to experiment by considering different ways of applying those rules, or even having different rules. This is not just an asset to artistic endeavours, or to flights of fantasy, but is fundamental to problem-solving and to the formation of strategies.

The illusion of causality extends to our mental activity since thoughts and feelings can trigger other activity, either mental or physical. When a decision is made through our executive faculty then it appears to have no causal antecedent, and this is the basis of what we think of as free will. The mind may have some autonomy of operation, but its state is built up over time through a combination of experience and cognition; it grows rather than appearing out of thin air. A causal connection is there but we are blindsided by our own subjectivity.

The complexity of our interaction with the environment, and with other living species, means that our choices cannot be made purely upon the basis of quantitative assessment or hard-and-fast logic. The criteria we need are not signposted in unambiguous terms, and since they will involve the non-physical as well as the physical then we need a different scheme. Our emotions provide this subjective assessment, but in an active manner; a passive assessment might yield a simple rating, or analogue response, but emotions provide an active assessment that we would find difficult to ignore. In essence, we 'feel' the assessment rather than simply having it available to do with as we please.

Although we have given these faculties specific names, and they are neatly delineated in Fig. 6-2, their interactions are far more complex. We have identified them from an empirical analysis of the mind's functionality, but the conscious mind is an emergent non-physical entity that encompasses those faculties of qualia, emotions, world-view, creativity, planning, pattern recognition, memory, and the executive. Consciousness cannot be equated to any linear combination of these faculties, yet the interplay between them gives rise to an awareness of our spatial environment, of the changes in this environment from moment to moment, of patterns that appear to make those changes predictable, of ourselves as independent entities, of our own thoughts and desires, of our involvement in the evolution of events and relationships, and of apparent choices we have in this involvement. It is truly incredible that our subjective reality can be shared, and that the consciousness emergent in different entities (and in different species) conspires to deliver a collective experience so rich with structure, meaning, and intent.

On what grounds, though, do we claim that the phenomenon of consciousness is 'real' when we say that the conscious mind is an emergent non-physical (and hence non-material) entity? *Materialism* holds that matter is fundamental, and hence that everything is rooted in our material world. *Physicalism* is similar in holding that there is nothing beyond our physical world. In essence, these beliefs are taken to imply that non-physical notions must be either supernatural, of a religious or spiritual nature, or simply immaterial and so not real at all. This is <u>not</u> the argument made in this chapter.

The mind is an emergent entity that comprises a layer 'parallel to' the physical, rather than somehow separate from and independent of it, and it is real in the sense that it is causally connected. The idea of 'strong emergence' is usually criticised by people who cannot conceive of a causally connected entity that is not physical, and if it has a physical dependence then why should the pair be considered separate? In other words, if the mind depends upon the brain then is the brain not the causal trigger for everything that we consider emanating from the mind? Choosing the brain as the causal trigger, rather than individual chemical or electrical signals within it, or even the associated fundamental particles, is a matter of convenience. But the mind also has its own elements of cause and effect, each of which may be non-physical, e.g. a thought triggering an emotion and a new mental state. That ecosystem of non-physical causation is intertwined with physical ones via the brain: a non-physical cause may yield a physical effect (e.g. I move an object because I feel like it), and *vice versa*. Hence, such an emergent entity has emergent properties that are not measurable and emergent behaviours that are not observable, but both of which supervene on the physical world; this being the main difference from the physical properties and behaviours arising during 'weak emergence'.

Emergent structure is usually equated with emergent pattern, but this is not quite correct. A pattern is some regularity, or predictable relation, and an emergent pattern is one where some regularity of smaller components manifests as a simple regularity at a larger scale; for instance, Truchet tiles. They do not require any causal interaction or interconnectivity between their components; only that the pattern associated with the smaller components aligns in some constructive or destructive fashion to yield the pattern associated with the bigger components. Emergent structure (discussed further in §8.3) may exhibit patterns, but emergent pattern is a more general concept. The importance of this is that, in a *block universe*, all properties, behaviours, and structures are simply patterns in the objective reality, and the self-imposed constraints of *physicalism* are inappropriate when considering that these same patterns may manifest physically or otherwise, and that the concept of physicality does not apply in the objective reality.

Consciousness and its components, such as qualia, emotion, thought, etc., are therefore part of our real world — our subjective reality — since ignoring them would leave holes in our causal explanations of events, and deterministic paradoxes in our apparent free will. We take this for granted without a second thought in our everyday lives, but it is contentious in the worlds of physics. So intent is it in exploring 'fundamental' aspects of the universe — meaning things that are part of the measurable world, and which are therefore susceptible to objective study — that it ignores virtually everything with a non-physical status. While it is true that these emergent entities are not part of the objective reality, and science deals primarily with our subjective reality, science still does not accept their non-physical status as in any way fundamental. There are important non-physical precedents in physics, such as the concept of semantic information, but the sticking point here is the assertion of causal influence (discussed further in §8.2 and §8.3).

A strongly held belief in the world of physics is that all causation is bottom-up, meaning that its influence flows from microscopic scales up to macroscopic scales. This belief can be linked with *reductionism*: the belief that everything can be considered in terms of the smaller entities that it is composed of. In other words, the movements of atoms and molecules, and their behaviours under the action of forces, completely explain all instances of causation observed at our scale, or beyond. According to this view, if we cited the environment as an example of top-down causation then we would be wrong because the effects attributed to that aggregate entity can be deconstructed into the effects of its constituents.

We have already argued against this view in several chapters here. For instance, that the mind has a top-down causal influence, but as a non-physical emergent entity then it can only be deconstructed into other non-physical components such as faculties and instances of subjective experience — we have no basis to describe instances of experience in terms atoms, etc. Irrespective of whether we include free will (§6.4), it is clear that causality as we observe it involves a mixture of macroscopic (aggregate and/or non-physical) and microscopic entities. So is there a problem with interpreting it as involving both bottom-up <u>and</u> top-down influences? Does this not clash with *reductionism*? Not if we accept that all causality is an illusion (§4.1), in which case it is only evident in our subjective reality, and primarily involving objects of our macroscopic scale. Our reductionist approach to a description of the physical world means that we extrapolate this notion of causality down to those microscopic scales, effectively applying *reductionism* to causality, yet we know that this eventually breaks down at the quantum scale because the rules are no longer those of our experience.

Whether we say that a storm blew down a house, rather than the motions of the individual molecules in a localised area of the atmosphere pushing against the molecules in its walls, is largely a matter of convenience since in a *block universe* neither statement is correct. This is important for our evaluation of mental causation and free will as there is no real conflict with the *reductionist* view. In just the same way that it is not entirely satisfactory to attribute the demise of the macroscopic house to molecular motions in the air, it is not entirely satisfactory to attribute a voluntary contraction of a muscle to neural signals in the brain. The storm is a case of 'weak emergence' because both the small-scale and large-scale components are part of the physical world, but the conscious mind is a case of 'strong emergence' because its larger-scale components are non-physical. We will examine this aspect of causality more deeply in §8.2 and §8.3.

A *non-reductive physicalist* is said to be someone who believes that the mind cannot be reduced to the physical brain, that the mind supervenes on the brain, and that mental causation exists. Korean-American philosopher Jaegwon Kim proposed a 'causal exclusion argument' that would appear to render mental causation ineffective and redundant. According to this argument, if such beliefs are combined with the notion that every physical effect has a sufficient physical cause, and his 'causal exclusion principle' which states that "No single event can have more than one sufficient cause occurring at any given time—unless it is a genuine case of causal overdetermination",[74] then it leaves no room for mental causation. In other words, if all physical effects have a specific physical cause, and no physical effects have multiple distinct causes (physical or mental), then there is no place for mental causation. The flaw in this argument is the long-held belief that 'sufficient reason' is both a unique and fundamental principle. We will see later (§8.2 and §8.3) what underpins our identification of physical cause, but causality in general is a phenomenal concept that we see where we want to see it.

A common argument for the existence of mental causation is the production of tears. This is a physical effect that could have either a physical cause (an irritation) or a mental cause (emotion), so what is the difference between these two scenarios? Well, they are not unlike the movement of a limb: the movement might be a reflex reaction to some stimulus, or it might be a voluntary movement. Whether such a movement is the result of a physical cause or a mental cause is simply a matter of perspective that best befits the explanation to be given. To claim that every such movement has a low-level physical cause is not an explanation that makes sense under all circumstances, and is simply a roundabout way of saying that all interacting components in the physical world are of material composition, but this reductionist approach can have only one consequence as it approaches the quantum reality: the realisation that causality is a merely phenomenon of our subjective reality.

We have made the case that mental causation not only exists but that non-physical causes and effects are not fundamentally different from physical causes and effects, and that all combinations are demonstrated (see Fig. 6-3). The one proviso being that the crossover between mental and physical only occurs between the mind and the brain (i.e. there is no evidence of telepathy or telekinesis). So there must be a notional causal transference at the mind-brain interface — such that an act of will or volition can cause electrical and chemical activity in the brain, which in turn can activate motor functions — but what form would this take? Although this is normally considered to be a sticking point, it is not so if all causality is notional. It is the term that we use to describe a direct or indirect interaction between two entities in the direction of our subjective time, and the mind-brain interface is no different.

So what about the *block universe*? Fig. 4-2 illustrates consciousness as a sort of world-line, akin to a particle world-line, because it only has a temporal dimensionality. Every instant along that world-line corresponds to a moment of awareness regarding events to one side of it only, and yet all of those instants are equally real and hence also our moments of awareness. We cannot have an ever-evolving consciousness in such a universe; nor can we have lost historical events; nor can we have unknown or yet-to-occur events. Since there is no single cosmic '*now*' moment then every instant on that world-line corresponds to such a '*now*' moment in our experience.

This may be as hard to accept as it is to explain, but it means (after reversing the last statement) that every moment of your conscious experience is on such a static world-line; none is lost and none is gained, and each is informationally connected to an adjacent one resulting in an experience of flow. Each is also connected to physical events through our senses and the apparent causation around us. Hence, although we cannot directly relate the experience of subjective time (or any qualia) between two conscious minds, the fact that their associated brains and bodies exist in the same universe means that their subjective times are metered by the experience of shared events (assuming that they are within each other's *causal horizon*), and so we appear to have a shared subjective reality.

This difficulty in accepting this is primarily because it means abandoning our experience of time, but look at it another way: every perception we have of something moving or changing is a consequence of this perception of subjective time. If one of these two dynamical phenomena is an illusion then so is the other. Our consciousness appears to be driven in one direction simply because of our awareness of events having occurred prior to (in the subjective sense) each '*now*' moment, and the fact that this gives the impression of unfolding change, and hence of causality. Note that it is not quite correct to say that we are aware of past events — we are aware that they have occurred only because our memory has recorded associated information, but each '*now*' moment corresponds to our experience of the environment at that instant. Implicit in this is that all differences in the objective reality between adjacent instants along the time dimension are smooth and continuous, and that these are manifested as similarly smooth and continuous changes in our observables.

The following diagram illustrates this by depicting a walking person within a *block universe*, a little like the cannonball example from Fig. 1-1.

Fig. 6-4, Person walking within a block universe.

It shows the person in different positions and at different locations for each instant along the time axis. It also shows the different face settings of an associated clock. However, rather than it implying any movement, or other change, it illustrates that both entities have a continuous evolution of their form over time and space. For instance, the sweeping of the hands of the clock actually forms a continuous shape through all the possible settings, and the diagram has merely selected five snapshots along that extended shape. Similarly with the disposition of the person: their form will have a continuous shape and the diagram has just sampled five cross-sections through that shape.

Now the conscious mind is slightly different in that it stretches over time, but not space. Each cross-section of this person's brain will harbour a temporal cross-section of the emergent consciousness; all such moments are extant, and each will have an *awareness* connected with the instant immediately prior, thus forming a chain that appears to be directed. This directedness is then responsible for the overall consciousness being aware of apparent change and movement in the environment.

An implication of this is that our whole field of scientific study is tainted by our everyday perceptions. This is not an issue when the science deals with aspects of our subjective reality, but as we get into fundamental physics then the difference is hugely important. There are so many phenomena that we take for granted and yet apply to fields outside of our direct experience that it must certainly present a skewed idea of what the objective reality might be like. Of all the events around us, we are only aware directly of ones that produce a spur-like causation capable of stimulating our senses, directly or indirectly; all others are inferred based upon experience and our knowledge of the laws of nature. Measurement of an event with equipment, as opposed to direct observation of it, involves inferences based upon our direct observation of the measuring equipment. We will take this up again in Chapter 8 where we will try and find a mechanism that accounts for the psychological view of time that we are here calling subjective time.

In Chapter 9, we will look at the relationship between our thought processes and time, showing that they are irreversible and yet would have occurred in the other direction of time had conditions been different.

Quantum Reality

What is the true nature of the wave function, especially in a block universe? Does it bias one direction in time?

The terms *quantum theory* and *quantum mechanics* are generally synonymous and interchangeable, but we are imposing a slight semantic difference here for convenience: *quantum theory* will imply a broader range of interpretations than *quantum mechanics*, which we will use for the more mathematical approaches.

Underpinning *quantum theory* is a wave-particle duality demonstrated by nature: sometimes an entity behaves like a particle whereas in other circumstances it behaves like a wave. The following sections will look at the origin of the wave-like character, but they will also use the term *particle*. This should not be interpreted using the smooth billiard-ball image that you may have been taught at school. To be honest, the true nature of these discrete entities is still unknown. Terms such as quanta or corpuscle might have been better, but each has alternative semantics that could lead to confusion.

Isaac Newton believed that light was composed of small units, or 'corpuscles' (little particles), but, in 1803, English physician and polymath Thomas Young conducted an experiment with two narrow slits that demonstrated the wave-like character of light. When shining light on a pair of slits whose separation was in the order of the light's wavelength then an interference pattern was obtained, similar to that formed by two sets of ripples on the surface of water. The waves from each slit interfered with each other constructively and destructively to create a banding of light-dark fringes on a screen, rather than just two bands of light corresponding directly to the two slits. In 1894, German theoretical physicist Max Planck was looking at how the intensity of the electromagnetic radiation emitted by a black body (an idealised opaque non-reflective body) depended upon the frequency of the radiation and the temperature of the body. He found that electromagnetic energy could be emitted only in multiples of a fixed unit that depended upon the frequency, but he still believed in the wave-like nature of such radiation. In 1905, Einstein explained experimental results of the photoelectric effect in terms of discrete quantised packets (photons[75]), and he was eventually awarded the Nobel Prize for this in 1921 (received 1922) — his only one.[76] In his 1924 PhD thesis, French physicist Louis de Broglie (pronounced 'de broy', rhyming with 'destroy') postulated that all matter (such as a beam of electrons) exhibits wave-like properties, termed *matter waves*. In 1961, the double-slit experiment was repeated with electrons, reinforcing the wave-particle duality that lay at the core of *quantum theory*. Although American theoretical physicist Richard Feynman was apparently unaware of this when his famous physics lectures were first published in 1963 (even today it is hard to put a definite name to the associated experiment),[77] he believed that the equivalent conceptual experiment captured all the fundamentals of *quantum theory*.

> In this chapter we shall tackle immediately the basic element of the mysterious behavior in its most strange form. We choose to examine a phenomenon which is impossible, *absolutely* impossible, to explain in any classical way, and which has in it the heart of quantum mechanics. In reality, it contains the *only* mystery. We cannot make the mystery go away by "explaining" how it works. We will just *tell* you how it works. In telling you how it works we will have told you about the basic peculiarities of all quantum mechanics.[78]

In the original Young experiment, the effect was explained as two wavefronts leaving the slits and interfering with each other.

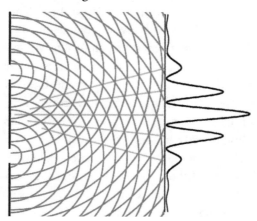

Fig. 7-1, Interference between wavefronts passing through two holes.

Two peaks or two troughs would reinforce each other (as shown by the lines joining them), while one of each would cancel out and leave a blank area on the detector screen. So the problem was that this effect could also be demonstrated with a particle beam (e.g. electrons), where two single bands directly corresponding to the slits would be expected, and so it was no longer clear whether the experiment involved particles or waves.

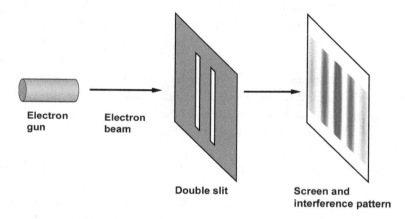

Fig. 7-2, Interference between electron beams passing through two close slits.

Placing a non-invasive (or, to be realistic, a minimally invasive) detector at one or both of the slits (before or after them) reverts the pattern to the classical two bands by losing the interference. It is said that because the experiment deduces 'which-path information' — either by directly detecting the particle at a given slit, or inferring that it must have gone through the other slit — then the interference is destroyed, yielding the classical result. Much controversy exists over the nature of this 'which-path information', and how the experimental apparatus appears to know of its acquisition and availability.

This banding even occurs when the intensity of the emitter is so low that only single particles are emitted at a time. Although each particle appears at a precise point on the detector screen, over time they build up the same interference pattern as would be observed as if they were transmitted *en masse*. It is sometimes said that each particle appears to go through both slits and interferes with itself, but this is inaccurate as we will see.

There are a couple of important thought experiments that need to be mentioned here as they emphasise the non-local nature of quantum reality, and they have since been verified in the laboratory: (1) In the 'delayed-choice experiment', attributed to John Wheeler, the non-invasive detector is placed far after the slit, so far away that even light would take a significant time to get from the slits to the detector. And yet, switching the detector on and off would still flip the pattern on the screen between the interfering and classical displays, suggesting that the result is nothing to do with each particle somehow going through both slits; (2) In the 'quantum-eraser experiment', attributed to American physicists Marlan O. Scully and Kai Drühl, tagging devices are placed before each of the slits that allow the particles to be associated with a specific slit. The device changes the axis of spin of the particles to one of two specific alternatives. This is effectively a different type of 'which-path information' that allows a better detector screen still to build up a pattern but also record which route each particle took. The interesting point is that having this information available destroys the interference pattern, as before, yet if those tags are removed from the particles before they hit the screen then the interference pattern is restored.

More recently, in 1999, a team at the University of Vienna, Austria, observed this wave-like behaviour using a beam of complex C_{60} molecules, informally known as 'buckyballs'. Even more recently (September 2019), an international team of researchers demonstrated this with molecules containing up to 2000 atoms.[79] This reveals that the phenomenon is a matter of scale rather than the properties of individual elementary particles, and that the effects eventually disappear as the size reaches that of everyday macroscopic objects.

So what is going on? How does the apparatus know to flip between a wave-like interference pattern and a classical particle-like two-band pattern? How can it possibly be aware that 'which-path information' is available? Although there are many interpretations of *quantum theory*, the mainstream ones try to interpret these results within the context of our subjective realities, and so propose that all the possibilities actually occur (e.g. each particle going through both slits), or that each particle is somehow 'smeared out', or that there is something special about the act of measurement, or even that consciousness plays a role. What these interpretations have in common is, as you might have guessed by now, causality; we find it hard to let go of this notion, and would probably feel disorientated or shaken by the repercussions of losing it.

In order to understand this wave-particle duality, including the 'mysterious behaviour' demonstrated in the double-slit experiment, and specifically in the context of a *block universe*, then we first need to look at the mathematics of *quantum mechanics* and see how this has shaped both our understanding of reality at this level and our questions. In other words, that the mathematics has been largely responsible for our interpretation of the experimental evidence, rather than *vice versa*, and that we may be forgiven for forgetting how we got here.

7.1   Quantum Mechanics

In a universe of uncountable numbers of fundamentally indistinguishable particles, it is hard to conceive of a descriptive mechanism other than probabilities. But probabilities have no real place in a *block universe*. They imply that events may have more than one outcome, due either to unknown details or some inherent unpredictability, and so must be applicable only within our subjective realities. *Quantum mechanics* deals with probabilities, but not the usual classical ones that apply to our world of experience.

Following a prompt from Dutch-American physicist Peter Debye during a conference, Austrian physicist Erwin Schrödinger was persuaded to give an account of de Broglie's *matter waves* at a subsequent conference. However, Debye then remarked that he thought his approach was rather "childish", and that any wave must be subject to some wave equation describing its evolution.[80] Just a few days before Christmas 1925, Schrödinger spent a two-and-a-half-week secluded vacation at a villa in the Swiss Alpine town of Arosa. He took a copy of de Broglie's thesis with him, and also wrote to "an old girlfriend in Vienna" (whose identity still remains unknown) to join him there, leaving his wife, Anny, in Zürich.[81] Surprisingly, this worked! By the time of his return, on 9 January 1926, he had formulated his famous wave equation based upon classical conservation of energy using *quantum operators*, and he then began a series of four celebrated papers on the subject.

Classical mechanics originally described the motion of bodies under the influence of forces, and this included Newton's work. Important abstract methods were later developed that allowed reformulations of classical mechanics, known as *Lagrangian mechanics* (due to Italian-French mathematician and astronomer Joseph-Louis Lagrange) and *Hamiltonian mechanics* (due to Irish mathematician William R. Hamilton). Central to their approaches were functions describing the state of a dynamic system, known as a *Lagrangian* (expressed in terms of space-time coordinates and velocities) and a *Hamiltonian* (expressed in terms of space-time coordinates and momenta), respectively.

The differential equations of motion for a system can be determined using the *principle of stationary action*, where a variational principle is applied to an attribute of the dynamics called the 'action'. There are different formulations of this principle, but *Hamilton's principle*, developed later, used the *Lagrangian* function as the basis of that variation. In effect, whereas the *Hamiltonian* or *Lagrangian* function described the evolution of the system directly, the *principle of stationary action* involved some quantity, S, which could be computed for each possible path, $x(t)$. The classical path was that for which S was 'stationary': usually meaning a minimum but generally meaning unchanged in the first order for small deviations to the path. Hamilton used a time-integral of the *Lagrangian* as the 'action'. Although sounding more complicated, this gives deeper insights into the reasons why certain paths would be taken in preference to others. To summarise this in a different way, if we take it for granted that things naturally travel in straight lines, which is the shortest distance between two points, then under the action of forces Newton's equations of motion would determine how things deviate from their inertial motion. The *principle of stationary action* treats these cases the same way, and says that the paths taken are the one for which this calculated (not measured) 'action' quantity is minimised.

Schrödinger began with the *Hamiltonian*, which basically embraces the conservation of energy, and replaced observable quantities with differential *quantum operators*. Technically, these were *Hermitian operators* because their *eigenvalues* had to be real if they were to represent something measurable. However, the resulting equation confusingly referred to something that seemed to appear from nowhere; the thing that those operators acted upon.

His equation is a linear partial differential equation, which means that any linear sum of solutions is also a solution. This admits the possibility of something called *quantum superposition*: if ϕ_1 is a solution representing one event outcome (say a particle going through the left slit and arriving at the screen), and ϕ_2 is a solution representing an alternative outcome (say going via the right slit) then $\phi_1 + \phi_2$ is a solution representing arrival at the screen via either route.[82] What his equation did not do is indicate the physical significance of the complex-valued wave amplitude, ϕ, since it is not an observable quantity. It exists only in a multidimensional mathematical *configuration space* with generalised coordinates that might include continuous ones (such as location or momentum) or discrete ones (such as spin). It effectively describes the potentiality of an event, and the coordinates capture the degrees of freedom in the system's state. It should be noted that *quantum superposition* is primarily a mathematical device rather than a fundamental property of the system since if a different basis is chosen for the representation in the *configuration space* (e.g. by position, or by momentum) then the superposition may not be there.

In 1926, German physicist and mathematician Max Born formulated a rule (the *Born rule*) that gave the probability that a measurement on a quantum system will yield a given result, and the probability of actually observing our particle in this scenario is the real-valued $P = |\phi|^2$, i.e. the absolute square of ϕ.[83] The quantity ϕ is therefore termed the *probability amplitude*, but this will be confusing in the context of this book, given that probabilities are not applicable in a *block universe*, so we will use the less-common variant *quantum amplitude* from here on. This amplitude is additive, which means that the observed probability cannot be additive because of an interference term (i.e. $|\phi_1 + \phi_2|^2 \neq P_1 + P_2$). So this *quantum amplitude* is determined by Schrödinger's wave equation, and it behaves like a wave with peaks and troughs that interfere in the normal way.

The *wave function* (ψ) is just a *quantum amplitude* that represents the total quantum state of a system, irrespective of its possible histories. In other words, it represents all the alternative ways that the current state could have occurred. For our double-slit scenario, the probability of a hit at a particular location on the detector screen (x) would be given by the *probability density*, $|\psi(x)|^2$. It is claimed to encapsulate everything that <u>can be known</u> about that system before an observation or measurement, with no additional unobserved parameters ('hidden variables'). The emphasised phrase reflects the fact that the *wave function* deals only in observables, and allows a prediction of future observables from a state of prior observables. Whether the inherent unpredictability of future ones is a consequence of fundamental indeterminism or of 'hidden variables' is still debated.

Although the evolution of the *wave function* over time is deterministic, the evolution of the observables that it describes is not; it is only when a measurement is made that we have a definite real-valued property of a system. It would be a fair question to ask, therefore, whether those observables constituent a fundamental description of any system.

The interpretation of the *wave function* has been debated ever since Schrödinger devised his wave equation. An exchange between Schrödinger and Dutch physicist Hendrik A. Lorentz in 1926 illustrates the main issues quite well. Lorentz preferred Schrödinger's *wave mechanics* over German physicist Werner K.Heisenberg's alternative *matrix mechanics*, "... so long as one only has to deal with the three coordinates x, y, z. If, however, there are more degrees of freedom, then I cannot interpret the waves and vibrations physically, and I must therefore decide in favor of matrix mechanics."[84] But Schrödinger was also concerned and responded in some detail, "You mention the difficulty of projecting the waves in q-space [position space[85]], when there are more than three coordinates, into ordinary three dimensional space and of interpreting them there ... the physical meaning belongs not in the quantity itself but rather to a *quadratic* function [$\psi\psi^*$, square of absolute value] of it ... What is unpleasant here, and indeed directly to be objected to, is the use of complex numbers. ψ is surely fundamentally a real function."[86] As well as the fact that his wave equation did not relate to real space, Schrödinger was so concerned with the use of *complex numbers* to describe the evolution of ψ over time that he reworked the equation to describe only a real-valued quantity and its space-time derivates. A bigger question, surely, would be why the world of our experience can be described using real-valued quantities.

The *Born rule* came as a shock to both Einstein and Schrödinger because it suggested that *quantum mechanics* could be understood via probability, and without any causal explanation. Einstein famously rejected this interpretation, and in a letter to Born, dated 4 December 1926, he wrote: "I, at any rate, am convinced that He [God] is not playing at dice".[87] Given that some observable was describable via a probability distribution, rather than being entirely random, then he rightly believed that there was some underlying mechanism responsible for the measured bias.

In effect, *quantum mechanics* is unable to assign specific values to properties prior to a measurement, and this led to what is known as the 'Copenhagen interpretation', conceived primarily by Danish physicist Niels Bohr, and also Heisenberg, during 1925–1927. According to this interpretation, physical systems do not have definite properties prior to being measured, and they exist in a superposed state of all possibilities. The act of measurement somehow selects just one of these possibilities, and all the associated probabilities reduce to 1, or 100%, for that specific case; a phenomenon described as *wave-function collapse*, or the 'measurement problem'.

But Einstein was a realist, and so believed that nature exists independently of any conscious entity's thought, knowledge, or observation. In order to express the absurdity of the 'Copenhagen interpretation', he once asked

Dutch-American physicist Abraham Pais whether he really believed that the Moon existed only when he looked at it.[88] He was correct in that there is an objective reality, but obviously struggled to accept that it could be so different from his subjective reality. In 1948, he wrote to Born, saying "However, if one abandons the assumption that what exists in different parts of space has its own, independent, real existence, then I simply cannot see what it is that physics is meant to describe".[89]

In 1935, Schrödinger highlighted the problems of the 'Copenhagen interpretation' in the context of everyday objects. His thought experiment put the life of a poor unfortunate cat (or at least one of its nine lives) in the balance, determined by some random quantum event external to a box enclosing the cat. The quantum event might be in a state of *superposition*, with both outcomes being simultaneously possible, but this surely cannot apply to the cat, who must be either dead or alive but not both, and independently of whether someone looks inside the box. Earlier that year, Einstein had written to Schrödinger with a similar thought experiment involving an unstable keg of gunpowder, pointing out that there was no intermediate between exploded and unexploded.

To be accurate, the *wave function* represents the situation between measurements, rather than simply prior to a measurement. The result of some measurement is a starting point for a *wave-function* description of subsequent events, which may or may not involve a *superposition* of states, but this leads to some contradictions. The *wave function* is blind to our perceived difference between past and future, and since the wave equation is deterministic then it can be run backwards from one measurement to describe the situation at the time of a prior measurement. That description might again involve *superposition* but it will never identify the result of that prior measurement. It is reasonable, then, to suggest that it is not a fundamental description, and that there are other, hidden factors at play. Einstein was adamant that this was the case, but (for reasons to be explained later) his arguments were gradually overtaken by a probabilistic description and by the 'Copenhagen interpretation'.

So the evolution of the *wave function* not only fails to predict future measurements but fails to describe measurements of prior circumstances leading to the current one. If future states are deemed to be a consequence of prior states, then the wave equation implies that prior states can be considered to be a consequence of future states, i.e. retrocausality. If we harboured any vestigial notion of causality then this should be enough to destroy it.

A popular belief is that if the *wave function* also described the measurement apparatus, and the observer, and everything else that might have a causal influence upon the measurement operation, then it would be more precise. There is even a concept called *quantum monism* in which the evolution of the whole universe could (in principle) be described by a single *wave function*. But by themselves, neither the deterministic wave equation nor our time-symmetric laws of physics seem to account for the 'causal asymmetry' observed all around us.

Since *quantum mechanics* is most often described in terms of probability then this apparent transition from quantum to classical during a measurement presents further interpretational problems. In a static acausal *block universe* there can be no spontaneous collapse, and nothing can be induced by the measurement itself. Neither can there be any alternative outcome, which then means that there can be no probabilities.

7.2   Uncertainty Principle

In 1927, Heisenberg devised a set of mathematical inequalities that placed fundamental limits upon the precision to which certain pairs of properties (called *complementary* or *conjugate variables*) can be measured simultaneously. It is sometimes called the *indeterminacy principle*, and there is some history behind the term selected in the English translations of his textbook, *The Physical Principles of the Quantum Theory* (1930). There are some semantic differences between the terms that even Heisenberg used, and so it is important for us to understand the fundamentals of this principle. In 1974, Israeli physicist Max Jammer wrote:

> The term used by Heisenberg in these considerations was
> *Ungenauigkeit* (inexactness, imprecision) or *Genauigkeit* (precision, degree of precision). In fact, in his classic paper these terms appear more than 30 times (apart from the adjective *genau*), whereas the term *Unbestimmtheit* (indeterminacy) appears only twice and *Unsicherheit* (uncertainty) only three times. Significantly, the last term, with one exception (p. 186), is used only in the Postscript, which was written under the influence of Bohr.[90]

The historical discussions of *quantum theory* also led to this principle being confused with what is called the 'observer effect': the fact that we cannot measure something without perturbing it, and so affecting the results of our measurements. This principle, however, is more fundamental, and would be relevant irrespective of whether a measurement was being performed. What it means in reality is that when one variable of a conjugate pair is determined through measurement, the other appears to have a fluctuating, imprecise value.

The two most commonly cited *complementary variables* are position and momentum, and the corresponding inequality may be expressed as:

$$\Delta x \, \Delta p_x \geq h \, / \, 4\pi$$

In other words, the uncertainty in the position (x) multiplied by the uncertainty in momentum along that dimension (p_x) cannot be smaller than *Planck's constant* ($h = 6.626 \times 10^{-34}$ J s) divided by 4π. Heisenberg's original equations used *matrix mechanics* and demonstrated non-commutation of these quantities.

$$Q\,P \, - \, P\,Q \, = \, ih \, / \, 2\pi$$

where the matrices P and Q represented momentum and position, respectively. We expect basic arithmetic to demonstrate commutation (e.g. $a * b = b * a$), but this is not true for matrices, nor for many other mathematical structures.

In fact, Heisenberg's principle applies to the properties of any wave-like system, and in the quantum case that would be the *quantum amplitude*.

In the *Planck–Einstein relation*, the energy of a photon is related to its frequency (Eq. (7.1)). De Broglie generalised the *Planck–Einstein relation* to relate the wavelength of his *matter waves* to a particle's momentum, termed the *de Broglie relation* (Eq. (7.2)). This pair of relations can be used to relate the energy (E) and momentum (p) of any particle to the frequency (v) and wavelength (λ) of its equivalent wave-like character.

$$E \, = \, h\,v \tag{7.1}$$

$$\lambda \, = \, h \, / \, p \tag{7.2}$$

Eq. (7.2) may be considered a generalisation of Eq. (7.1) since, for a photon, $p = mc = mc^2 / c = E / c$, and $\lambda = c / v$.

Rearranging these equations gives multiplication relations between energy and period ($T = 1/v$), and between momentum and wavelength.

$$E\,T = h$$

$$p\,\lambda = h$$

This allows us to interpret Heisenberg's inequalities in terms of wave-like properties. When we consider a particle's *wave function* then it actually behaves like a *wave packet*, or short wave train, and this means that multiple frequencies must be present.

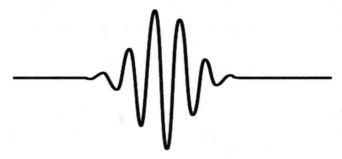

Fig. 7-3, Wave packet.

When multiple waves of different frequencies are superposed then it is possible to get this shape. If you are familiar with Fourier series then this is the same basic behaviour, with simple sine waves interfering either constructively or destructively with each other. In the case of a *wave packet*, they interfere constructively over a small, localised region, and progressively interfere destructively at positions away from that region.

In order to increase the localisation of the packet, and so make its position more refined, we would have to introduce more wavelengths, and this would make the momentum determination less precise because it depends upon wavelength. Fewer wavelengths, making the momentum determination more precise, would cause the packet to spread and have a less-precise position. A similar relationship exists between the energy and an instant in time. It is therefore a fundamental trade-off between the location of the *wave packet* in space-time and the spread of the frequencies (and wavelengths) making up the packet (i.e. its bandwidth).

But when the *uncertainty principle* is invoked, it is taken to imply that the world is fuzzy or random at the quantum level, whereas we have just explained that it is a trade-off in the measurement of certain pairs of observables; observables that we believe are intrinsic properties of all discrete particles. It would be much more accurate to describe it as an *indeterminacy principle* than an *uncertainty principle*, and the common view of it describing a seething random fluctuation of nothingness is very misleading.

In de Broglie's *matter waves*, the *wave packet* was considered to be a representation of an actual particle. It was shown that its *group velocity* (v_g) corresponded to the particle's velocity, and the *phase velocity* (v_p) came out as c^2/v_g, which although greater than the speed of light (c) is not in conflict with *special relativity* since nothing physical is being transmitted that fast.[91]

An interesting thing happens to the *wave function* as a consequence of the *uncertainty principle*: the representation of a particle spreads over time. In essence, the *complementary variables* are observables, and observables are the parameters of the wave equation, which results in the uncertainty increasing with time from some point of measurement. This effect, known as dispersion, is also involved in *quantum tunnelling*. When the *wave function* approaches a potential wall (a mathematically defined barrier) then some of the wave function penetrates the barrier and some of it rebounds, thus illustrating that the *wave packet* involves a multitude of possible energies. But note that a single particle will not divide in this way — it must do one thing or the other — and the extent of a single particle does not spread as it travels. There is clearly a difference between the particle and its *wave function* representation.

7.3   Sum Over Histories

In the late 1940s, the theory of *quantum electrodynamics* (QED) — the relativistic *quantum theory* that described how light and matter interact — ran into serious trouble with infinities. Three distinct solutions were submitted by Japanese physicist Shinichiro Tomonaga, and American physicists Julian S. Schwinger and Richard Feynman, but in 1949 English theoretical physicist and mathematician Freeman J. Dyson demonstrated the equivalence of their different formulations. The 1965 Nobel Prize in Physics was awarded jointly to Tomonaga, Schwinger, and Feynman for "their fundamental work in quantum electrodynamics".

Feynman's approach, using *path integrals* — informally called 'sum over histories' or 'sum over paths', and famous for its use of *Feynman diagrams* — was rather different from the operator approaches of the other two. It is his approach that we will look at here as the description would appear, from the name, to favour histories over futures.

In order to explain this concept, note that the mathematical operation of integration involves summing over infinitesimally small intervals of one or more independent variables, or — graphically — calculating the area under a curve, or surface, by summing infinitesimally narrow strips along one or more axis. *Path integrals* (or *line integrals*) involve summing some quantity over infinitesimally short segments of a curve or path. However, a Feynman *path integral* actually sums over a space of paths, or a space of functions describing paths, and so is technically a *functional integral.* Their importance was in handling the *superposition* of all the possible ways that something could happen in order to determine the probability of that particular outcome. Since the wave equation is linear, and a sum of solutions is also a valid solution, then an integral (which is a generalisation of a discrete sum) is also a solution.

Quantum mechanics was originally formulated from an analogy with *Hamiltonian mechanics*, but in 1933 English theoretical physicist Paul A. M. Dirac suggested that a *Lagrangian* approach might be more fundamental, and would also be more consistent with *special relativity*. In trying to find the *quantum mechanical* equivalent of the *principle of stationary action*, he had noted a correspondence between the *quantum amplitude* of a path and the equivalent classical 'action'.[92]

$$\phi[x(t)] \ = \ const \ e^{(i/\hbar) \ S[x(t)]} \tag{7.3}$$

where ϕ is the transition amplitude between two points on the path $x(t)$, and $\hbar$ is defined as $h/2\pi$. S is the classical 'action' for the path, and the square brackets emphasise that the argument is a function rather than some specific value (S is then termed a functional). The 'action' is actually calculated as the *line integral* of the *Lagrangian* over time for the path. This is one solution of the wave equation, and exhibits wave-like characteristics due to the e^{ix} term.[93] When a *quantum amplitude* varies with time then it can be viewed as two orthogonal sinusoidal waves with magnitude r and phase angle θ (with phase difference of $\pi/2$), or a helical rotation in the complex plane, known as a *phasor*. A common example of the relationship between sinusoidal oscillation and rotation is the pistons and crank of a vehicle engine.

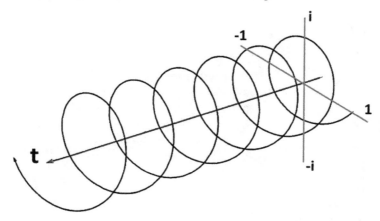

Fig. 7-4, Phase rotation associated with a world-line (phasor).

Any linear sum of these solutions is also a solution, and the constants are usually normalised so that the probabilistic interpretation yields an exhaustive total (i.e. accounting for all outcomes) of 1, or 100%. Feynman later uncovered this paper, tucked away as it was in a Soviet journal, and developed it into a full theory by applying his method of *path integrals*.

Fig. 7-5 shows the path of a particle between two points, A and B — technically in a position *configuration space*, but that is not particularly relevant here. The so-called classical path is the one for which the 'action', S, is a minimum. However, the interesting thing about Eq. (7.3) is that the $1/\hbar$ factor in the exponent is huge (nearly 10^{34} when using SI units). So, considering just macroscopic cases for a moment, the 'action' multiplied by this factor results in a similarly huge phase angle, as though the little arrow rotating in the complex plane (that we will refer to as a 'phase arrow') had undergone a massive number of rotations. This means that a slight displacement from a path, δx, results in a further massive number of phase rotations, leaving neighbouring amplitudes being effectively random with respect to each other, and so they cancel out. It is only when we look at quantum-level displacements from the classical path, where the 'action' is stationary and does not change much, that the 'action' balances that factor and we see some coherence in the calculated amplitudes. This is the reason why the classical path is the one that works, and it is the quantum equivalent of the *principle of stationary action*.

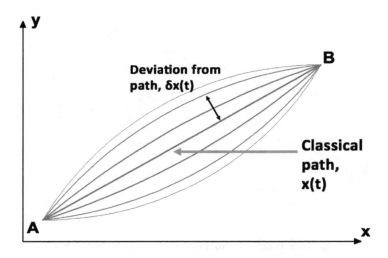

Fig. 7-5, Deviations from the classic path between two locations.

The following sample case was used by Feynman in his lectures and books, and the computer-generated illustrations used here are strongly based upon those he used himself.[94] It considers photons from a monochromatic light source that are reflected by a mirror and reach the same detector. At school, we are taught that rays of light are reflected symmetrically ('angle of incidence equals angle of reflection'), and so only the path marked by the label 'G' would be significant. However, when we look at the 'phase arrows' for all the possible paths of reflection then we see how this *quantum mechanical* principle explains the familiar wave-like phenomenon in terms of particles.

Fig. 7-6 shows a group of potential reflections if this 'equal angle' principle was ignored. The paths on either side of 'G' get progressively longer, and so the associated 'action' — which is the *line integral* of the *Lagrangian* over time — also gets larger. Below the figure is the equivalent 'phase arrow' for each path, and these illustrate how the phase rotations get progressively more wild either side of 'G' (which itself is shown with an arbitrary value here).

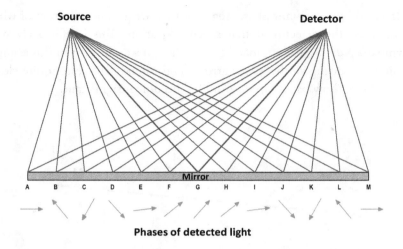

Fig. 7-6, Different paths and phases associated with reflected photons.

When we look at the time taken for each of these paths (which is proportional to the path distance because all the photons travel at the speed of light) then we see how it has a minima (or stationary point) at 'G'. All these potential paths contribute equally (well, nearly, which is why we have drawn the 'phase arrows' of equal length), but the phase rotations are proportional to the time taken. NB: the constant of that proportionality is chosen here for effect rather than being realistic.

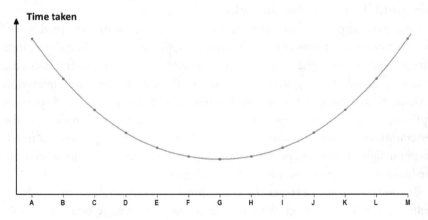

Fig. 7-7, Time taken for alternative paths of reflected photons.

If we add the resultant phases together then we get an indication of which paths reach the detector at that specific location. This is effectively what Feynman's *path integral* approach does, although we can do it in this example by simply drawing all the 'phase arrows' end-to-end. The result quite clearly demonstrates how paths distant from 'G' become insignificant.

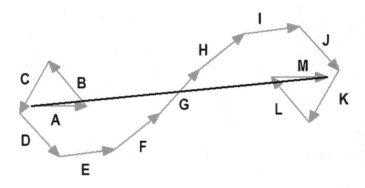

Fig. 7-8, Summing the incident phases from the alternative photon paths.

Around 'A' to 'C', and 'K' to 'M', the 'phase arrows' form tight loops that do not go anywhere. If we added even more paths then those loops would get even tighter. The main contributions to the composite 'phase arrow' come from paths 'E' to 'I' in this illustration.

Feynman's approach has been used to explain commonly accepted wave-like phenomena in terms of particles, such as reflection (including the strange effects from parallel glass panes such as iridescent colours), diffraction (the spreading of light passing around an object or through an aperture), refraction (change in direction of a wave passing between different media), dispersion (splitting of light into a spectrum of colours), focusing of lenses, and the generation of a spectrum from a mirrored diffraction grating. It gives a much deeper insight into what is really happening in these cases, and allows accurate predictions of further, less intuitive optical effects.

But what of the 'histories' in the informal name for this approach? It really means 'paths' rather than temporal histories, and it does not imply any asymmetry in time. Everything described here could be calculated in reverse; for example, by summing over potential futures instead of histories.

The *Lagrangian*, used to calculate the 'action' is a deterministic function of time, and the Feynman *path integral* approach can be transformed into an equivalent Schrödinger equation, which — as we have already mentioned — would be fully deterministic.

Is a photon a *wave packet*? A *wave packet* is a localised version of a wave, and was originally postulated in *quantum theory* as a wave-like representation of a particle (de Broglie's *matter waves*), but do *wave packets* really exist? A fundamental question that rarely gets asked goes like this: if a photon has a definite energy related to its frequency by $E = h\nu$, but a *wave packet* must have a range of frequencies in order to reinforce locally and cancel remotely (see Fig. 7-3), then what frequency is ν? Well, we know that the photon has a definite energy due to Einstein's work on the photoelectric effect and Planck's work on black-body radiation, so the associated frequency, as given by $\nu = E/h$, is of the phase rotation associated with the photon's world-line. In the case of monochromatic light then there will be no other frequencies, and given that the world-lines (as defined here) would be a static extent from one electron to another then there can be no *wave packet* along that world-line.

The *wave packet* is effectively the distribution of frequencies associated with a cross-section through the world-line at a given time, and represents the potential paths (as described above), each of which will have a slightly different 'action'. Heisenberg's *uncertainty principle* relates to the fundamental problem of such a packet not having simultaneously precise values for certain quantities, as explained in §7.2, and hence to the localisation of the particle amongst those potential paths. In an ensemble situation, with vast numbers of photons of equal energy, then interference between these *wave packets* spreads them out, resulting in a purely wave-like manifestation with a precise frequency and completely undefined particle-like position.

7.4   Measurement Problem

When a measurement or observation occurs (including via our detector screen) then something interesting is deemed to happen: the deterministic complex-valued *quantum amplitudes* are replaced with a set of specific real values, but these values are not singled out or predicted by the wave equation. This means that we have to describe observable outcomes in a non-deterministic (stochastic) fashion using real-valued probabilities. This is known as the 'measurement problem', or more specifically as *wave-function collapse*, and more formally as *state-vector reduction*.

In a way, this phenomenon would appear to separate our observation-dependent subjective reality from the observation-independent objective reality, but more on that later. It is mysterious in a number of ways: it appears to occur instantaneously, even over very large distances; it is not predicted by the wave equation, and in fact is incompatible with it; it singles out only one of the possibilities described by the *wave function*; and it is irreversible (because quantum information is lost). The wave equation can be used to model forwards or backwards from a measured state, but it never yields a precise prediction for measurements, either future or prior ones. The fact that a measurement selects just one of the possibilities, rather than zero or many, is often ignored because we take it for granted that measurements always yield specific and reproducible results. This must mean that the *wave function* has to collapse to a single spike representing the measured state, but this is not a natural consequence of the wave equation. Mathematically speaking, *wave-function collapse* is said to occur when a *wave function* irreversibly reduces from a *superposition* of several *eigenstates* to a single *eigenstate*.

Whichever way the deterministic wave equation is run, in order to describe either future or prior states, the probabilities for the superposed states are all conserved; they do not vanish. This is termed *unitary time evolution* because all the probabilities add up to 1, or 100%. So what happens during a measurement? How can the state of a system have a fully deterministic evolution, and yet be punctuated by non-unitary and irreversible measurements? This is why the apparent *wave-function collapse* is deemed incompatible with the wave equation. Note that the 'many-worlds interpretation' deals with the collapse by treating it as a branching point, and asserting that each of those alternatives continues independently, in their own 'world', forming a branching 'tree' of unimaginable complexity — which is why we dismissed that interpretation back in §5.3.

In 1970, German physicist H. Dieter Zeh proposed a mechanism to help explain the apparent collapse.[95] He showed that the system under measurement became entangled with its macroscopic environment, and that quantum information leaked away into the environment in an irreversible process known as *quantum decoherence*, or more specifically *environmental decoherence*. He showed that the haphazard phases of the environment effectively destroyed the interference between the superposed states of the *wave function* (i.e. they decohered), revealing distinct alternatives that could be modelled using classical probabilities.

But not all physicists agree that *environmental decoherence* solves the 'measurement problem'. In 2001, American physicist Stephen L. Adler wrote a paper, intended as a response to views expressed by American theoretical physicist Philip W. Anderson, stating that decoherence is a step in the right direction but does not fully explain the 'measurement problem'.[96] *Environmental decoherence* only removes the interference terms from between the superposed alternative states, not any of the states themselves. So, going back to the double-slit experiment, before a measurement is made at one of the slits, the states describing the two alternatives — left slit or right slit — appear to interfere with each other, and we see the multi-banded pattern on the detector screen. Introducing some macroscopic detection apparatus at one of the slits supposedly destroys that interference and we then see just the two-band pattern again, although we still cannot predict which slit any given particle will go through. NB: it is not clear how this explains the 'delayed-choice experiment' or the 'quantum-eraser experiment' as they involve non-locality.

But why is one specific alternative singled out by a measurement? Although each particle leaves a discrete mark on the detector screen, showing that it came via a specific slit, *Quantum mechanics* cannot provide an answer to this, and so its state descriptions carry around all the superposed alternatives. This is why the probabilistic interpretation was added, and why Einstein passionately believed that something determined which of those possible states was selected, and hence that we merely have insufficient knowledge to determine it ourselves.

The problem appears to leave only a few options for an explanation. Either, (a) the wave equation does not describe the act of measurement, and it needs to be modified in some way, (b) the *wave function* also needs to include the state of the apparatus, and possibly that of the global environment too, or (c) the *wave function* is not describing a fundamental state, and there is more at play than mere observables. But it is not clear how to interpret a *wave function* when it represents superposed states of a macroscopic object. This is just the same issue as with 'Schrödinger's cat': the alternative states of the quantum event can be represented by a single *wave function*, but the cat can only be either dead or alive.

There is also a subjective issue to this. Imagine that we have some test on a quantum system that has just two possible outcomes. In quantum terms, each of those states is 'coupled to' some detection apparatus, meaning that the apparatus is correlated with the quantum system, and will have corresponding states indicating each of those outcomes (we will discuss *quantum entanglement* in the next section). What happens now if we add in an observer, say Alice? Her observation will have apparently singled out one of the alternatives, and the *wave function* description will have collapsed to a 100% probability for it.

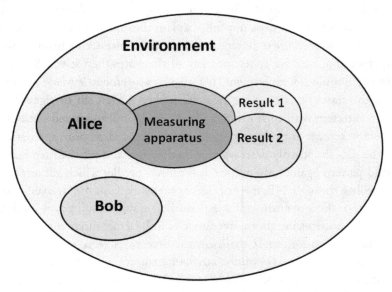

Fig. 7-9, Entanglement of observer, apparatus, and results.

If we introduce a second observer, Bob, he would see the composite system of Alice, her apparatus, and her test system, but Bob would not be aware of any collapse. That is, until he interacts with any part of that composite system, at which point he should then share the same observation as Alice.

In 2019, a team at Heriot-Watt University in Edinburgh claimed to have performed this thought experiment (also known as the 'Wigner's friend paradox'), but demonstrating that Alice and Bob would disagree, and that reality is therefore subjective. However, at the time of writing, this result is very controversial.

There is still no unanimous agreement upon how such things should be interpreted. There are even physicists who say that we should just use the mathematics (which works very well) and not bother about why it works. We will try and resolve this, and other issues, in §7.6, below.

7.5   Entanglement

Quantum entanglement is a phenomenon that occurs when a group of particles are described by a single *wave function*, and they cannot be described separately. Their state is correlated, or connected, but it is not the case that any information is instantaneously passed from one to another when a measurement is made; this is a common misunderstanding. For all intents and purposes, such a system must be considered a single composite system. Mathematically speaking, a composite of two non-interacting systems (e.g. two particles) can be represented as the *tensor product* of their states, $\psi_A \otimes \psi_B$. Such states are then termed separable, but the states of an entangled composite system cannot be factored apart.

Entanglement occurs as a result of direct interactions between particles. Two-particle examples include the production of identical pairs of photons when one of high energy is converted to two of lower energy, the creation of electron-positron pairs from a photon, and the decay of particles. Such entanglement is broken when a measurement is made on one of the particles.

Einstein believed in what is known as *local realism*. This involves two principles: *locality* and *realism*. *Locality* (or *local causality*) means that objects are directly influenced only by their immediate surroundings, thus limiting cause and effect to the speed of light in accordance with *special relativity*. The alternative would be 'action at a distance', which even Isaac Newton was unhappy with in his theory of gravity. We have already heard that *realism* is generally the belief that there is an objective reality that exists independently of any conscious entities. In this specific usage, however, it is the belief that every particle must have a pre-existing value for any measurable property, again independently of conscious entities. There is a related term, *counterfactual definiteness*, which is subtly different from this version of *realism*, but is also more precise: if no measurement of a given physical property is performed (i.e. *counterfactual*), then the physical property still has a definite value (i.e. *definiteness*), and it is meaningful to deal with the unmeasured values on an equal footing with the measured (i.e. *factual*) ones.

In 1935, Einstein collaborated with Russian-American physicist Boris Y. Podolsky and Israeli physicist Nathan Rosen on an article designed to show that *quantum mechanics* was incomplete: "Can Quantum-Mechanical Description of Physical Reality Be Considered Complete?".[97] It described a thought experiment, later known as the 'EPR paradox' (using their initials), where the properties of an electron-positron pair created from a photon (an 'EPR pair') could be separately measured in order to determine values for *complementary variables*. According to Heisenberg's *uncertainty principle*, one could not measure, say, position and momentum simultaneous to an arbitrary level of accuracy, but in this experiment the particles are identical (albeit with opposite charge, and travelling in opposite directions) and so it should be possible to measure the momentum of one and the position of the other, and thus infer the unmeasured properties of their partners.

In order to support the logic behind their deduction, the authors defined a condition for the completeness of a physical theory: "Every element of the physical reality must have a counterpart in the physical theory", and also a criterion for physical reality: "If, without in any way disturbing a system, we can predict with certainty (i.e. with probability equal to unity) the value of a physical quantity, then there exists an element of physical reality corresponding to this physical quantity". Since the thought experiment suggested that a complementary variable can be predicted with certainty for one particle of the 'EPR pair', and without disturbing it, by measuring the variable on the corresponding particle then that variable must be an element of reality. However, since the mathematics disallows this then either (a) the description of reality given by the *wave function* is incomplete, or (b) these two variables cannot have simultaneous reality. They showed that if (a) is false then the only other alternative, (b), is also false, and so *quantum mechanics* must be incomplete.

When Schrödinger wrote to Einstein, very shortly after the article appeared, sharing his own reservations and insights, he used the German term *'verschränkung'*. This is usually translated as 'interweaving' or 'interlocking', but was later translated by him into English as 'entanglement'.[98]

Bohr responded within a few months of the EPR article, in the same journal and under the same title, refuting their combined challenge to *quantum mechanics*.[99] He resorted to his 'principle of complementarity': objects having certain pairs of complementary properties that cannot be observed or measured simultaneously. In particular, he maintained that the EPR criterion for physical reality was ambiguous in the phrase "without in any way disturbing a system" since, as well as the normal mechanical disturbance, there is "an influence on the very conditions which define the possible types of predictions regarding the future behavior of the system", and that these conditions must constitute an inherent element of reality. In this argument, Bohr had introduced a subjective aspect to the notion of reality, implying that the conscious choice of the measurer, or of the designer of the measurement apparatus, somehow changes the outcome of the measurement.

The EPR authors' belief that such properties had specific values that could be simultaneously measured, or predicted, meant that they were simultaneously real. The 'EPR paradox' was that *quantum mechanics* showed they had only a specific value once measured, and yet a physically separated pair would acquire the same value (or correlated values) upon the measurement of just one. As a result, the authors believed that either there was some non-local interaction between the particles, or that they already shared some properties due to their prior interaction or shared creation.

These are termed 'hidden variables' and are common in classical physics when statistics must be employed to explain large-scale behaviours where there are known to be smaller-scale details that are inaccessible or too complex. For instance, describing the behaviours of gases without considering the position and momentum of every single molecule. The instantaneous nature of *quantum entanglement* would mean that any signal from one particle to the other would have to violate *special relativity*, and so would have repercussions for causality. The EPR authors therefore preferred the alternative that there was a deeper level to reality, and that *quantum mechanics* must be extended to become a *local hidden-variable theory*. A *local hidden-variable theory* maintains consistency with *local realism*, and so is also consistent with causality. There are *non-local hidden-variable theories* that do not imply faster-than-light interactions, but we will come to them in the next section.

In the 'Copenhagen interpretation' of the 'EPR paradox', the properties in the composite system are always correlated resulting in a single overall measurement, although if either particle is measured individually then the result would still appear random. The moment an observer measures one particle, they know the value of the same property of the second particle, but an observer of the second particle cannot benefit until the results of that measurement have been communicated to them. That communication cannot exceed the speed of light and so *special relativity* would not be violated. So, just as with measurement on a single particle, an observer cannot simultaneously measure *complementary variables* on the composite system. In effect, this interpretation means that there are no 'hidden variables' and there is no 'action at a distance'. It may sound strange to many people that the *wave function* describing the superposed states (the alternatives) of the composite system is said to collapse for the whole system when a measurement occurs.

In a private letter to Born, on 3 March 1947, Einstein mocked the concept of *quantum entanglement* as "spooky":

> I cannot seriously believe in it because the theory cannot be reconciled with the idea that physics should represent a reality in time and space, free from spooky actions at a distance [German: *spukhafte Fernwirkung*].[100]

In 1932, Hungarian-American mathematician, physicist, and computer scientist John von Neumann produced a proof that all *hidden-variable theories* were incapable of reproducing the same predictions as *quantum mechanics*. In 1935, German mathematician Grete Hermann published a critique of von Neumann's 'proof', pointing out a circularity flaw that meant non-local theories could be valid. Recognition of her observation could have changed the course of *quantum theory*, but her work, unfortunately, was ignored for decades. While it is undoubtable that this was partially due to von Neumann's formidable reputation, and to the momentum of the 'Copenhagen interpretation' combined with Bohr's reputation, it has also been suggested that her work was ignored because she was a female mathematician and unknown to the male elite of the physics community.[101]

It was not until 1964 that Northern Irish physicist John S. Bell rediscovered this flaw, inspired as he was by the 1952 work of American theoretical physicist David J. Bohm, which we will cover in §7.6. Bell devised a theorem showing that specific classes of *hidden -variables theory* would not result in the same statistical predictions as *quantum mechanics*.[102] More specifically, it was the requirement of locality — that the result of a measurement on one system be unaffected by operations on a distant system, separated by a space-like interval (i.e. beyond the *causal horizon*) — that was considered responsible for the difference. The theorem included a mathematical inequality that, if violated by experimental results, would rule out *local hidden-variable theories* as an explanation of the correlations in *quantum entanglement*, although it still allowed for *non-local hidden-variable theories*.

> In a theory in which parameters are added to quantum mechanics to determine the results of individual measurements, without changing the statistical predictions, there must be a mechanism whereby the setting of one measuring device can influence the reading of

another instrument, however remote. Moreover, the signal involved must propagate instantaneously, so that such a theory could not be Lorentz invariant [i.e. it would violate *special relativity's* lack of absolute simultaneity].[103]

Later, in 1971, American mathematical physicist Henry P. Stapp showed that *counterfactual definiteness* was also an implicit concept in *Bell's theorem*.[104] Violation of *Bell's inequality* would therefore imply that *counterfactual definiteness*, or locality, or both, were false.

In 1972, American physicists Stuart J. Freedman and John F. Clauser became the first to test *Bell's inequality* in a laboratory. In 1982, a team led by French physicist Alain Aspect demonstrated more conclusively that *Bell's inequality* was violated by *quantum mechanics*.[105]

Classical (non-quantum) correlation is something that occurs all around us. A common illustration is that of a pair of gloves: having only one in your possession means you know whether the other is left-handed or right-handed, without any physical or informational connection between them.[106] In 1981, Bell wrote an article called "Bertlmann's socks and the nature of reality"[107] where he used the case of the odd socks worn by an eccentric colleague (Austrian physicist Reinhold A. Bertlmann) to explain correlation in the classical world. Bertlmann always wore odd socks, as a sort of protest against the establishment, so if you saw the colour of one sock then you instantly knew that the other sock was not that colour. This would be true no matter how distantly the socks were separated, and so simply demonstrated a correlation of information rather than anything being physically transmitted.

Yet in *quantum mechanics*, the prevailing 'Copenhagen interpretation' would mean that neither sock (or rather some quantum-level analogy of the socks) has a definite colour until observed: both socks would be in a *superposition* of possible colour states. This then leads to an anomaly because observation of one would instantaneously — in the true sense of the word — cause that and the other to collapse to the same colour-combination state; the measurement causing collapse of the *wave function* describing the composite system. But what type of causal connection could force both into the same state, instantaneously, and independently of the separating distance?

Some interpretations suggest that the first particle has a random, fluctuating value until the measurement is performed, at which point *wave-function collapse* magically gives the second particle the same value. If this was an instance of local causation then it could not be transmitted at greater than the speed of light, but if the particles are separated by a space-like interval then it would have to exceed that speed, and this would violate the principle of causality as it would also be impossible to say which occurred first (cause or effect). This problem of local causality also applies in circumstances not involving entanglement. If two distant detectors were trying to detect the same particle then there would be a race condition: they cannot both detect it at different locations and so the result of one being successful must instantly prevent any paradoxical detection by the other.

One of the ways of experimentally demonstrating the violation of *Bell's inequality* is by generating two photons, both travelling in opposite directions, that have an entangled polarisation. Each photon is passed through a polarisation filter (a little like your polarising sunglasses) before being incident on separate detectors. The generated polarisations of the photons are random, but they are also identical within each specific pair. The experiment involves changing the relative orientation of the two filters and then correlating the separate detections. If the filters are parallel (0^0 between their directions) then the detections are perfectly correlated as both the photons either pass the filters or they do not. If they are orthogonal (90^0) then the detections are perfectly anti-correlated since if one photon gets through then the other will be blocked, and *vice versa*. When the angle is 45^0 then the detectors are uncorrelated as there is a random 50:50 chance of them agreeing (or disagreeing). This all makes normal sense so far as it would be the same with a classical correlation.

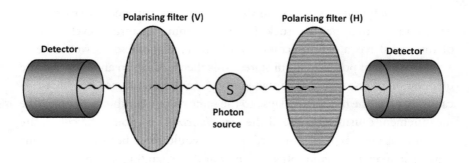

Fig. 7-10, EPR experiment with polarised photons.

Note that the essential reason for varying the angle between the detectors is that the *uncertainty principle* restricts precise measurement of spin or polarisation along more than one of the orthogonal axes. Measuring the property of one particle leads to a distribution of possibilities for different detector angles at the other. The difference between the classical correlations (where local causality prevails) and the *quantum correlations* occurs at any other angle, and it arises because the classical correlation is a simple triangular relation (straight gradients with singularities at the change of gradient) whereas the *quantum correlation* is smooth. If we define a correlation value, *C*, as +1 for correlated, -1 for anti-correlated, and 0 for uncorrelated, then the *quantum correlation* for this polarisation case is calculated to be $C = cos(2\theta)$.[108]

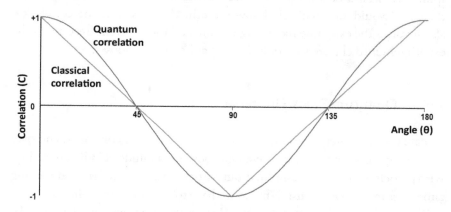

Fig. 7-11, Difference between quantum and classical correlation.

The perceived mystery arising from this scenario is to do with those differences of correlation: the gaps in this graph. If the experimenter is free to choose the angle between the filters (θ), and the correlation depends only upon the chosen angle, then how can the agreement (or disagreement) be consistently greater than the classical expectation associated with *local realism*? It may sound like some type of conspiracy between the photons and the detectors, or between the photons themselves. However, note that the result is independent of the distance between the two detectors, and of the distance of the detectors from the source of the two photons. This means that (in principle, at least) the setting of the angles could be changed after the two photons have been sent on their way, and yet the result would still be as described here.

There is a variation of this experiment that measures the spins of an electron-positron pair. Although effectively random, each pair will have identically opposite spins (i.e. one up and one down). Given that measuring one component of the spin (say, in the x direction) would mean that the other two (y and z directions) would have fluctuating imprecise values, then we are finding that it is the same x component that has a definite value for the second particle. Not only that, if we change the angle of what we are calling the x direction in the detectors, after the particles have begun their journey, then we still see the correlation with the second particle.

So it is not just a matter of properties acquired by the particles when they were created; for instance, that one particle had up-spin and one had down-spin. That would be a normal classical correlation because if you knew one then you would automatically know the other. In this case, the correlation also involves the experimental configuration, and the apparent freedom of the experimenter to change the configuration as he or she chooses.

7.6   Quantum Block Universe

Debate over the interpretation of *quantum mechanics* still continues, and over the consequences of the topics presented above for an understanding of reality: is it a particle, or a wave, or a smeared-out particle, or a *wave packet*, or something altogether more mysterious? Why do we have to resort to probabilities?

There are respected scientists who even believe that consciousness plays a crucial part, particularly in the 'measurement problem', including von Neumann; Hungarian-American theoretical physicist and mathematician Eugene P. Wigner; and American mathematical physicist Henry P. Stapp. This view is sometimes referred to as the 'consciousness-causes-collapse interpretation'. Given the ubiquitous nature of *wave-function collapse*, as exhibited by the vast macroscopic world around us, and the rather rarer phenomenon of consciousness, then we will not entertain this viewpoint any further here.

Although Einstein had originally proposed the quanta of light known as photons in order to explain the photoelectric effect, and Bohr had originally disliked this because of the arbitrary duality of wave-particle solutions that it appeared to offer within physics, their roles turned around as the quantum revolution unfolded. Einstein was shocked by Heisenberg's *uncertainty principle*, and then again by Born's probabilistic interpretation of the *wave function*. His strong belief in *local realism*, and hence in causality, meant that he could not countenance superpositions of possibilities, fundamental randomness (as opposed to applying statistics in the case of 'hidden variables' or unknown processes), non-local effects, or the importance placed upon the role of the observer. They embarked upon a prolonged debate, lasting the rest of their lives (and beyond[109]), consisting of exchanges of argument and counter-argument that helped shape our modern understanding of physics. They remained lifelong friends, and respectful colleagues, but they never found agreement on these matters of reality. The 'EPR paradox' was probably the strongest of Einstein's arguments as it would be several decades before it could finally be proved incorrect, but the modern consensus is that Bohr triumphed in their debates from a philosophical standpoint.

In the 'Copenhagen interpretation', physical systems cannot be said to have definite properties prior to being measured, and we can only predict the probability distribution for a given measurement. This makes *quantum mechanics* more a theory of phenomenal knowledge than of physical objects. But the *quantum amplitude* (and hence the *wave function*) is a mathematical device — it is defined in an abstract mathematical space,[110] and it cannot be observed in our space and time — so the question becomes whether the amplitude is ontic (representing something real or physical) or epistemic (representing a state of knowledge about something). The probabilistic interpretation makes *quantum mechanics* an epistemological theory, and the EPR resort to 'hidden variables' attempted to make it an ontological one. Unfortunately, these distinctions are rather blunt in this context, and are accepted to be mutually exclusive, but this section will also make a case for the amplitude having both ontic and epistemic qualities.

In the 'ensemble interpretation' of *quantum mechanics*, the *wave function* is said to apply to a many-particle system rather than to specific individual particles, and hence justifies the probabilistic interpretation. However, this view has difficulty in explaining the gradual build-up of an interference pattern when particles are allowed through the double-slit one at a time.

One of the most common interpretations is that the superposed states are all real, and that the individual particles somehow take (or 'explore') all of the alternative paths available to them, thus interfering with themselves in the double-slit scenario. This would account for the gradual build-up of the interference pattern for single particles, but it would not really explain how the presence of a detector at one slit, or the availability of 'which-path information' acquired by some other means, eliminates all but one of those alternatives.

A central problem with most of the interpretations of *quantum mechanics* is the presumption of causality. In a *block universe*, there can be no *wave-function collapse*, or non-local correlation, happening 'in response to' a measurement. If we imagine taking a step back, and looking at a system in retrospect — thus helping us to forget causal expectations — then all the world-lines of the particles, and all the correlations of *quantum entanglement*, are consistent with each other; everything is effectively 'sketched out', and there are no alternatives, no superpositions, and no probabilities. So where does the wave-like character come from?

What we need is an interpretation of the mathematics of *quantum mechanics* that is consistent with the concept of a *block universe*: that unchanging universe involving objective time, no motion, no choice, and no causality. Let us call this the 'quantum block universe': a type of *block universe* that will hopefully take us one step closer to describing the objective reality. We have already backed away from the term 'probability' (as in *probability amplitude*) in order to avoid a presumption of indeterminism, but we must similarly back away from the term 'knowledge' since it may be taken as implying 'knowing for a fact' or presuming the participation of conscious entities.

We will start with the premise that individual particle entities — as vaguely described at the start of this chapter — have an independent objective existence. Quantum-level phenomena such as particle decay, hadron collisions, and the photoelectric effect, all yield discrete effects and artefacts that may be traced back to such discrete entities. Without such effects then we could not have detectors such as Geiger counters. The apparent collapse of the *wave function* to just one specific *eigenstate* (which we queried earlier) must therefore be so because there is just one consistent possibility for the particle entity at that instant.

In 1929, English physicist Sir Nevill F. Mott formulated a paradox (the 'Mott problem') concerning the source of discrete particle tracks in a cloud or bubble chamber when many such situations are described mathematically by a spherically symmetric (in space) *wave function*.[111] His specific example was the emission of an alpha particle from a decaying nucleus, and the issue was that the detection chamber records discrete directed particle tracks whereas the *wave function* describes a "spherical wave". If this wave were real then you might expect random ionisation of the gas throughout the chamber. It is possible to consider each ionisation to be a case of *wave-function collapse*, and so consider the emanation of spherical waves from each of the ionisation positions, but an obvious alternative conclusion would be that there is a real particle there, and that it causes a sequence of ionisations along its trajectory. Although Mott's paper solved the problem in terms of multiple waves, and showed that a straight ionisation line of indeterminate direction is overwhelmingly probable, we will consider that the *wave function* is purely a mathematical description of our ignorance, and so incompatible with the observation of the specific particle path.

It is important to remember that mathematics is not physics. As obvious as this may be, there is always a temptation to give physical meaning to mathematical abstractions, and to assume that a given mathematical framework is a unique and accurate way of modelling some phenomenon. The *quantum amplitude* represents superposed states in a *configuration space* of possibly infinite dimensionality. This heavyweight mathematical framework is actually trying to carry around all possible scenarios, and rapidly becomes unmanageable for many-particle scenarios, but it does not mean that they are all equally real and contemporaneous; we are interpreting it too literally. Feynman's *path integrals* approach to QED illustrates this quite clearly since it integrates over all possible paths for a discrete particle, and yet is mathematically equivalent to the Schrödinger equation.

A very good illustration of the difference between *wave-function* mathematics and an actual scenario can be found in a book by English physicist and mathematician Sir Roger Penrose.[112] It involves high-energy photons individually sent from a source (S) to a half-silvered mirror (M). Assuming a 50:50 probability for the photon going through the mirror to the detector (D) — route S-M-D — or reflected into the ceiling (C) — route S-M-C — then the wave equation nicely describes both of the alternatives together as superposed states.

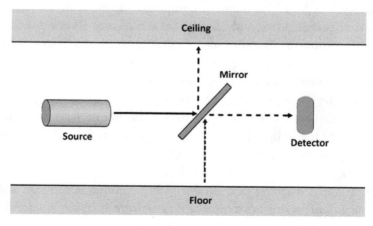

Fig. 7-12, Wave function blind to causal asymmetry.

However, instead of looking at probable outcomes after S, the wave equation can also be used to look at possible histories prior to D. Under those circumstances, it would describe a 50:50 chance of the photon coming straight through the mirror — route S-M-D again — or being emitted by the floor (F) and reflecting off the mirror — route F-M-D. Clearly the latter is an unrealistic event as it excludes so many aspects of the configuration, but the *quantum amplitude* <u>would</u> describe a valid scenario if those aspects were suitably modified. Although presented as an example of 'time asymmetry' by Penrose, it is actually a case of 'causal asymmetry' (§8.2). It is not unlike the cannon example in §1.3: the mathematics does not say that the cannonball went from the cannon to the floor, or *vice versa*; it only describes the shape of its path and is ignorant of what we deem to be the causal connections.

Much has been made of the 'measurement problem', but the 'quantum block universe' accommodates a different interpretation, given our assessment of *quantum superposition*. It is mixing a mathematical treatment of the possible outcomes with the physical nature of specific measurements, thus mixing potentialities and actualities (or *apples and oranges*). A measurement yields a single real value, but the *quantum amplitude* describes multiple possibilities because *quantum mechanics* is unable to predict that measured value from the observable properties available to us. This then results in a messy situation as the wave equation is fully deterministic (allowing calculation in either direction from a given time), continuous, and unitary, but the measurement appears to be discontinuous and irreversible.

One aspect of Bohr's 'principle of complementarity' holds that the wave-particle duality is exclusive, and that each view cannot be observed at the same time as its counterpart. Another way of phrasing this is that things behave as particles when measured, or directly interact with something else, and behave as waves in between those events. So this suggests that the *quantum amplitude* (and hence the *wave function*) is epistemic, and describes the potentiality of scenarios that we are unable to confirm without a measurement, but the measurement process itself is ontic, and so incompatible. This does not yet explain why we observe the consequences of some wave-like property, and where it originates, but we are getting there.

So what about *quantum entanglement*? The correlation is accepted as being instantaneous and evident as soon as a measurement is made, but this is true irrespective of whether the particles are separated by a time-like interval (not requiring super-luminal speeds, and so allowing *local realism*) or a space-like interval (outside of their *causal horizons*). Within a time-like interval, *special relativity* shows that there is no such thing as absolute simultaneity, although the ordering of events is preserved. Hence, a causal interpretation sounds feasible, if using a *local hidden-variable theory*, but *Bell's inequality* provides testable constraints on this that ultimately show the correlation is not a classical one and cannot involve local 'hidden variables'. Within a space-like interval then the concept of causality would break down because any signals propagated faster than the speed of light would mean that the ordering of cause and effect would depend upon the observer.

If we accept non-locality — which Bell showed as being a viable class of *hidden-variable theory* — then this only requires super-luminal communication speeds if we deem there to be a causal aspect to the correlation, i.e. some mediating signal. Also, any associated 'hidden variables' would have to remain permanently hidden since if they were observable then we could take advantage of their speed to create situations that would violate our apparent causality. It has been suggested that von Neumann's 'proof' wrongly regarded the concept of causality as equivalent to the concept of *determinism*, hence making indeterminism a violation of causality.[113] The most popular interpretations of *quantum mechanics* are causal and non-deterministic[114], but we have abandoned causality for the *block universe* and so we want a solution that is both acausal and deterministic.

One approach to having a non-local theory that is *Lorentz invariant*, and so the same for all inertial observers, is to have an external all-pervading influence on the particles that is related to space-time itself. Physicists reading this will immediately think 'oh, you mean *pilot-wave theory*', and there is some common ground so let us just review what it means in order to determine how much common ground exists.

In 1952, Bohm presented a deterministic non-local interpretation that was in complete agreement with standard *quantum mechanics*.[115] It posited that all particles had precisely definable states, but that their motion was guided by a separate wave-like concept involving a *quantum potential*. Although he used the term potential, the effect of this wave depended upon its form rather than its magnitude, and it did not fall off with distance.[116] Also, the potential demonstrated non-local connections because it was defined in a *configuration space* and reflected the known circumstances, or total state, described by Bohm as a 'quality of wholeness'.[117]

Unbeknown to Bohm, he had rediscovered a theory previously presented by de Broglie in 1927, known as *pilot-wave theory*. Although de Broglie's theory was never developed as far as a multi-particle formulism, its 'pilot wave' was essentially the same as this *quantum potential*. His theory had been quickly abandoned because it received strong criticism from Austrian theoretical physicist Wolfgang E. Pauli, and it was not revisited because von Neumann's 1932 paper was taken to seal the fate of all *hidden-variable theories*.

Bohm's refinement is therefore known as the *de Broglie–Bohm theory*, but it was initially criticised too. Although the intention of Bohm's paper was primarily as a counterexample to von Neumann's 'proof', and so to demonstrate that deterministic *hidden-variable theories* were possible, this point seemed to get lost, and his example was considered to be contrived.[118] Rather surprisingly, Einstein was not impressed with the theory, and wrote to Born on 12 May 1952 "Have you [Born] heard that Bohm believes (as de Broglie did, by the way, 25 years ago) that he is able to interpret the quantum theory in deterministic terms? That way seems too cheap to me. But you, of course, can judge this better than I."[119]

Worse still, Bohm had become *persona non grata* in the McCarthyite America of the 1950s. There was a concerted effort to ignore both him and his theory. Dutch-American theoretical physicist Max Dresden recounted some of the reactions to a seminar he gave to explain Bohm's work: "juvenile deviationism" (Abraham Pais), "public nuisance" (other), and "if we cannot disprove Bohm, then we must agree to ignore him" (American theoretical physicist J. Robert Oppenheimer).[120]

Luckily, the theory gained renewed interest when Bell was inspired by it to investigate whether its non-locality could be eliminated, resulting in the publication of his *Bell's theorem* in 1964.

In the context of the double-slit experiment, this guiding wave (or potential) is defined at both slits, but the particle only goes through one particular slit. The conditions of generation of the particle beam can never be fully specified and so the true initial positions and motions of the particles constitute the 'hidden variables'. The wave passes through both slits and creates an interference pattern on the other side. The peaks and troughs of this interference define a greater or lesser potentiality for the particle to be guided in the associated direction. This also applies in the case of particles sent one at a time, where the variable potentiality causes banded distributions to emerge on the detector screen over time. The source of the theory's 'non-locality' was described as follows by Bell:

That the guiding wave, in the general case, propagates not in ordinary three-space but in a multidimensional-configuration space is the origin of the notorious 'nonlocality' of quantum mechanics. It is a merit of the de Broglie–Bohm version to bring this out so explicitly that it cannot be ignored. [121]

A problem with the *de Broglie–Bohm theory* is how to identify the 'pilot wave' in physical terms. The fact that it is defined in a *configuration space* rather than our real three-dimensional space is the same interpretational issue as with *quantum amplitudes*, but the 'pilot wave' appears to have an additional causal guiding influence on physical particles, as opposed to being simply an evolving state description. If the 'pilot wave' is an independent entity to the particles under its direction then how is it synchronised with the conditions that define their classical paths? It cannot be independent if it is 'aware' of their starting conditions and actions. It also leads to some interpretational issues such as 'ghost waves' (or 'ghost fields'), which are hypothetical cases of the 'pilot wave' in the absence of any particle.

The 'quantum block universe' shares some aspects with the *de Broglie–Bohm theory* since both would generate exactly the same predictions as standard *quantum mechanics*, both assign precisely defined states to particles, both have a separate concept responsible for the wave-like variations between particle paths, and both are deterministic. But, the 'quantum block universe' is acausal, and there is no propagation of any physical 'pilot wave', nor of any type of wave, because everything is static and the equivalent of the wave is a property of space-time.

Until this point, we have used the term 'potentiality' (the possibility of something happening in the future) to describe the variant outcomes induced by the 'pilot wave'. While describing the 'quantum block universe', though, we will use the less dynamic term 'propensity' (an inclination or natural tendency to behave in a particular way) to describe the apparent weighting of the possible world-lines. This slight semantic shift is simply to distinguish possibilities that imply any notion of change or choice (i.e. potentialities) from possibilities that are static and deterministically consistent (i.e. propensities). This may sound like a pointless exercise but although there are no alternative outcomes in a *block universe*, there is still a distribution of world-lines (observed as paths) that would be consistent with some set of conditions involving 'hidden variables'.

Note that it makes no sense to discuss particles in the absence of space-time, and there is little point in discussing space-time in the absence of particles; they are effectively part of the same thing. Using the double-slit experiment as an example, the initial conditions of the particles are 'hidden' (meaning that their positions and momenta are not precisely defined), but also the space-time starting positions and subsequent paths for every single particle are fundamentally different: there is no absolute space-time positioning, and even when described relative to the apparatus then any distinctness of the particles demands that their space-time world-lines are all unique. This means that our equivalent of the 'pilot wave' cannot be a specific property of space-time — as a metric[122] would be — but of those endpoint conditions, and hence of the individual world-lines. Moreover, it also applies to hypothetical world-lines.

But that is basically what the mathematics of Feynman and Dirac already describes. A metric is a property of a specific space-time location, the integral of which provides the length of an interval between two locations, and inertial objects appear to move along the shortest paths between locations (but see note 160). When using *Hamilton's principle* in classical mechanics then an object follows the path of stationary 'action', but if the endpoint conditions are imprecise then we have a distribution of possible paths, or rather a density of possible world-lines over the associated space-time locations. The propensity of these classical world-lines is manifested to us as additive probabilities for observable paths.

When using *path integrals* in *quantum mechanics* then the *quantum amplitude* for a potential path is related to the classical 'action' in such a way that the world-line has a phase in the complex plane. These amplitudes are not just additive but may also cancel as a result of that phase, and so the propensity of possible quantum world-lines is 'clumpy' because they exhibit wave-like inference. The probability of an observed path is then related to this propensity by the *Born rule*. The essential point is that the non-locality afforded by the *de Broglie–Bohm theory* is attributed here to a description of possible world-lines, and with no physical wave to explain, no wave-like propagation, and no causal influence. It is highly likely that this is a clue to the true nature of space-time since the world-lines (both factual and counterfactual) are inseparable from their hosting space-time, but the nature of this connection is still unknown. We will take a slightly different look at 'emergent space-time' in §11.5.

Let us just approach this again with a little more detail. *Quantum amplitudes* are defined in a *configuration space*, but if we make this a position space then they can be directly related to both world-lines and to what is observed by folding the spatial dimensions[123]; the other non-space-time dimensions of the *configuration space* (e.g. momentum) would become the 'hidden variables' by rolling them up. Each world-line is described by an amplitude related to the classical 'action' of a corresponding particle — Eq. (7.3) — and so if we deem that amplitude to be a fundamental property of possible world-lines then we have the 'quantum block universe' equivalent of the 'pilot wave', and without its interpretational issues. The amplitude defines the propensity of each possible world-line, and we know that this has a wave-like character because of its phase. Furthermore, this character causes interference effects, resulting in a bunching of that propensity (i.e. increased in some regions and decreased in others). This is not a physical interference, as with propagating waves, but is a notional interference resulting from the simple summation of complex-valued propensities.

We accept that simple real-valued non-negative probabilities are additive in a similar way, but these are strongly tied to our subjective reality. The best way to envisage this static reality is to consider the propensity as a complex-valued weighting of possible world-lines. Each particle world-line is determined by its endpoint conditions (which are partly hidden from us), and so given a continuous distribution of particle initial positions, directions, and velocities then we can say that more of them will have world-lines in the vicinity of increased propensity. This not only results in the banding seen in the double-slit experiment, but also the banding that is built up over time as individual particles are sent. Furthermore, it is then obvious why such wave-like effects are only observed under aggregate conditions: ensemble collections (sent together) or multiple particles sent over a protracted period.

You might be thinking 'surely this is just the probabilistic interpretation again', but that would be missing an important point. The mathematics of probability theory stands on its own terms, and is blind to our experience, yet our interpretation of that mathematics involves the relative likelihood of a particular outcome given certain sets of initial conditions, even though the mathematics itself does not say that. So natural is our assessment of the likelihood of future outcomes that we frequently apply the forecasting paradigm to cases where subjective time is not even relevant. For instance, the fact that there are more decimal integers that begin with one than with two, and more that begin with two than with three (*Benford's law*), is a mathematical certainty and nothing to do with probability, but it is common to see it explained as 'if I randomly sample integers from the interval so-and-so then there's more chance ...'. The reality is that there are simply more instances.

In a *block universe*, our general probabilities would correspond to a density of observable possibilities, either of outcomes or of contributing factors — depending upon which temporal direction we were looking at — but we will revisit this subject in more detail in §10.3. An analogy that might help to visualise the difference is to consider an irregular watercourse, making its way through sand and stones. The water will fork and take different paths depending upon which is easiest given the ('hidden') parameters of each part of the flow, and we might describe this as some paths being more probable than others. Now imagine the flow frozen in time, so that the individual parts of it (which we are assuming to have little or no effect upon each other) have some similarity with the possible world-lines in a 'quantum block universe'. We would then see the difference between the alternative paths in terms of the volume of flow having taken them rather than in terms of any probabilities, and hence in terms of the concentration of possible 'flow lines' per path.

There is another take on *quantum mechanics* that we have neglected to mention, known as *decoherent histories* (or *consistent histories*), which is based upon a slightly different notion of *quantum decoherence*. Each potential transition is effectively constrained by the preciseness of its starting and ending conditions, as determined by interactions with other particles and forces, such that the number of possible alternatives is reduced accordingly. These alternatives are categorised according to 'fine-grained histories' (accounting for every possibility) and 'coarse-grained histories' (accounting for distinct overall outcomes). The entanglement with not just the previous histories but also with what might follow leads to a paring down of these possible alternatives, and a decohering of the coarse-grained ones, until just one of them is left: the only one still consistent with the conditions, and hence the one apparently taken. These consistency criteria allow classical probabilities to be assigned to the various coarse-grained alternatives while still being consistent with Schrödinger's wave equation.

A strong advocate of this approach, American physicist Murray Gell-Mann, wrote of the determinism of 'fine-grained histories' as follows:

> It is mind-boggling to consider, instead of those decohering coarse-grained histories, an extreme case of fine-grained histories with non-zero interference terms and no true probability.[124]

This is almost a picture of our 'quantum block universe' with 'fine-grained histories' corresponding to its world-lines. The consistency criteria — as represented mathematically by an entanglement with prior and future histories — effectively impose non-causal constraints upon those world-lines. It is certainly the case that the aforementioned dependency upon the endpoints corresponds mathematically to Gell-Mann's "extreme case" of decoherence.

This 'quantum block universe' is actually a variation of what is known as *superdeterminism*. In its conventional interpretation, this posits that the results of all measurements are predetermined by the causal chain going right back to the 'big bang', or however the universe originated. In other words, that all those prior correlations that we deem to be causations are responsible for the universe as we see it now. The fact, then, that the experimenter and the experiment have a shared history, going back to the beginning of time, would mean that they are correlated — in fact, absolutely everything would be correlated in this way — and so the experimenter's choices would not be statistically independent of the system being measured. Such theories are sometimes described as 'conspiratorial theories' because of the fanciful notion that the universe could conspire to prevent you doing anything other than what you actually did. In the case of the *block universe*, however, the *determinism* is not causal, instead being the result of a static pattern, and this puts an entirely different perspective on it: the difference between *mathematical determinism* and *causal determinism*.

One of those to recognise the significance of *superdeterminism* was actually Bell, who admitted that it was a way around his *Bell's theorem* with a *hidden-variable theory* that did not require superluminal speeds. On 11 May 1984, during a BBC Radio 3 interview organized by Paul C. W. Davies and Julian R. Brown, Bell confirmed that *superdeterminism* could explain the correlation results of *quantum entanglement* without the need for superluminal signalling.

> *... I was going to ask whether it is still possible to maintain, in the light of experimental experience, the idea of a deterministic universe?*
>
> You know, one of the ways of understanding this business is to say that the world is super-deterministic. That not only is inanimate nature deterministic, but we, the experimenters who imagine we can choose to do one experiment rather than another, are also determined. If so, the difficulty which this experimental result creates disappears.

Free will is an illusion -- that gets us out of the crisis, does it?
That's correct. In the analysis it is assumed that free will is
genuine, and as a result of that one finds that the intervention
of the experimenter at one point has to have consequences at
a remote point, in a way that influences restricted by the finite
velocity of light would not permit. If the experimenter is not free
to make this intervention, if that also is determined in advance, the
difficulty disappears.[125]

But in relation to the mind having a fundamental role in physics, Bell
was less sure: "I neither believe, nor disbelieve that. I think that mind is
a very important phenomenon in the universe, certainly for us. Whether it is
absolutely essential to introduce it into physics at this stage, I am not sure."[126]

Bell's theorem assumes that the observer is free to make whichever
measurements they choose, and that this choice is independent both of other
measurements and of 'hidden variables'. Not only that, it assumes that it is
meaningful to speak of results that might have been obtained if different
choices had been made — this is the *counterfactual definiteness* that we defined
earlier. This assumption is implicit whenever we employ probabilities as
a measure of the ways that something can happen compared with the number
of ways that it cannot happen: we are then grouping eventualities according
to whether they are consistent with the choices made or not. In a fully
deterministic theory then no choices are actually possible since everything
is predetermined, and repeating an experiment to test alternative outcomes
will involve different conditions (despite our best intentions), and different
space-time locations.

An advocate of *superdeterminism* is Dutch theoretical physicist Gerard 't
Hooft (pronounced 'geerar-dut-hoft'), who had discussed this loophole with
Bell and recalled that:

I think it was in the early '80s. I raised the question: Suppose that
also Alice's and Bob's decisions have to be seen as not coming out
of free will, but being determined by everything in the theory. John
said, well, you know, that I have to exclude. If it's possible, then
what I said doesn't apply. I said, Alice and Bob are making a decision
out of a cause. A cause lies in their past and has to be included in
the picture.[127]

Superdeterminism is not a popular view as it is believed to entail abandoning free will (which is very hard for most people), and to have potential repercussions for science if the experimenter is not truly free to make choices (say by destroying falsifiability), so let us consider its implications in the light of our bipartite reality. Firstly, the *superdeterminism* associated with our 'quantum block universe' is entirely acausal, and so subtly different from the conventional interpretation. States at different times are correlated by virtue of mathematical determinism rather than causal determinism. This is also the biggest difference between our propensity of future states that correlate with prior states, and the *de Broglie–Bohm theory* with its causal guiding wave; David Bohm initially referred to his theory as the 'causal interpretation' of *quantum theory*.[128] Secondly, we abandoned free will as an illusion of our subjective reality in §6.4. Thirdly, the notion of *counterfactual definiteness* must remain intact because it is borne out through experience and science, and is encapsulated in our laws of physics. We find predictability if we repeat an experiment at different places and at different times. Lastly, the fact that the difference between classical correlation and a *quantum correlation* is predictable, and measurable, would suggest that it has nothing to do with the shared history between the experimenter and the system being measured, or with any lack of options open to the experimenter. This would be better explained as classical probability being appropriate only to our subjective observables, and not to the underlying world-lines.

So what of the fear that experimenters do not have the freedom to establish configurations of their own choice, and hence that the experimental set-up is no longer statistically independent of the measurement goal? This is easily the biggest obstacle to the concepts of both *superdeterminism* and a *block universe*, no matter how much sense those ideas make mathematically, but it is ill-founded, depending as it does on our world of experience. Science has a huge part to play within our subjective reality, including utilising concepts such as choice, free will, and even measurement itself, but at some level then we have to accept that these are illusory. Both the goal and the capabilities of scientific study must shift markedly as we get closer to fundamental physics. Inanimate apparatus do not make measurements; they demonstrate a specific correlation between some properties, or effects, where we know there to be a generic correlation that is deterministic and repeatable.

In our subjective reality, we can observe one variable in order to gain what we deem to be insights into the variation of the other (as in the case of the mercury in a thermometer bulb expanding in response to a temperature increase). In the objective reality, however, then we have only static acausal correlations. Their relative changes along the time dimension could be mathematically modelled (if we had access to them), and this 'pattern of change' is the basis of our laws of physics; but we are also just a bundle of ever-changing world-lines, and those correlations extend to include them too. It is inappropriate to consider that this has any bearing on our apparent choices, and a far more important consideration is that *counterfactual definiteness* is honoured by that underlying determinism. We can repeat tests *ad infinitum* to cover different settings, or we can create massive parallel combinations of tests with variant settings to achieve the same coverage at a particular time, but we have to assume that the results will be independent of whether we achieve them at a different time or a different place. From this, we can speak meaningfully of configurations that we could have done but did not, and hence that our role in being a part of the experiment is much overrated. Had the settings been chosen by some unpredictable quantum event then it would still be consistent with the mathematical description.

In summary, having previously proposed that the objective reality is based upon a *block universe*, we have examined the consequences of that at the quantum level and found that it admits both an acausal form of *superdeterminism* and a *non-local hidden-variable theory* along the lines explored by Bohm. This 'quantum block universe' consists of acausal world-lines (real and hypothetical) that are characterised by a rotational phase in a complex plane, and the *wave function* describes the propensity of these world-lines given classes of conditions representing their endpoints (i.e. either prior- or future-bound). Because the phase of these world-lines interferes constructively and destructively, irrespective of whether they are actual or hypothetical (just like additive probabilities for hypothetical observable possibilities) then it gives the impression of a non-local theory,[129] just as the *de Broglie–Bohm theory* was. Also, the 'measurement problem' is not really a problem because the *wave function* is only utilising as much as we can know (or have observed) about a system.

Something we have not mentioned in this section so far is 'which-path information'. Why is it that placing detectors near either of the slits in the double-slit experiment changes the results to the classical non-banded version? In both the 'quantum-eraser experiment' and 'delayed-choice experiment' scenarios there is no possible causal connection, yet the results will still be changed. It is important to note that in all of these configurations, everything is perfectly determinate and consistent: particles go through one particular slit, the 'which-path information' confirms this, and the results on the detector screen are consistent with it. **This is important because it is one of the strongest pieces of evidence that we really do exist in a *block universe*.** In an ensemble collection of particles, where we have no 'which-path information', then the apparent motions of the individual particles will be determined by the *quantum amplitude* describing the propensity of the world-lines that are consistent with the experimental configuration, and the associated interference causes the striated display on the detector screen. As we described above, this amplitude is closer to a density of those world-lines in space-time rather than any probabilities of observable paths. When we insert a detector at one slit then that is a non-causal constraint and the world-lines of the *block universe* must be consistent with it, as you would expect where *superdeterminism* rules.

Quantum correlation is another example of *superdeterminism* in action, and so is additional evidence that we exist in a *block universe*. Again, everything is consistent. In fact, *quantum correlation* is less mysterious in the absence of independent particles, causality, and the associated probabilities.

A small digression before we leave this section: if *quantum mechanics* was all-encompassing then it should also describe the measurement apparatus and the effective environment, and also be able to predict with some accuracy rather than with probability. Whether it can predict with total accuracy (e.g. predicting the direction of an alpha particle from a decaying nucleus) depends upon what we have access to — what we can measure — and that will always be limited.

Quantum superposition describes independent possibilities that cannot be specifically predicted, and yet a measurement — or, allegedly, any interaction with the macroscopic environment — yields only one precise state. So, given that the state at any instant of time in a *block universe* is fixed, what possible significance (beyond our own calculations) could there be in dividing it into superposed linearly independent states?

Let us take a very simple scenario. When representing a particle that may have a spin of up or down then *quantum superposition* can be used to form a linear sum of the two states, which is then also a solution of the wave equation (written here using Dirac's Bra-Ket notation).

$$|\psi\rangle = \frac{1}{\sqrt{2}}|\psi_U\rangle + \frac{1}{\sqrt{2}}|\psi_D\rangle$$

The factor of $\sqrt{2}$ is so that when associated probabilities are calculated, the total comes to 1 because there are no other possibilities. This implies that up and down are distinguishable, which presumes the existence of some frame of reference and hence of other particles. If this particle was in total isolation, with nothing else around it, then up/down, left/right, clockwise/anticlockwise, etc., would be meaningless, and the breakdown of the particle's state into two superposed states would be pointless. More than this, though, the *wave function* for such a particle would be undefined because neither its position nor its momentum could be quantified, and the *uncertainty principle* could not apply.

If we now consider two particles then the associated configuration space would normally include three spatial (or momentum) dimensions per particle, plus a common time dimension (i.e. $\psi(x_i, x_i', t)$). But if they are far apart — beyond any causal connection — then that mathematical representation has no advantage over two completely independent configuration spaces; it is only when there is a potential interaction that the cross-product of their states is at all relevant. If, though, we accept the reality of a *block universe*, and its total lack of all things dynamical, then the representation in configuration space is at least inappropriate.

We are, here, further questioning the fundamentality of the *wave function*, and of the associated wave equation. Schrödinger's derivation was an attempt to describe the evolution of de Broglie's *matter waves*, but they were not a well-understood concept at the time, and the resulting equation is rather vague in terms of what is actually evolving. Only by relating it back to hard-and-fast particles, and by employing probabilities, has any useful interpretation been given to it. If the above scenarios can be deemed unrealistic then it suggests that space-time itself is not fundamental, and is dependent upon the presence of those interactions (§11.5).

This section has approached the problem from a quite different direction: deconstructing the wave-particle duality to find a possible explanation that is consistent with a *block universe*. This is a huge constraint to impose upon any aspect of physics, or our subjective reality, but the resulting 'quantum block universe' proposes an entity from which it should be possible to reconstruct the mathematics of *quantum mechanics* (which we know agrees with measurement to a very fine degree).

We have dismissed the concept of *quantum superposition* as incompatible with a *block universe*, and the 'measurement problem' as a consequence of the *wave function* not being a fundamental description of a physical state and so clashing with a measured state. It must be stated, though, that the concept of something having particle-like properties on a measurement and wave-like properties in between is compatible with a hidden objective reality. Every macroscopic event can be deconstructed to the interactions of individual particles, including force-carrying ones. Anything in between two such interactions is absolutely inaccessible as it would require another interaction to probe there, and no such option is available in a static reality. This is another way of saying that our physical world is defined by these discrete events that simply appear to us as 'interactions', and that they might have a special significance within the objective reality. This is not a line that we are following since there is evidence of a smooth and predictable determinism linking those interactions, and we are interpreting that as the existence of continuous world-lines.

— 8 —

Arrow of Time

What underpins the apparent flow of time from past to future? Where is the asymmetry in the laws of physics?

We have so far dismissed the apparent flow of time as an illusion, albeit one that goes hand-in-hand with consciousness (see TAP), but we have not tried to explain why it occurs in just one particular direction. There are several phenomena that have been claimed to demonstrate an apparent asymmetry in the direction of time, and it is reasonable to suggest that there is a single underlying reason. For nearly 100 years, the prevailing thinking has been that this is the result of the *second law of thermodynamics*, but in Chapter 3 we explained that this law is both time-symmetric and yet irreversible — thus solving 'Loschmidt's paradox' — because it is of mathematical (or algorithmic) origin rather than physical, and hence has no direct connection with time.

In order to dig any deeper here then we need to clarify what we mean by a temporal asymmetry since reversing the perceptions of our subjective reality is not quite the same as a mathematical physicist changing the sign of their 't' variable from positive to negative, especially given that there is no objective flow of time that can be captured mathematically.

In physics, a symmetry of a system is a physical or mathematical property that remains unchanged under some transformation. Since the laws of physics are expressed by equations that represent the observed relations between measured properties then a symmetry amounts to an invariance of those equations under some mathematical transformation. These transformations may yield continuous symmetries such as invariance under the following:

- Coordinate transformations.
- Changes between inertial frames of reference (*Lorentz transformations*). This can also be considered a rotational symmetry in the *Minkowski space-time* (Fig. A-1).

- Spatial translation. Change of location, expressed by $x_i \mapsto x_i + a_i$.
- Spatial rotation.
- Temporal translation. Change of instant, expressed by $t \mapsto t + a$.
- Changes to the quantum mechanical phase (§7.3).

They may also yield discrete symmetries such as invariance under:

- Spatial inversion (P-symmetry, or parity transformation). Expressed by $x_i \mapsto -x_i$. May apply to individual dimensions, or to all of them. Application to any odd number yields a mirror image.
- Temporal inversion (T-symmetry). Expressed by $t \mapsto -t$. This is sometimes known as 'time reversal', but that term comes with implicit baggage that we want to avoid here.
- Charge conjugation (C-symmetry). Interchange of particle with antiparticle.
- Interchange of identical particles or atoms.

Notice how many of these symmetries are related to space-time transformations. This is connected with the special status of space-time in our concept of measurement (§5.4).

CPT-symmetry is a combination of C-, P-, and T-symmetry that is obeyed by all known phenomena, and is the only combination of those separate symmetries that is not violated.[130] By implication, a positron behaves — mathematically — like an electron travelling backwards in time. We have to stress that this is a mathematical description, and that no particle actually travels in time since all particles are simply static world-lines with two endpoints in a *block universe*.

In 1918, German mathematician Amalie <u>Emmy</u> Noether (pronounced 'noi-ter'), described by Albert Einstein as a "creative mathematical genius",[131] published a theorem (*Noether's theorem*) that linked conservation laws to symmetries. According to this theorem, for each continuous symmetry there exists a conserved quantity, i.e. one whose total in an *isolated system* remains constant over time. This is conservation of linear momentum in the case of spatial translation, conservation of energy in the case of temporal translation, and conservation of angular momentum in the case of spatial rotation. An interesting case occurs in *quantum mechanics* where invariance under a phase rotation (a type of *gauge symmetry*) is related to the conservation of electrical charge.[132]

So what does temporal-inversion symmetry really mean, and how does it relate to a reversal of what we experience (e.g. when watching a video played in reverse)? We have noted that it involves changing 't' in our equations to '$-t$', but the important aspect is not that the values then become negative — negative versus positive is simply an arbitrary choice of the origin — it is that the equations are ambivalent with respect to the sequencing of events along the time dimension. Imagine the simple case of a force acting on an object and causing it to accelerate. If we were to play the sequence backwards then we would not see an accelerative force; we would see the same force, acting in the same direction, slowing an object down rather than speeding it up. In other words, rather than seeing, say, the object accelerate from right to left, we would see a fast-moving object coming in from the left and being slowed down as it moved to the right. Both the force and the acceleration would be unchanged, but the velocity would be reversed.

Note that it is a characteristic of all physical quantities that they either flip their sign under temporal inversion, because they depend upon an odd power of time, or their previous sign is retained (including the case of a time-independent quantity, which is effectively a power of zero on time).

Let us just visualise this case of a force with the aid of a graph because it is hard to sidestep our perceptions in this matter.

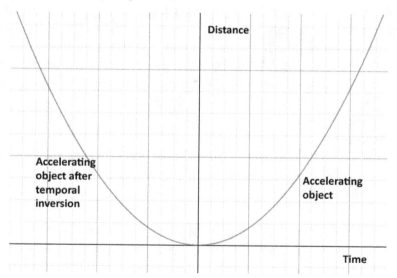

Fig. 8-1, Temporal inversion for accelerated object.

The curve on the right side of the graph represents the acceleration of an object in the vertical direction (i.e. moving faster up the page as time increases to the right), and the curve on the left side is simply a mirror image of this having undergone a temporal inversion. By changing the sign of all the time values and then considering them in our conventional numeric order (from negative to positive), this means that it describes a fast-moving object approaching from above and being brought to a standstill at the origin. However, there is no motion in a graph and so we are actually considering this scenario from the perspective of a *block universe*.

The velocity of the object is represented by the slope of the curve (dx/dt), and differs in sign for the two cases, but the acceleration is the rate of change of this slope (d^2x/dt^2), and is the same for both. As noted above, the fact that the temporally inverted curve uses negative values on the time axis is irrelevant; if we had moved the origin some arbitrary distance over to the negative side (taking advantage of temporal-translation symmetry) then the graph would be entirely unchanged. In fact, the form of the curve and its inverted version are identical (despite not being able to superimpose them): the slopes and rates of change are actually the same in magnitude. The essential difference is whether we deem t_1 to have occurred before or after t_2, and that is nothing more than a bias in our consciousness. For instance, consider the average velocity between t_1 and t_2. Whether we represent it as $\Delta x/(t_2 - t_1)$ or $\Delta x/(t_1 - t_2)$ is only a matter of our chosen sign convention, and has nothing to do with physical law. We choose the former purely because, in our subjective time, t_1 appears to occur before t_2.

The T-symmetry is a mathematical expression of this equivalence that is not fundamentally different from the P-symmetry for space: they both relate to inverted dimensions of the *block universe*. We do not have this interpretational problem with the spatial dimensions since the ordering of x_1 and x_2 is not related to our consciousness.

The rate of change of the slope (i.e. the acceleration) is identical for both curves, and happens to be a constant in this example. The applied force is proportional to the acceleration and so is also identical. Although these quantities are unchanged during temporal inversion, a spatial inversion would flip their sign. This can be thought of as the nature of the force being interpreted as a pull-from rather than a push-to, and would correspond to our graphs being inverted top-to-bottom.

But how can we relate temporal inversion to our experiences and to our subjective time? We mentioned, above, that negating the time variable is a mathematical way of sequencing things in the opposite direction, just as changing the sign of a distance variable could represent your position progressing in the opposite direction, but if there is no progression other than the one we perceive then is this a realistic operation? We might distinguish two facets in the search for an 'arrow of time': examining any disparity between the juxtapositions of states either side of some instant (including the preponderance of those two states), and looking for reasons why we only remember events from one temporal direction (i.e. the past). The latter is effectively our subjective time, and we have stated that it is the only place where there is any real flow. Although this has to be explained, accepting its illusory status is the reason for avoiding the experiential term *reversal*. The reason why the differentiation of the above facets is important is that they are regularly conflated, and this leads to physics chasing reasons why things appear to evolve differently. There must be some lopsidedness in our universe, but the apparent flow of our subjective time is a consequence of it rather than a fundamental component of it.

Surprisingly, maybe, there are already different opinions on what 'time reversal' means. In terms of mathematical operations, there are two classes of transformation: passive, where the coordinates are manipulated (such as with our temporal inversion), and active, where things are rearranged or re-sequenced without changing the coordinates.[133] Richard Feynman also made remarks about the paths of electrons and positrons that could be interpreted as a simple illustration of a CPT transformation, or that electron and positron paths represented in four dimensions have some sort of temporal direction built into them, i.e. that particles have independent paths through space-time as opposed to time having a global flow of its own (or, of course, that all temporal flow is illusory).[134]

A backwards-moving electron when viewed with time moving forwards appears the same as an ordinary electron, except it's attracted to normal electrons—we say it has "positive charge." (Had I included the effects of polarization, it would be apparent why the sign of j for the backwards-moving electron appears reversed, making the charge appear positive.) For this reason it's called a "positron." The positron is a sister particle to the electron, and is an example of an 'anti-particle'.

This phenomenon is quite general. Every particle in Nature has a [quantum] amplitude to move backwards in time, and therefore has an anti-particle [meaning even a neutron and its equivalent antiparticle would annihilate, but cf. Majorana fermions which are their own antiparticle].[135]

American philosopher of science David Z. Albert took exception to the idea of simply inverting the sign of a time coordinate, and the implication that each instant could be reversed rather than a sequence of instants being reversed: "What can it possibly mean for a single instantaneous physical situation to be happening 'backward'?"[136] He presented an alternative active time-sliced model under which magnetic fields do not invert during time reversal because: "Magnetic fields are not—either logically or conceptually—the *rates of change* of anything".[137]

A few years later, American philosopher of science David B. Malament criticised Albert's approach because such vector fields would effectively "just lie there" in each slice, remaining intact when the slices were re-sequenced, and instead presenting a more conventional four-dimensional geometrical approach where magnetic fields do invert.[138] But Albert was not alone: American philosopher of science Craig Callender had independently conceived a similar time-sliced model, arguing that "It just doesn't make sense to *time-reverse* a truly *instantaneous* state of a system".[139] Their time-sliced models have since been collectively termed the 'Albert-Callender pancake account'.[140]

Yet this time-sliced approach is not too far removed from the *block universe*, as presented here. Rather than there being any progression, reversal, inversion, or re-sequencing, the *block universe* has all the time slices there together, and it is a consequence of our conscious minds that we experience any directed change. This puts the question of symmetry over time much closer to our experience of it since we can observe, say, whether scenario-1 can both follow and precede scenario-2, and assess the preponderance of the two possibilities.

Using our notation from Chapter 3, we would express this as $s(t_1) \ll\gg s(t_2)$, meaning that the state at t_1 can transition to the state at t_2, and *vice versa*. Both are complete states of some *closed system*, rather than simply visible states, and the relation similarly expresses the symmetry but without the implication of a specific law, or reliance upon the negation of a time variable. The usage of this notation is driven partly because it helps with the static geometrical view required for a *block universe*, and partly because it can be applied to cases not involving time at all. In the case of the card shuffle (Chapter 3) then it described algorithmic transitions — steps unrelated to time — rather than physical ones. The geometrical requirement is because a static *block universe* has no actual flow of time, and so 'time reversal' would be a meaningless concept, as would any re-sequencing.

However, even the concept of temporal inversion, where the sign of the time variable is flipped, may not accurately correspond to a geometrical view where we can compare the juxtaposition of states in either temporal direction. There are really just two types of potential arrow in a block universe: cases where the shape of change (i.e. the interrelation between the world-lines, and hence our equivalent laws of physics) is asymmetrical over time, and cases where the change is symmetrical but the specific conditions at some different time were exceptional (e.g. not in equilibrium, or space and time being different to now).

Let us examine some of the phenomena that are held to indicate an 'arrow of time' with the goal of determining which are related to each other, and which are red herrings. Ideally, all the genuine arrows should boil down to just one, which should be capable of explaining our subjective time.

- *Psychological arrow*: This roughly corresponds to our subjective time. It usually refers to the evolution of time from past to future, rather than *vice versa*, but our subjective time embraces why it appears to evolve at all, the concept of '*now*', and the differences between a knowable past and an unknown future.
- *Thermodynamic arrow*: We have already seen that the *second law of thermodynamics* does not constitute an 'arrow of time', but this does not preclude the possibility of a cosmic energy gradient where the availability of usable energy diminishes over time from some 'initial condition' where it was incredibly high.
- *Cosmological arrow*: This equates to the expanding universe, and hence to the so-called 'big bang'. The primary evidence for this is still the 'red shift' in distant starlight, but we must consider a geometrical perspective on it for a *block universe*. In §8.3, we will consider a couple of specific geometrical models, but Chapter 11 will question the notion of a 'big bang', as well as space-time itself.
- *Causal arrow*: In a nutshell, this is our perception that every effect is preceded (in subjective time) by an associated cause. Although David Hume proposed that what we really perceive is a repeated conjunction of certain events, this does not distinguish causation from correlation. In §4.1 we abandoned causality as a fundamental part of the objective reality since it depends upon subjective time, and although the psychological arrow is responsible for our inference, there must be some evident asymmetry that we base it on.

- *Gravitational arrow*: When we watch events happen at the surface of the Earth then we see things that would look totally unrealistic if reversed. A typical counter to this apparent arrow is to mention a stable planetary orbit, which looks the same in both time directions, but something is still asymmetrical so what is it? We will expand upon this in §8.1.
- *Quantum arrow*: This is basically the loss of quantum mechanical phase relations (coherence) known as *quantum decoherence*. The *wave function* is unitary and fully deterministic, but its reversible nature appears to be punctuated by instances of an irreversible process that we describe as the *wave-function collapse*. Some physicists believe that interactions with the macroscopic environment cause this *wave-function collapse*, and so establish an 'arrow of time', but §7.4 points out that it is only the fine-grained alternatives that are weeded out by *quantum decoherence*, and hence that classical probabilities are still required for the coarse-grained ones. Also, §7.6 argues that the apparent collapse is unreal, and the result of an inappropriate mixture of a mathematical framework for potentiality (actually the propensity of world-lines) with physical measurements of actuality.
- *Weak nuclear force*: This is the interaction between subatomic particles that is responsible for the radioactive decay of atoms. It was shown, in 1964, to violate the combined C- and P- symmetries, together known as CP-symmetry. Since CPT-symmetry still holds then this means that T-symmetry must be violated by weak nuclear interactions. However, these violations are rare and unlikely to contribute to a global 'arrow of time'.
- *Radiative arrow*: This is the difference between waves propagating away from some central point rather than converging on it. For instance, from a light source, a radio transmitter, a sound source, or even ripples from a point on a surface. As a case of temporal asymmetry, it is usually presented in terms of waves because the associated wave equation would be symmetrical, and so would admit convergent instances, but since waves are an ensemble or aggregate phenomenon then the true reason must be at a lower level.
- *Environmental arrow*: The proportions of particles in the universe, and the prevalence of matter over antimatter, both constitute obvious environmental asymmetries, but there may be others too. Although the laws of physics may be symmetrical across time, the conditions either side of our current epoch might not be. We will expand upon this in §8.3.

8.1   Gravitational Arrow

We must spend a little time reviewing the apparent gravitational arrow. It was included above only because many people infer that it has an arrow since reversing a film of an object falling would apparently show it being repelled by the Earth. It is actually time-symmetric, but understanding how will be instructive in relation to the reversal of other aspects of our experience.

When we consider a stable planetary orbit then we can see that gravity is time-symmetric: running events in reverse would show an indistinguishable elliptical orbit with the planetary motion in reverse. When we consider the hyperbolic deflection of a moving body as it passes a large gravitational mass then we again see that the reverse motion is symmetrical. Even if someone on the surface of the Earth throws an object into the air, and then catches it as it falls back, the resulting parabolic motion is basically symmetrical (neglecting air resistance). What is harder to understand is the fundamentally attractive nature of gravity. Surely, if two objects, initially at rest relative to each other, are allowed to attract one another then would the reversed events not show a repulsion? The answer is no because we would only be observing part of the theoretical motion. If the attracting objects could somehow pass through each other without colliding then they would both continue passed each other to similar positions on the far side, at which point they would attract again and so continue to oscillate about their centre point. Even if there was a totally elastic collision between them then their rebounds would return them to their original positions, at which point they would attract again and continue oscillating. A simple pendulum demonstrates the same basic phenomenon without the risk of a collision.

So in idealised scenarios with elastic collisions (or non-colliding entities) then the states either side of the instant of their coincident position would be symmetrical. But we do see an asymmetry; if we did not then we would not have the formation of (nearly) stable stars and planets. The thing to note is that real, non-elastic systems experience dissipation, where energy is lost through radiation or transferred to other matter as heat, stress, etc. This can only happen where there are many objects (or particulate constituents), and it is an irreversible statistical change (Chapter 3), but also time-symmetric. It would happen if the attraction of the masses was viewed in either direction of time.

The pertinent question is where all those components — macroscopic and microscopic — were before they came together. At the macroscopic scale, the masses had a gravitational potential between them, and hence a separation that must be treated as an initial condition. But this also depends upon (at the microscopic scale) the formation of atoms, molecules, crystals, molecular chains, etc., having already occurred. The idea of an environmental arrow will be picked up in §8.3.

8.2   Causal Asymmetry

We have used the term 'causal asymmetry' in these chapters to refer to the temporal disparity associated with what we deem to be causal relations. When looking at idealised mechanical systems with relatively few components then everything is mathematically symmetrical, and we can only identify cause and effect through some arbitrary perspective on the conjunction of events; viewing an elastic collision in reverse looks exactly the same, and there is no fundamental difference between the impetus of one object and the recoil of the other. But when we look at systems with a massive number of (interacting) components then the identification of cause and effect seems simpler, and it is somehow tied to an apparent 'arrow of time'. But what is the essence of causality?

There are two quite different models for interpreting causality: deterministic — if A causes B, then B must always follow A (in the direction of subjective time) — and probabilistic — if A causes B, then there is a greater probability of B following A. A much-quoted example of the latter being that smoking is deemed to cause cancer, and yet not all smokers develop cancer. Although philosophically debated, the probabilistic interpretation is simply an extension that applies in macroscopic cases of aggregate events. If we could model all the individual micro-events associated with smoking then we could identify specific causal cases of a chemical agent being associated with the development of a cancer, but that is impossible and so we have to resort to overall probabilities. Causality is still evident but is not fully predictable.

Some philosophers have argued that causality is not about events at all, citing cases such as a letter or taxi having not arrived leading to specific outcomes. These are also macroscopic cases related to aggregate events but at a much bigger scale. In the absence of the expected event, there would be a natural cause of other events that would be changed by the introduction of that missing event. In other words, causality is associated with events and not with their absence. We only think of such scenarios differently because of our misguided sense of free will, and the illusion of some counterfactual dependence (or 'if only ... then ...').

Most readers will be aware of the maxim 'correlation does not imply causation', but what is their essential difference? A classic example is data that shows a correlation between the sales of sunglasses and ice-cream — it does not imply that the wearing of sunglasses is necessary for the eating of ice-cream. In this case, both are a consequence of a prior cause: a sunny day. So, in our subjective reality (we will introduce the *block universe* in a moment), a correlation is a probabilistic dependence between two measurements or observations: the probability of one is related to the occurrence of the other.

Hume suggested that we infer causation from the repeated conjunction of events, i.e. from their correlation, but if not all correlations are causations then how do we distinguish them? It is not obvious, as evidenced by superstitious beliefs. In fact, the misidentification of causality from apparent correlations has been shown to occur in other species. In 1947, B. F. Skinner recorded behaviours in pigeons that were akin to our superstitious behaviours (although without any supernatural connotation): turning a particular way in their cages, or moving their heads and bodies in a pendulum fashion; behaviours that they thought were connected with the release of food from dispensers that were merely programmed on regular timers.[141] Conscious entities are clearly geared up to spot patterns of repeated conjunctions, but there is something else that leads to an identification of causality.

You may think that because we have different terms for the components of causation (i.e. cause and effect) that the asymmetry is obvious, but they merely reflect the fact that we see one type of event before the other, and more specifically that some dynamical change is correlated with a prior one, thus demonstrating some fundamental connection between our notions of causality, change, and subjective time.

All instances of causation are also instances of correlation, but not *vice versa*. The correlation may be coincidental, or may be the result of an 'identity relation' (i.e. where you are observing two aspects of the same thing). Even when we have classified a particular correlation as causal, there are different causal relations that might be implicated. It might be direct (A causes B), indirect (A causes B causes C, etc.; also called a causal chain), common effect (A and B converge to cause C), common cause (A causes both B and C), sufficient cause (either A or B are sufficient to cause C), and necessary cause (B implies prior cause A, but A does not guarantee B will follow). In fact, all of these have symmetrical possibilities with mirror-image relationships, and so enumerating such relationships does not help in separating causation from correlation, or finding some inherent asymmetry that might account for an 'arrow of time'.

Causal reasoning in the sciences involves testing the reproducibility of a correlation, and also investigating the result of changes to the supposed cause on the observed effect. The predictability arising from such results can form the basis of scientific laws, the lowest levels of which are the laws of physics. So rather than it simply being a matter of the repeated conjunction of events, causal reasoning here involves an experimental study of a process and its variations, as driven by the goals of predictability and understanding (§1.3).

In particle physics, causation is a more direct association that may result from some local mechanism (e.g. collision, or particle decay) or non-local mechanism (i.e. a field of force), although some changes (e.g. atomic electron transition) appear to have no discernable cause. But if the juxtaposition of two particles results in their properties (such as their position or momentum) being different to normal then we can say that they interacted, but the specific identification of cause and effect would remain subjective. In the non-local case, the mediating agent cannot transmit its efficacy faster than the speed of light, which in turn helps preserve a consistent illusion of causality.

When considering the dynamics of a small number of fundamental particles then we observe a symmetry that makes the choice of cause or effect somewhat arbitrary, and this also applies to idealised macroscopic scenarios in Newtonian mechanics. For instance, consider two billiard balls that experience elastic collisions and are immune from environment effects. Their motion before and after a collision would be symmetrical, and the collision itself would have no distinct cause or effect since it would depend upon how we — the observer — sequenced those events. As they are idealised then we would probably have assigned a causal role quite arbitrarily to one of them by virtue of its motion relative to some chosen frame of reference.

In real-life situations that involve a great many entities, or are aggregates of many smaller ones (e.g. atoms or molecules), then we observe effects such as friction and dissipation, and these add a dampening aspect to those mechanics; but they still do not define an 'arrow of time'. They effectively reduce the usable energy — that capable of doing work — through multiple contacts and interactions that even it out. But being a statistical phenomenon, these changes would occur in either direction of time, and so the difference must be the initial conditions: what gave these entities their initial kinetic energy before the dampening occurred? This would probably be a billiards cue in our illustration, but there will always be something befitting the description of a cause.

A working definition of 'cause' at the physical level may be a change originating from useful energy; energy that for some reason has not yet been evened out, and so is not in a state of *thermodynamic equilibrium*. This would imply an infinite causal chain because such a non-equilibrial state cannot be bounded by equilibrium on both sides of the time dimension. Such a working definition seems natural because we interpret all dynamical change in terms of cause and effect, but that infinite regress is unavoidable and leads us to metaphysical questions. Our experience of cause and effect will additionally include non-physical causes, as described in Chapter 6 (e.g. consciousness), but the principle is not fundamentally different.

In the 1950s, German philosopher Hans Reichenbach introduced his 'common cause principle' (RCCP). If two events, A and B, are statistically correlated such that $p(A \cap B) > p(A)\,p(B)$, i.e. that the probability that A and B both occur is greater than the product of the individual probabilities, then there are three explanations: A causes B, B causes A, or both A and B are caused by some prior event, C. By contrasting what he called 'conjunctive forks' that are open to the future (C causes both A and B: common cause) or open to the past (A and B both cause C: common effect), he argued that in nature there are many more forks open to the future than to the past, and hence that this asymmetry was the basis of the direction of cause and effect.

Reichenbach tried to demonstrate that his RCCP and the *second law of thermodynamics* could be derived from similar principles, and that they were analogous to each other. Just as a state of low entropy is widely believed to imply a prior state of even lower entropy (see Chapter 3), he maintained that finding a correlation between two events implies a prior event that caused both of them. But this is based upon a misunderstanding between asymmetric physical processes and irreversible statistical changes.

Consider a gas in almost *thermodynamic equilibrium*. We can imagine a single molecule hitting two others, and each of those hitting two more, etc.; this corresponds to his 'open to the future' conjunctive fork. But we can equally imagine two pairs of molecules hitting two other molecules, which in turn hit the same single one; this corresponds to his 'open to the past' conjunctive fork. In that gas, there is equal opportunity, and so equal probability, that both of these scenarios could happen. Now if the gas were placed in an initial low-entropy state then the opportunities for change would be skewed due to the distribution of energy, but the same statistical changes will occur, and they are blind to any direction of time. The essence of the argument, then, is how a system gets into that state of low entropy rather than its inevitable (and irreversible) progression from there to equilibrium.

When we discuss causality, we have to admit that it is entirely subjective, that the distinction between cause and effect is a purely experiential one, and hence that it appears to progress in the direction of our subjective time. Returning to the thought experiment of gas molecules in an equilibrial state, if we saw molecule A_1 hit B_1 (which then bit C_1 followed by C_2) followed by B_2 (which then hit C_3 followed by C_4), etc., then we might label that a chain of causation, even though each individual collision is symmetrical. But if we considered this all in reverse then we could also say that C_4 hit B_2 (which then hit A_1 followed by A_2) followed by B_3 (which hit A_3 followed by A_4). In other words, it is only through the identification of one particular entity, and the following of its events in preference to all others, that can infer any causation; otherwise, the motions within the gas are symmetrical both at the individual level and when viewed *en masse*.

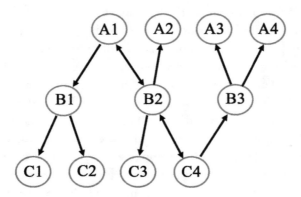

Fig. 8-2, Causation in symmetrical collisions.

So are these conjunctive forks important? In a word, evidence. If event A caused event B then we would be unable to directly observe it unless it also caused an event C that we could connect to, and so observe or measure. We can illustrate this at the macroscopic level as follows. Imagine that you hear a door close in the next room. You know that it was closed because you heard it. Some action by another person not only closed the door but made a recognisable sound that you connected to. Had you gone into that room without hearing this and observed the door as being shut then you would not be able to form the same knowledge. Even if you knew that the door was previously open, you would not know the instant at which it was shut, or how many times this event had occurred. The difference is knowledge by direct observation (or measurement) and conclusions or inference based upon circumstantial information. In other words, that spur, or side effect, of the causation is a prerequisite for us being able to infer and record prior events.

But what of Reichenbach's assertion that there is an asymmetry in the types of conjunctive fork exhibited in nature? There is a definite energy differential that permits change to occur, and this implies that prior conditions (using the direction of our subjective time) were quite different from those at our current epoch. We have to be clear, though, that when we say the laws of physics are time-symmetric that we are describing our observation and interpretation of dynamical change, and not the static change inherent in the *block universe*. If we observe a preponderance of a given change in one direction, rather than its inverse, then this can be linked to the difference of conditions. For instance, proximity might be associated by a greater tendency of 1-to-N particle decays than N-to-1 particle building. This makes sense because if all things were very widely separated then there could be no causation between them.

But a very important point was missed by the likes of Reichenbach, Hume, Kant, and others studying causality at our own scale: it is really about entities and not about events. An entity is deemed to cause multiple effects, just as in Fig. 8-2, and this is then strongly connected with our ability to assign identity. We do not think of discrete unconnected events representing cause or effect; the causal agent will have an identity that persists over some period of time (e.g. a storm, a person, a vehicle, etc.), and this naturally leads to an observable asymmetry in the types of conjunctive fork in nature.

8.3   Environmental Arrow

Let us just recap on some of the potential clues to the 'arrow of time' that we have uncovered so far.

- In Chapter 2, we noted the importance of the continuity of all change in supporting a 'persistence of form', and hence the concept of identity.

- In Chapter 3, we explained that the *second law of thermodynamics* is about usable energy — energy that can effect a relative change of position or motion — and not about order or disorder. Also, that it does not favour any particular temporal direction; real-life dissipative phenomena cause energy to be evened out irrespective of the direction of time, but there is an extant usable-energy differential across time.
- In §5.5, we noted that all forms of energy are a relative concept, and that it is related to the relative orientation of world-lines in a *block universe*.
- In this chapter, we have seen that 'time reversal' is not a realistic concept as it presupposes a temporal flow, and so we have, instead, adopted the view of a super-observer capable of comparing the states either side of some instant of time to assess an asymmetric pattern.
- Also in this chapter (and §4.1), we have suggested that a low-level physical cause can be defined in terms of the energy differential, but it is the concept of identity that underpins a true distinction between cause and effect, and that we need this in order to cognise change.

There are two distinct opinions on a cosmic source for the 'arrow of time': initial conditions (e.g. a prior cosmic state of low entropy) or dynamical processes (e.g. 'spontaneous symmetry breaking' during the early stages of the universe). In a *block universe*, there is little distinction between these, and so when we use the term 'environmental arrow' from here on then we are implicitly including contributions deemed to be either static or dynamic.

Given the importance of usable energy, and so of non-equilibrium, then a simplistic way of looking at things is that the universe was initially wound-up, like a giant spring, with inherent potential to effect change in the face of a statistical evolution to equilibrium. What we would then be observing is a winding-down of the universe, and an evolution to the so-called 'heat death' where there is no more usable energy. But things have to be more complicated than this. Consider the transition of an electron in an atom from an excited state to a lower-energy or ground state. When described by a *wave function* then there is virtually no difference between this and the reverse process, but there is a difference: opportunity. In order to go to a higher-energy state then we need an energetic photon to interact with the electron, which is a less probable condition than having the excited electron emit a photon, through some unknown trigger, and so transition to a ground state. Without knowing the nature of that trigger then there would seem to be a favouring of particle interactions that have more outputs than inputs.

Consider, too, the formation of atomic nuclei from separate protons. Their electrostatic repulsion would keep them apart unless their kinetic energy was sufficient to overcome it, but to allow the strong nuclear force to take over at shorter distances then we also need to force their proximity. This is one of the mechanisms described as nuclear fusion that is responsible for the creation of heavier element. Clouds of interstellar gas ('molecular clouds'), containing predominately hydrogen, are almost balanced between the gravitational attraction and the pressure of the energetic constituents, but the inherent 'clumpiness' is believed to result in the formation of stars through gravity winning over. As the gravitational potential energy of the constituents is replaced by kinetic energy (increased motion), and their proximity becomes squeezed, then the fusion processes can occur. Energy is released during the creation of the heavier elements, and this is a massive source of usable energy at our planetary scale.

We have direct evidence for these mechanisms, but only indirect evidence for the very early stages of the universe. Did it really begin with a massively dense plasma of fundamental particles, or even their lower-level constituents? If it was in a smooth and even state of low entropy then how could the current 'clumpiness' arise? We may never know for sure, yet the apparent evolution of the universe from that initial state demonstrates multiple 'cohesive influences', and at almost every scale. This can be viewed as a sort of condensation, or precipitation, that results in the stable and semi-stable structures that we observe around us, including both ourselves and our creative efforts.

The loose term 'cohesive influences' was introduced in Chapter 3 to reflect the fact that our universe exhibits this tendency for the formation of structure, including atoms, molecules and molecular chains, crystals, stars and planets, galaxies and galaxy clusters, life forms that grow and reproduce, and even the endeavours of those life forms. That same chapter explains that such structures cannot always be viewed as a lowering of entropy, although some of them do involve a localised lowering of energy (a 'binding energy' or 'bond energy') that effectively makes them stable, and with that energy being lost into the greater environment. Beyond a certain scale, the structures have a semi-stable form rather than constitutes, and this may be the result of changes to aggregate structures being both smooth and relatively small, or of repair mechanisms (as with life forms). Having recognisable large-scale forms supports our concepts of distinctness, 'persistence of form' (§2.1), identity, semantic information, and memory. At any point in the existence of such structure, it may erode due to the processes of decay, degradation, dissolution, and disintegration, but the randomising effect associated with the *second law of thermodynamics* would be applicable in either direction of time (Chapter 3), and so the 'arrow of time' must be related to the formation of these structures rather than to their demise.

The universe appears to have a balanced number of electrons and protons (i.e. a net charge of zero), but no one really knows why. They are two of the four known stable particles, the other two being their antiparticle equivalents: the positron and the antiproton, but where are they? Also unexplained is the asymmetry between *baryonic matter* (basically atoms as we know them) and *anti-baryonic matter* (atoms formed from the equivalent antiparticles). This is known as the *baryon asymmetry*, and reflects the asymmetry between matter and antimatter in the observable universe. It is good that there is such an asymmetry because matter and antimatter would otherwise annihilate each other, but why is there such a disparity?

A process called *baryogenesis* was proposed to account for the disparity, and in 1967 Russian nuclear physicist Andrei D. Sakharov proposed a set of three necessary conditions that a baryon-generating interaction must satisfy to produce matter and antimatter at different rates. These conditions were inspired by the discoveries of the cosmic background radiation and of CP violation in the decay of neutral kaons. The three necessary 'Sakharov conditions' are:

- That the conservation of baryon number (B) be violated in some interaction. This is effectively a conservation of quark numbers but the terminology predates the quark model.
- The interaction that violates B must leave *thermodynamic equilibrium* at some point (e.g. as a result of the expansion of the universe) so that it stops and leaves an asymmetric result rather than oscillating between excesses of baryons or anti-baryons.
- C- and CP-symmetries relate particles and antiparticles, so this must be violated if the production of either is to be biased over the other.

Although these all occur in the *standard model* of particle physics, the effects are too weak to account for the observed asymmetry.

An interesting alternative was published in 2018 that is informally described as the 'big separation'. This posits that rather than there ever being a violation of symmetries, that the universe "... after the big bang is the CPT image of the universe before it, ...".[142] In other words, that there is an anti-baryonic universe on the other side of the 'big bang'.

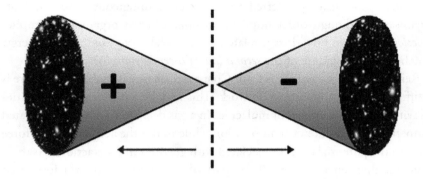

Fig. 8-3, Cosmic symmetry: 'big separation'.

Although this paper is mired in the notion of subjective time, and talks of the "contracting half" in contrast to the accepted expanding half, this model could fit very cleanly into a *block universe* as it would restore structural symmetry with no expansion or contraction to account for.

Another interesting variation on this suggestion was published in 2014; it is interesting because it considers the possibility that the 'arrow of time' is actually local rather than global. The researchers showed that a complex system, such as a number of masses exhibiting mutual Newtonian gravitational attraction, would eventually demonstrate a unique point of lowest entropy, irrespective of the initial conditions. This point could then be considered the origin for two symmetrical progressions of complexity: one in either direction of time. It is suggested that this effect could occur at different points in the universe, each resulting in two local, and opposite, arrows. As the complexity grows irreversibly in each direction, structures are created that may store dynamical information and so act as records of a corresponding past.[143] Another reason that this paper is interesting is that it associates the 'arrow(s) of time' with the formation of structures through which memory, and hence a subjective time, could emerge. However, given that this would have to occur at the subatomic level (rather than this idealised model) in order to account for subjective time, then the unimaginable size of the associated *phase space* would imply a near infinite period of time would be required for it to occur — a period after which there would be little or no usable energy left.

If we accept that there is an 'arrow of time' exhibited by the formation of structure — usually referred to as either 'spontaneous order' or 'self-organisation', though order implies *structural* whereas organisation implies *functional* — then how does it relate to the availability of usable free energy, which is the true nature of the *second law of thermodynamics*?

Reiterating our conclusions from Chapter 3, energy is usable when there is a differential that allows it to do work. This may be a difference in velocities (as with the kinetic energy of molecules in a gas deemed to have an associated temperature) or a difference in position while under the action of some force (as with the potential energy associated with gravitational attraction). As these even out then energy may still be part of the system, but in a form that cannot be put to use (i.e. making a specific or deliberate change somewhere). The availability of usable energy appears to decrease in the direction of our subjective time — nothing to do with order or chaos — yet the random change causing this loss is not in itself a physical process, and the loss would apply in either direction of time. The fundamental arrow is, in fact, that a differential exists at all. In a *block universe*, both kinetic and potential energy can be identified with the relative positions and orientations of world-lines, and energy can be considered more a measure of associated changes than a source of them.

The loss of this energy differential does not follow a smooth path. Many physical and chemical processes are *exothermic*, meaning that they release energy in forms such as heat, light, and sound. This occurs because transitions from one stable (or semi-stable) state to another involve a decrease of potential energy, almost as though there were some ladder of energy levels that the universe descends. We have already heard that gravity provided the proximity of matter that allowed nuclear fusion to proceed in stars such as our Sun. Fusion forms heavier and heavier atoms, each with a higher nuclear binding energy, and with a corresponding loss of energy as heat, light, and elementary particles. This occurs about as far up the periodic table as iron and nickel since the binding energies start to decrease after that, and this is the reason why iron and nickel are so common in the cores of planets. That heat and light constitute free energy, but some of this will become trapped making it usable.[144] For instance, our Earth's flora will capture heat and light by chemical processes allowing it to grow. Our fauna at the bottom of the food chain will digest some of the flora using other chemical processes, releasing energy as the chemical bonds change, and fauna further up the food chain will digest them. Although some of these chemical reactions will be *exergonic* (releasing energy) while others will be *endergonic* (consuming energy), there will always be an overall net loss of usable energy. Some energy will also become trapped in a complex combination of kinetic and potential energies in changes to the tides, waves, and winds — situations that would eventually quieten down if it were not for continued perturbation from the Sun and the Moon. But at each and every stage some energy is lost, so the trend is for less and less usable energy: energy that could create new energy differentials, change the state of something, change the path of something, or simply move something from one place to another.

We have thus far attributed all dynamical concepts (change, motion, etc.) to the conscious mind and to its experience of a subjective time. We have also attributed the direction of this subjective time to some asymmetry in the initial conditions of the universe, rather than in the physical laws that we know of (which, in a *block universe*, simply describe the static changes of these conditions between instants of time). The fact that we are not currently in *thermodynamic equilibrium* is justification for the existence of such initial conditions at a finite time in a particular direction from our perceived '*now*'.

This is important for several reasons: firstly, we need usable energy in order deliberately to record something, whether it involves computer bits, analogue sound or image, or our own memory. Secondly, without the exothermic nature of such processes then we would not have the spur from which we infer causation; we would require direct physical contact in all cases. Thirdly, without some sort of structure then we have no medium on which to record events, and no distinctness whose identifiable traits could be recorded. Hence, we must be close to proposing a reason why our conscious moments appear to progress in a particular direction. There may be no real objective flow of time, nor of any dynamical change, but being on some sort of 'downward gradient' could certainly support that illusion, and the laws of physics can still be time-symmetric if this gradient is a result of specific conditions at another time.

It cannot be unexpected that this proposal would be multifaceted, rather than identifying some 'magic bullet', since the problem has remained unsolved for so long, and so any solution must be anything but straightforward. Astute readers will notice that we have taken time, here, to find the right questions to ask, and not simply wheeled out solutions based upon the *second law of thermodynamics*.

Identifying subjective time as a phenomenon connected to our consciousness not only tames all those mysteries and paradoxes associated with time, but narrows our search to one explaining our conscious experience of time.

So let us bring together those facets:

- *Usable energy*: Our environment is not in *thermodynamic equilibrium*, so we have energy that can be used to effect change. Moreover, since the progression to equilibrium is time-symmetric then there must have been specific conditions some finite time from now (into our subjective past) where this availability was maximal.

- *Cohesive influences*: The progression of usable energy towards equilibrium is punctuated by the formation of various stationary states through to stable or semi-stable aggregate forms. The continuity of all change means that the evolution of these identifiable structures gives conscious entities the impressive of dynamical change, of subjective time, and of a yardstick by which the apparent flow of time can be measured. These structures also provide the means by which we can record events (or other data), e.g. through writing, video recording, sound recording, static images, computer memory, and our own memory — all of which are (in a *block universe*) merely static correlations between the properties of objects separated in space-time and the arrangement of structures in some medium.

- *Causality*: The presumption of a unique fundamental cause for every effect is a millstone for both physicists and philosophers. At the physical scale then we can identify a cause as a change brought about through usable energy, and against the natural paths of entities and natural progression of a state to equilibrium. A basic premise of our experience, though, is that certain correlations appear to have direct connections: you hit something and it moves; you drop something and it falls; the Sun comes out and we feel warmth; etc. This scale of cause and effect is related to identifiable entities rather than to discrete events. On the one hand we try to upscale these perceptions, attempting to identify bigger reasons, and attributing causation to bigger phenomena (as with the storm example),[145] but on the other hand we try to downscale these perceptions, taking them apart through analysis to find smaller-scale component causations. Our scientific knowledge is largely a product of this latter application of *reductionism* to causality, but the 'principle of sufficient reason' is also part of the illusion of causality, and both upscale and downscale approaches eventually run out of steam. The conscious mind is an emergent non-physical entity, comprising non-physical properties and behaviours, to which we attribute higher-level causation, i.e. that it is responsible, through access to motor functions, for explicit changes in our environment.

- *Causal asymmetry*: Whether a photon is generated by the transition of an electron from a higher to a lower energy state, or generated by radioactive decay, we have no way of knowing in which direction it will travel. With many instances of this occurring together, we can say that they will be radiated in all directions, and an ensemble of such photons can be modelled as a wave that would give the appearance of a radiative arrow. We have many other instances where something is radiated in all possible directions from a source location through some medium, including sound, waves, vibration, oscillation, disturbance, heat, and projectiles (as in an explosion) — all of which involve the transmission or dissipation of energy resulting from changes in an aggregate source. The apparent radiative arrow is therefore associated with the general progression to equilibrium. The important common features in all of these cases are that (a) the radiated change provides us with our perception of causality because the effects are manyfold, any one of which could be observed; and (b) it takes a finite time for the change to get from the source to our senses. This means that our sense of causality can only be correlated with events within the light cone of our past (ones connected to us by time-like intervals), and hence we can only affect events within the light cone of our future.

It is proposed that these facets, together, support our conscious mind, our perceptions of dynamical change, and our experience of subjective time. For time, this includes both the direction of its apparent flow and our concept of '*now*'. What has not been proposed, so far, is the mechanism by which our sensory data is processed per instant, thus allowing us to be aware of moment-to-moment changes. We have described this as a temporal sense, but we have not analysed why it is so rather than us being able to process temporal blocks of such data.

A possible explanation is that the micro-events between any two instants are discrete, and there is nothing in between them that could possibly be associated with sensory input (i.e. no apparent causation). In other words, it is never the case that our sensory inputs are smooth and amorphous, and hence needing to be divided according to instants, but that they are naturally distinct and they punctuate periods of time. Even in the absence of external stimuli, we are still aware of internal changes such as our breathing and heartbeat so there will always be a temporal sense if we are alive.

The time-symmetry of our laws of physics can only be confirmed over the periods of time for which we have evidence, but if we assume this to be true for all times (or at least with suitably adjusted laws) then it leaves us with an explanation that must involve an asymmetry of conditions. If the universe had been around for an infinite period of time then everything would now be in *thermodynamic equilibrium*: there would be no usable energy, nothing we could describe as causation, and no consciousness. But since this is not what we see then we can infer that conditions were once hugely different to that of equilibrium, although this is not the same as saying that there was a singularity, as we will explain later.

You may have noticed that this explanation sits entirely within our subjective reality. This is valid, but we also need to consider things as they might be in a *block universe*. Returning to the gaseous example of Chapter 3, the atoms and molecules are deemed to be in random chaotic motion, and that this accounts for the levelling out of different energies. If a hot gas is mixed with a cold gas then the many collisions will eventually cause all the particles to have a different average speed. When any two particles collide then there will be a transfer of momentum that will not be one-dimensional (i.e. a simple recoil that perfectly mirrors their approach); the transference will depend upon the *sin/cos* of the angles involved, and so for massive numbers of particles (in three dimensions) then their scalar speeds will gradually settle down to what is known as the *Maxwell–Boltzmann distribution*.[146] But there is no random motion, nor any motion, in the objective reality. Our Glossary defines non-temporal algorithmic steps as involving the repeated application of rules to a system, and in this case they can be considered to reflect the statistics of an idealised collision, thus resulting in an irreversible but time-symmetric phenomenon. But what does this say about the world-lines of a *block universe*? It may be hard to visualise but they would demonstrate, after enough of these steps, a more even distribution over space, and a greater alignment along the time dimension (averaged speeds), and those rules are responsible the individual kinks in those world-lines.

But there will be some reader, one who maybe was not convinced by the argument in Chapter 3, who will ask what the difference is between these rules and the laws of physics — surely the *second law of thermodynamics* is a law of physics and we are just making a distinction that does not exist. Well, that would be missing some essential points. Firstly, the rules are largely based upon statistics rather than physical processes. Secondly, the rules are independent of the nature of the particles, and would apply even for idealised uniform spherical entities. And lastly, but possibly most importantly, the sequencing of the rule application is non-temporal. There are many computer simulations that model the evolution of a system of gas molecules, and those simulations are performing precisely these essential points. The rules are codified (or 'scripted', as we will say in the next chapter) using a programming language. The entities being manipulated by that code would be given initial values, and the repeated application of the rules (or 'enactment') would demonstrate a levelling out of their relative positions and speeds. But if we had started from the final values then the same system would not have evolved back to the original initial conditions; it would tend towards the same equilibrial state, thus demonstrating that the algorithmic steps are symmetrical but irreversible.

— 9 —

Computing

*Why are computers not intelligent or conscious? Can we
learn anything by looking more deeply at them?*

Computers are neither intelligent nor conscious, but some insight may be obtained by considering the nature of computer operations. Computing is an irreversible manipulation of data. Although *reversible computing* is a genuine field of research, this irreversibility is usually blamed upon the *second law of thermodynamics*. As they derive data from prior data, this is sometimes considered to be a very simplistic model of what our brains do. Without restricting the scope of our arguments, we will restrict our analysis to computers that have a finite amount of storage and are not processing real-time data.

Rather than looking at the physical implementation of computer operations, which must be based upon reversible laws of physics, let us just look at the essence of these irreversible operations. Consider two sequences of bits: B_0 and B_1. In some cases, an operation that converts B_0 to B_1 has an inverse that can reverse the operation. Hence:

$$f : B_0 \mapsto B_1$$

$$f^{-1} : B_1 \mapsto B_0$$

An example of this might be a complement operation that just flips all the associated bits.

But there are also irreversible cases, such as a one-way hash — a surjective mapping that lies at the heart of indexing, and also of 'zero-knowledge proofs' as used in the software field of authentication. A cut-down example of irreversibility that might be easier to understand is the simple summation of a list.

$$sum : \{B_1, B_2, B_3, ...\} \mapsto B_0$$

There is no inverse that can decompose B_0 back to any or all of the summed sequences because information has been lost. This is an informational issue, and nothing to do with physical laws, or to the actual implementation of the algorithm.

Taking a simpler case: any of the binary logic gates. An AND-gate, for instance, takes two binary values and returns a single resultant binary value; there is no way to get from the output to the specific inputs used.

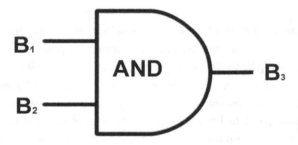

Fig. 9-1, Computer logic gate.

But an even simpler case is a 'copy' operation, where B_1 might be copied to a different storage location where it overwrites B_0. This is not reversible since moving B_1 back to the original location would have to uncover a B_0 sequence — a sequence algorithmically unrelated to anything else. We will later posit that nothing is random in the objective reality and that all things are part of a determinate pattern (see DPC in Chapter 10). So is this 'copy' example not too trivial? Expressed symbolically, we are saying that the transition $\{B_1, B_0\} \gg \{B_1, B_1\}$ is not reversible because $\{B_1, B_1\} \gg \{B_1, B_0\}$ would yield some random B_0 that cannot be deduced from any other data in the system.

What this line of reasoning leads us to realise is that there is no randomness possible in the physical world, but that it occurs when trying to reverse a sequence of algorithmic steps. In other words, the logical operations of the computer are fundamentally different from the workings of the physical components of the computer. Although this statement will be clarified below, it is basically the same observation that was made in Chapter 3: algorithmic steps are not related to time, and are generally irreversible. Putting this another way, an algorithm has a number of steps that can be sequenced on some medium (e.g. using printed words, or using a diagram) but that sequencing is not a temporal one. Because a *block universe* has no dynamical progression, then what is happening physically is that those algorithmic steps are sequenced (or 'enacted') on the medium that is the determinate pattern of the objective reality. The apparent temporal progression is simply a consequence of our subjective time when we operate the computer.

To illustrate this, consider a small (and arbitrary) piece of computer code that simply loops around four times and increments some location by 10 on each of the iterations.

```
for (int i = 0; i < 4; i++) {
    x += 10;
}
```

This code describes the algorithm and its steps (i.e. it is 'scripted'), but it could also be represented diagrammatically, using a flowchart.

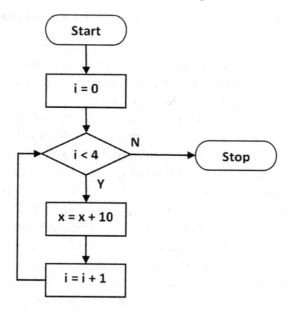

Fig. 9-2, Algorithm scripted diagrammatically.

Now when that script is enacted then each actual step is realised, and these steps can also be sequenced on a serial medium, as illustrated with the following bit of pseudo-code.

$0 \rightarrow i$
if $i \geq 4$ stop
$x + 10 \rightarrow x$
$i + 1 \rightarrow i$ (now 1)
if $i \geq 4$ stop
$x + 10 \rightarrow x$
$i + 1 \rightarrow i$ (now 2)
if $i \geq 4$ stop
$x + 10 \rightarrow x$
$i + 1 \rightarrow i$ (now 3)
if $i \geq 4$ stop
$x + 10 \rightarrow x$
$i + 1 \rightarrow i$ (now 4)
if $i \geq 4$ stop

Non-temporal sequencing

Fig. 9-3, Algorithm enacted using words and symbols.

If we want to go down to the level of the electronic components in the computer then each of the signals and state transitions that were responsible for the enactment of these steps are fixed in the 'fabric' of the objective reality: all the associated world-lines in the *block universe*.

Although the laws of physics are time-symmetric, we do require usable free energy in order to make a specific change, but this is not the same as the irreversibility exhibited by a computer program, its algorithm, or its logic. We see computers as a series of processing units, logic gates, etc., and with electrical signals propagating between them, yet in the objective reality all these signal paths are static patterns extending across time. The enacted steps of the algorithm are embodied in these static paths. An interesting point is that although an algorithm is generally irreversible, this enactment of the steps could be serialised in either temporal direction on the pattern of the objective reality (i.e. its world-lines and the relations between them). So the low-level physics does not demonstrate an 'arrow of time', and although an algorithm is a directed concept, it has no connection with time and could be serialised in either direction on an associated medium.

As with our observations on thermodynamics (Chapter 3), we have a situation where temporal symmetry and irreversibility are not mutually exclusive. The distinction, though, may be clearer now: temporal symmetry is a consequence of the objective reality, and so is reflected in the laws of physics we use to describe it, whereas irreversibility is an algorithmic issue, independent of time but simply enacted over the instants of time in this scenario.

In summary, no determinate algorithm, including logical and mathematical deduction, is related to the apparent passage of time. They can all be scripted using symbolic logic, mathematical equations, computer code, pseudo-code, etc., or even represented pictorially (e.g. by a flowchart), which means that their script could be physically enacted (i.e. mechanically or electronically) in either time direction. This even applies to our own decision-making, however illogical it may be, which is physically implemented via our complex neural pathways. The ability to reason does not define an 'arrow of time'.

This is a crucially important point worth going over again. We think of computers as operating in the direction of our subjective time, and building upon past data to generate new data. Because this implicit arrow is akin to our own then we extrapolate and suggest that they are like a primitive brain, and might eventually exhibit consciousness. But if we strip things back to the world-lines of the electrical signals in the underlying *block universe* then none of that would be evident; there would be a deterministic pattern (see *superdeterminism* in §7.6) but no copying, adding, or any of the other operations scripted in software and enacted via those world-lines.

By separating the algorithmic from the physical then we are left with an electronic machine that relies upon time-symmetric laws of physics, and a set of algorithmic steps (i.e. decisions and actions) whose enactment is represented via those world-lines. Admittedly, this will be a huge leap of faith for most people. The two perspectives make total sense separately, and yet the mapping from one to the other is entirely non-trivial. In effect, computers are built to enact some scripted logic in the same direction as our subjective time, although that enactment is static and represented by the world-lines in the *block universe*. But this raises an interesting question: if computers could — in principle — be built to work in the inverse temporal direction, then could we? All conscious entities that we are aware of share the same direction of subjective time, and it seems likely that this is a universal correlation. In §8.3, we identified the factors that appear to support our conscious experience, including our subjective time, and of these, the availability of usable energy would also be an issue for computer implementation.

Note that the word 'algorithmic' was selected to represent all state transitions that are not a direct consequence of physical processes, meaning that it can be applied to observable changes that are a consequence of mathematics (as with the *second law of thermodynamics*, Chapter 3), or it can be applied to the discrete steps in any decision-making, such as logic, mathematics, and our very own reasoning. We take it for granted that the script defining such decisions (e.g. symbolic representation, computer code, or our neural pathways) can be represented in many forms, but the enactment of such steps — the branching paths actually selected — can also be represented in a similar way. All of the branching points in such decision-making could (in principle) be laid out using any of the same media.

In summary, the enactment of all real-time decisions is imprinted on the 'fabric' of the objective reality. All the branching points then correspond to what we term events, which are static points within the space-time of the *block universe*. All the apparent passage of time is providing is a directed sequencing of the distinct algorithmic steps.

9.1   Intelligence

Intelligence is one of those poorly defined concepts, just like consciousness, that may embrace a multitude of different elements, including learning, problem-solving, reasoning, understanding, creativity, and even self-awareness. Maybe this is because it is so hard for us to focus upon the nature of intelligence without consciousness. We have an intuitive feel for what it is, but only in the context of conscious entities. In what follows, we will not try to differentiate sapience (which is generally related to wisdom) from intelligence, and assume that they are simply different hues of the same phenomenon.

What intelligence is not is the ability to answer questions on popular culture, politics, or sport, despite wanting such a person on your side in a quiz. It is not even the ability to recite answers to historical questions, or provide names or values of concepts in science. It is not even the ability to do mental arithmetic. All of these things can be done by an unintelligent computer. So if it is not about the storage and retrieval of information (factual or otherwise), or the ability to calculate, then what is it?

It is often said that the human brain is a 'massively parallel processor', but this comparison with the technology of our everyday computers is at best misleading, and at worst totally wrong. A computer's central processing unit (CPU, or processor) sequentially executes a stream of instructions, and so is capable of performing just one task at a time. An operating system gives the appearance of running more than one task at a time in a processor by using time-slicing: cyclically processing a few instructions from here, then from there, etc., to give each task under its control a fair bit of consideration. To achieve genuine parallelism — truly doing things at the same time — then the computer must have multiple processors (or multiple cores within each processor) that have coordinated access to shared resources such as storage or devices. The operating system can then execute groups of instructions from more than one task at once, either in different programs or in the same program. When a specific program has multiple streams of execution, whether parallel or time-sliced, then it is called multi-threaded, as opposed to single-threaded. We have used the term single-threaded in the context of consciousness (both in §6.3 and below) but only as a phenomenological adjective; our technological steps are hugely primitive when compared to a brain. The components of a computer are very distinct and specialised, and the signals between them are discrete.

A brain is a network of neurons, and these interact quite differently from our linear digital circuitry, no matter how parallel it is. Although artificial neural networks can be modelled within a conventional computer, and are used in a range of applications from image recognition to business intelligence, they differ from biological neural networks in being limited only to 'learning' and recognising patterns or relationships within sets of data. For instance, they are successfully used in business to make predictions from new data using patterns learned from prior data, but they do not think, and they do not exhibit any type of consciousness.

A biological neural network is different again in that the usual division of code and data that we impose on our digital computers is inappropriate, and learning means a change to our logic, or reasoning, as much as to information recorded in our memories. Chapter 6 talked of the memory as a mental faculty rather than a physical repository, and noted that it is capable of not just storing and recollecting our qualia (subjective experience), but also static images, sounds, emotions, spatial organisations, events, mental creations, language, logic, and even our own thoughts. Computers are not even close to this.

The brain can coordinate many of our functions at once, including breathing, listening, smiling, walking, and chewing gum (well, in most cases anyway), but our train of conscious thought — our executive faculty — can be said to be single-threaded in some sense. For instance, to recall an image while paying detailed attention to an actual image or scene is difficult, if not impossible, and similarly with recalling one piece of music while listening to a different one. There are other interesting forms of contention between our faculties. Richard Feynman once conducted an informal experiment, while in graduate school at Princeton, to see whether he could mark time accurately, and to see what might affect it. He found that he could not speak while marking time because he was already 'talking' to himself while counting (internally vocalising the numbers). However, one of the other students found he could not read while marking time because he was already 'looking' at a tape going by with the numbers on it.[147] Two very different methods of marking time, but both exhibiting similar limitations in our faculties associated with reading and speaking.

The term 'artificial intelligence' (AI) is common in the world of computers, and it is worth considering what it means. In contrast to some shameless marketing claims of computer intelligence in cases of programming that simply 'learn' responses to be given in specific circumstances,[148] AI is better-defined although it is still a field of much research. Opinions may differ on what it embraces, but we will exclude applications such as speech recognition (difficult but still a straightforward application of computing resources), handwriting recognition, speech generation, and any other application that simply tries to simulate our communication skills, since computers still do not have anything of their own to communicate to us. Computers can organise and classify words and symbols, but they cannot associate them with categories of experience as they have none; their logic is missing something essential in respect of their goals and volition.

We can imagine a scale by which an entity relates to its environment:

- *Reactive*: An entity that responds directly to a stimulus from its environment.
- *Adaptive*: An entity that responds to an environmental stimulus by utilising previous experience of similar conditions.
- *Intelligent*: A goal-directed entity that uses knowledge of its environment, and of prior experiences, to both set and achieve its goals. The greater temporal range of past and future considerations must also be noted.

There are three ways that we can characterise the differences between AI and natural intelligence: the source of the goal, the nature of the goal, and the sophistication of the route to the goal. The most obvious difference is that the route to achieving a goal may be convoluted, involving planning, intermediate goals, and proxies necessary to reach a complex goal where a direct A-to-B would not suffice. However, the goal may be a product of the mind and not a direct result of environmental influence. Similarly, the goal itself may not be a physical change in the environment, and it may be related to creativity, reasoning, or even an emotional state. Embodied in these differences are the notions of free will, comprehension, creativity, and planning, which extend the scope of a naturally intelligent entity's 'environment' beyond the physical world. For instance, the desire to solve, say, a mathematical problem may be a product of the mind, as would be the solution, and the route to achieving it would demonstrate intelligence to a lesser or greater extent. This view necessarily connects natural intelligence with consciousness.

Whether computers can think depends upon your choice of definition for *thinking*. We are here interpreting it as exhibiting conscious thought, and so it depends upon the nature of consciousness (see Chapter 6). English mathematician and computer scientist Alan M. Turing, who played a pivotal role in the development of modern computer science, believed that machines could give the appearance of thinking (the *Turing Test*, or 'the imitation game'). He considered an objection that he called 'the argument from consciousness', as delivered by Sir Geoffrey Jefferson, then professor of neurosurgery at the University Manchester, in a speech entitled "The Mind of Mechanical Man" in June 1949.

> This argument is very well expressed in Professor Jefferson's *Lister Oration* for 1949 ... 'Not until a machine can write a sonnet or compose a concerto because of thoughts and emotions felt, and not by the chance fall of symbols, could we agree that machine equals brain — that is, not only write it but know that it had written it. No mechanism could feel (and not merely artificially signal, an easy contrivance) pleasure at its successes, grief when its valves fuse, be warmed by flattery, be made miserable by its mistakes, be charmed by sex, be angry or depressed when it cannot get what it wants.'[149]

Rather than invalidating the principle of his test, Turing decided that it was not possible to say that machines could 'think', unless we could become a machine and were aware of thinking, but then we could not communicate those feelings to anyone (or anything) else; such was the mystery of consciousness and of what thought really entailed.

> I believe that in about fifty years' time it will be possible to
> programme computers ... to play the imitation game so well that an
> average interrogator will not have more than a 70 per cent chance
> of making the right identification after five minutes of questioning.
> The original question, 'Can machines think?' I believe to be too
> meaningless to deserve discussion.[150]

Implicit in these statements is a fundamental point about the recognition of intelligence. Intelligence can only be demonstrated through physical change, including written and spoken language, and those changes can only be assessed for intelligence by another conscious entity. In other words, irrespective of whether you consider yourself to be intelligent, you can only demonstrate it for objective assessment by making changes in your physical environment. Also, the assessment of those changes in relation to the overall context (i.e. the why and what-for) requires another conscious entity endowed with an appreciation of subjective time. Outside of our subjective reality, then, intelligence has no meaning.

If we try to distil these notes on intelligence then we are left with two classes of behaviour:

- The creating, imagining, or thinking of things through our
  own volition. This is connected with free will, which in turn is
  a phenomenon experienced by conscious entities (§6.4).
- The level of sophistication that we employ in utilising past experience,
  and associated knowledge, in planning and reasoning (i.e. setting and
  achieving goals). Note that the inventiveness of the first point is a key
  part of this sophistication.

This leaves us with the conclusion that intelligence is associated with consciousness, and that computers will not exhibit natural intelligence until they exhibit consciousness. But we have also noted, at the start of this chapter, that there is a fundamental difference in the way our brains work and the way that our current computers work. Computers have no subjective time, and appear to operate in the direction of our time simply because we constructed them to enact their logic that way.

This claim is bound to be controversial, but this chapter started by explaining that the laws of physics are time-symmetric whereas algorithmic logic is irreversible. This irreversibility is independent of time since the scripting and enactment of the logic may be made using any serial medium. For computer logic, that medium is the 'fabric' of the objective reality, and the enactment we will deem to be the activities in the electronic circuitry and semiconductors when fully laid out in a *block universe*.

Yet our own algorithmic steps (to call them logic would be overly optimistic) may be described in a similar way: if the activities of all the neural and chemical signals in the brain were laid out in a *block universe* then we would have the enactment of our conscious mind. So where is the difference? Well, from the viewpoint of some super-observer, capable of seeing that *block universe*, none. But from our own subjective viewpoint, as a conscious entity, then we see ourselves and other such beings as emergent non-physical entities that have a special relationship with time (see TAP).

NB: 'emergence' is a phenomenon, and so is relevant only to our subjective reality. And yes, that means that the conscious mind exists in our subjective reality, which in turn is a product of our own conscious mind. Our awareness and experience of a flowing, subjective time gives rise to notions within our subjective reality that also include change, choice, free will, and causality. We therefore structure the things around us to help us with the evolution of that illusion, from the humble clock on the wall to a computer.

— 10 —

Mathematics

What is the relationship between mathematics and the physical universe?

Mathematics is usually lumped in with sciences during our education but does that mean it is a science? The answer is no, but the relationship that mathematics has with science, our everyday lives, and the universe as a whole is less than obvious.

Most people would say that mathematics is a tool that we use in science, and that it is the basis of our reasoning and logic. It is also the only subject where anything can be proved in the absolute sense. By contrast, in science, where nature, or the universe, dictates what is correct, our best theories and calculations are only 'true' until some future observation or measurement disproves them, and we can never be sure if and when that might happen.

So would we expect aliens from another world to share the same mathematical concepts as ourselves? Obviously their terminology and symbolism would be different, but what about concepts such as arithmetic, geometry, calculus, set theory, logic, topology, symmetries, etc? It is fair to assume that they would (or could) share them, yet does that mean there is some fundamental significance to those concepts as opposed to them simply being inventions? These two camps are usually referred to as *conceptualists*, who believe that we have invented mathematics to suit our needs, and *platonists*,[151] who believe that mathematics is inherent and that we are merely discovering it. But common to both is faith that the universe can be described using the tool of mathematics.

The philosophy of *platonism* posits that there are abstract objects that can be grasped by the mind through reason, but exist independently of both the physical world and the conscious mind. This would appear to suggest that there is another domain, separate from the objective reality, our subjective reality, and the mind, as depicted in Fig. 5-1. A simple example would be the countability of items, implying that numbers must exist independently of conscious minds, and so are abstract concepts separate from any physicality of those counted items. In this view — now described as *platonic realism* — Plato considered a wide range of these idealised transcendental ideas or forms, including geometric figures, relations, ethics, and even God. Some of these can be argued to be emergent concepts from our conscious minds, but the subjects of mathematics and logical reasoning must be considered in more detail.

10.1   Application of Mathematics

It is sometimes hard to separate, in our minds, those physical aspects of our reality from the mathematical tools that we use to describe them. A common *faux pas* in school science lessons goes something like 'momentum is a vector'. Although the intention is fairly clear, the statement is not strictly true. Momentum is a measurable physical quantity, but a *vector* is a mathematical concept. A *vector* can be used to model momentum under most circumstances, but it is not the only mathematical tool that can be used for that purpose; momentum might be alternatively modelled using *tensors*, *matrices*, or even *operators*. Another way of expressing this distinction is that mathematics describes the relations between concepts without any connection to experience, whereas physics applies mathematics to the description of the objects of experience (i.e. our subjective reality).

This is an oversimplification, though, since many mathematical concepts are tainted by our experience, and so are conceived or visualised according to our subjective experience. At its core, pure mathematics is a structured form of logic that may be expressed symbolically, but the use of graphical representations, simple arithmetic, and even basic counting, are really just applications tied to our subjective experience. Each of those fields can be described symbolically, without recourse to our perceptions of space, separation, or distinctness of objects in our environment, but the symbolic representations are fundamentally different to their application within our experience: the latter not being true mathematical fields. Some people reading this may be shaking their heads in disbelief, and so some justification will be necessary.

If you believe that mathematics can be roughly divided into symbols (algebra, etc.) and numbers (arithmetic, etc.) then think again. Numbers (for both measurement and counting) are one of the most fundamental concepts of our subjective reality, and so describing them in purely symbolic mathematical terms, divorced from our everyday usage of them, is quite hard. In other words, we are saying that mathematics is all about symbolism, and that our usage of numerical symbols (e.g. '9') is inextricably bound to our subjective reality.

Let us start with the concept of the *natural numbers*, 0, 1, 2, etc. We learn about them in an intuitive way rather than from an abstract perspective, and even hardened mathematicians might struggle to deal with them in a wholly symbolic form, without visualising them as representing groups of distinct physical items.

This set of numbers can be represented as a sequence of mathematical entities that have a fixed abstract relation between them: a rule that defines the successor for any given entity. This is a very general description, which could be applied to almost any sequence, depending upon our choice of abstract relation. We can define the addition operator for all such entities, a and b, and a successor function, S, as follows:

$$a + 0 = a$$
$$a + S(b) = S(a + b)$$

For instance, if we define 1 to be the successor of 0 (i.e. $1 = S(0)$) then $a + 1 = a + S(0) = S(a + 0) = S(a)$. That is, $a + 1$ is just the successor of a, and we have a representation of the sequence of *natural numbers*. A slight problem here is that this mathematical sequence is infinite,[152] and although our *natural numbers* are unbounded, they are not truly infinite. In fact, if a calculation in mathematical physics yields an infinite value then it is deemed unrealistic (i.e. wrong!) because nothing of infinite count or magnitude can ever be realised, but more on this in a moment. The (subtle) point is that there is a distinction between concepts in our subjective reality and the mathematical tools that we use to model them.

John von Neumann devised a representation of *natural numbers* using set theory such that each *natural number* is defined as the set of all *natural numbers* less than it, or $n + 1 = S(n) = n \cup \{n\}$. These 'von Neumann ordinals' would be represented symbolically as follows:

$$0 = \{\}$$
$$1 = 0 \cup \{0\} = \{0\}$$
$$2 = 1 \cup \{1\} = \{0, 1\}$$
$$n = n - 1 \cup \{n - 1\} = \{0, 1, ..., n - 1\}$$

The list of all these sets is also infinite, just as with our *natural numbers*, but the representation of each number as a set may seem somewhat circular: effectively defining it as the size of a corresponding set of mathematical entities when we already use it to represent the size of a set of real-world entities.

What this should convey (but probably doesn't yet) is that there is no fundamental concept of *natural numbers*, or of counting, and that the mathematics is simply modelling something from our subjective reality. For instance, we can define a symbol called '9', or even 'ix', as part of an abstract mathematical series, but this is not the same as counting some set of distinct items. This is admittedly a subtle point that seems to make little or no sense within our subjective reality.

It would be a fair response to ask what happens when we compare, say, a set of three objects with a set of four objects; surely, one is greater than the other, and we can extrapolate this to define a counting operation. We have stated that the *natural numbers* classify a system according to its elements of distinctness (§5.4), and that distinctness requires a space-time framework to support the conception of self-same identity (§2.1), but we know that it requires a physical operation to change one set to another, and a conceptual add or remove operation in the case that they are not physical sets. Without those operations then we simply have separate sets of distinct items to which we can apply this classification, but no way compare them. The above mathematics is modelling our notional increment operation as a rule that constructs a series of such classifications. Without some concept of a physical change to a set (or a representation thereof), or of a subjective time within which we can assess successive subsets (i.e. our counting operation), then all we have is the mathematical series.

But can we not relate countability to geometrical figures? Even a simple line has two endpoints. Yes, but such figures are defined symbolically; it is only when we conceptualise them that we imagine them in an actual space — one accessible to our world-view faculty — and then we are back to the same issues mentioned above.

Let us move on to a simple numeric scale. You may think this is also so obvious that it does not deserve any analysis. Numbers are basic to our everyday lives and are essential for all things countable or measurable. The *natural numbers* may be the ordinary whole numbers used for counting, but zero was not always part of this scale; it took time for that concept to form. Other integer scales, such as even numbers, prime numbers, etc., can all be derived from the concept of *natural numbers*. Although you might visualise them as a linear scale, as with a graphical axis, they should be visualised ideally as amounts, as with counting.

If we are measuring a distance then the *natural numbers* are no longer enough; you need a continuous numeric scale with indefinite subdivisions, or *real numbers*. Now we visualise this scale as a physical line, primarily because that is what it was designed to model. That set of numbers includes both *rational numbers* (i.e. quotients of two integers) and *irrational numbers* (e.g. π or √2).

If we are measuring forwards or backwards from some reference point then we need to make the numbers signed (positive or negative) in order to model the physical direction. Note that the sign is a mathematical attribute whereas direction is a physical one. Again, we visualise this signed scale as a physical line with an origin since that is how we are applying it. This is in contrast to a usage for measuring the distance from the centre of a sphere, which would necessarily be non-negative. Negative numbers are also useful with counting but are slightly harder to visualise. The mental model we use then depends upon the context of their application, e.g. profit/loss in accounting, or credit/debit in banking.

At this point you may be thinking 'OK, so all numbers lie on a continuous, signed, numeric scale and we simply pick a subset to suit our needs'. Well, no, that is an oversimplification. Consider *complex numbers*. These have a real and imaginary component, both of which are signed, continuous scales. Hence, we visualise them as a plane and represent the two components of the numbers using two orthogonal axes.

You should be able to see where we are going with this now. Our real numbers were designed to model the space we perceive around us — the framework for the physical world — and hence we visualise them using a similar mental model, even when each number has more than a single, signed component. There are generalisations of *complex numbers* with four components (*quaternions*) and eight components (*octonions*); however, what use would we have for a number system with a ternary sign taking the place of the binary positive/negative concept? How would we even visualise it?

Our subjective reality is formed from the inputs of an array of senses, and subject to our correlations and deductions, leading to perceived associations such as extent, separation, movement, and causality. We invent branches of mathematics to describe elements of that reality, but the visualisations associated with those branches are not part of the mathematics itself, which is defined symbolically; they result from the application of those branches feeding back into our assimilation of them, and so assisting us in their manipulation. It does not matter whether we are talking about graphs, Cartesian coordinates, sets, or even mere counting, we create these mathematical frameworks to describe our subjective reality, and so we naturally visualise them using perceptions from that same subjective reality. This may be hard to accept because we are taught so many of these branches with the aid of diagrams — just think of calculus, for instance. It is likely that other branches also have some form of 'visualisation' that may not be specifically connected to our internal world-view since history has shown that people who can internalise their mathematics wield it much more effectively.

Sometimes, the symbolism comes first and we employ our visualisations to understand it better, and sometimes the visualisation comes first and we only develop the pure symbolism later (as with numbers). Of particular note is the field of geometry, which is concerned with the shape, size, and relative position of figures in a mathematical space, and the properties of that space. This whole field was originally conceived as a way of describing and predicting relationships in the perceived space of our subjective reality, and so the relationship between the mathematics and reality is especially close. It has since been extended to include spaces of different dimensionality and topology (e.g. so-called curved spaces), but the adjective Euclidean is still reserved for 'flat' spaces in a mathematical context.

Our stance, then, is one of *conceptualism*, where branches of mathematics are created by us — usually for a specific purpose — but also that their conceptualisation is nearly always dictated by their application within our subjective reality (e.g. countability or spatial extent). There are certainly esoteric branches of mathematics that have no direct application, but the aspect that they all have in common is a consistency based upon logic.

10.2   Origin of Mathematics

German mathematician David Hilbert remarked that there is nothing arbitrary about mathematics. In fact, mathematics is a hierarchy of tools — each level built on the principles and foundations of others. Between 1910 and 1913, English mathematicians and philosophers Alfred N. Whitehead and Bertrand Russell published a three-volume work on the foundations of mathematics called *Principia Mathematica*. It was an attempt to derive all mathematical truths from a well-defined set of axioms and inference rules in symbolic logic, and moreover to prove that mathematics is just another form of logic. *Logicism* is the belief that mathematics is reducible to logic, and hence that mathematical deduction is not just founded upon logic but is a form of logic.

This endeavour ran into some difficulties as no complete and self-consistent mathematical hierarchy is possible (cf. the *incompleteness theorems* of Austro-Hungarian mathematician Kurt Friedrich Gödel, and the various paradoxes in set theory). However, we are here interested in neither mathematics as a standalone and independent hierarchy nor in branches of mathematics that have no application. The value of mathematics lies in its ability to describe patterns and relationships between properties of the measurable world, and so a hierarchy that is applicable to our subjective reality — and by implication to the objective reality — will have little or no need of extraneous concepts such as infinity. It is entirely possible for such a hierarchy to be consistent with a derivation based upon logic, but we need to dig a little deeper than this in order to see how it would arise.

The intuitive notion of propositional logic[153] ('if A then B', etc.) is not quite the same as the symbolic logic that would underpin such a hierarchy: the first is derived from our real-world perceptions of true and false, and we would use it in our day-to-day lives, while the second is invented to model those rules for mathematical derivation. This may be contentious, again, but consider that the notions of true and false cannot be derived via any mathematical route, and must be taken as given.

We also need a fundamental set of axioms to begin a mathematical hierarchy, but they need not be the same as our intuitive logical ones. If we renamed their bi-state truth-values to simply T and F — thus divorcing them from their application in the field of propositional logic — then the associated rules and axioms would still be valid. Relations such as the following, connecting T to F, and to *AND* ($\land$) to *OR* ($\lor$), would remain unchanged.

$$T = \neg F$$
$$x \land y = \neg(\neg x \lor \neg y)$$
$$x \lor y = \neg(\neg x \land \neg y)$$

We could, instead, begin with a different set of axioms based upon a tri-state, or even multi-state, truth-value, but the resulting mathematics would be of little practical use to us. This is a very important observation because it means that mathematical derivation is simply a set of algorithmic steps (see Glossary) that employ a formalised set of rules that model our intuitive notions of true and false.

So, if our notions of true and false can be modelled by symbolic logic, but are not a fundamental part of it, then where do they come from? It is impossible to conceive of them in the absence of our subjective reality, so we must look for something in the objective reality that would underpin them.

The answer to this was hinted at in §5.3 by labelling Existence a unitary concept. There is no alternative to Existence; it just *is*! Well, this is very similar to our notions of true and false. Everything in the universe is either true or false, even if we do not know which; nothing can be both, the status is immutable and cannot be changed, and there is no alternative to true and false (the term 'maybe' is a reflection of our subjective knowledge, and not a fundamental state). Everything in a *block universe* 'always' exists, and everything else will 'never' exist. Even our conscious reasoning and decisions are merely pathways mapped out in the 'fabric' of the objective reality. The true/false notions therefore map directly onto the 'is'/'is not' of the *block universe*, and the ultimate 'is' notion is Existence itself. All things within the *block universe* must have a status of 'is' and all things not within it have a status of 'is not'. Nothing can be a 'maybe', or 'might be later', or 'probably'; everything is therefore either an 'is' (i.e. its existence is true) or 'is not' (i.e. its existence is false). The importance of this connection is that it relates the core of mathematics to qualities of the objective reality, and our chosen hierarchy of mathematics to a logical conception that we use to model our subjective reality.

One more question here, 'can we ever be content with a purely mathematical description of reality?' This is a question that frequently comes up because as physics advances, and it describes the workings of more-and-more phenomena in an all-encompassing fashion, then its notions become increasingly abstract and describable only through mathematics, often introducing non-observable notions.

A related question was a cause of much debate in the early days of the quantum theory since some physicists — notably Bohr — believed that you could only describe the universe in terms of its observables, whereas others

— notably Einstein — believed that there was an underlying reality, and a physicality that could be understood. Einstein was troubled, for instance, by a probabilistic description of finding a particle at some location rather than understanding what a particle is, or what it was doing. Modern 'string theory' has been criticised for the cavalier way that it introduces non-observable notions, such as extra dimensions, in order to make a consistent mathematical theory.

What these issues have in common is the relationship between a mathematical and a physical description of the universe. We can make the mathematics give the answers we want, but at what point does it no longer represent reality? Can all aspects of reality be represented by mathematics?

The answer to this last question must be both yes and no: if you abandon any fundamentality of our experience of dynamical change, as we have done for the objective reality in these pages, then the answer must be yes; but if you require a full description of our subjective reality, including those experiential aspects such as change, movement, choice, causality, and consciousness itself, then the answer has to be no. Mathematics is ideally suited to describing static patterns or correlations between variables, but when applied to situations involving subjective experience then it is less applicable; we have to add those semantics to the mathematics based upon our knowledge or experience.

10.3 Mathematical Universe

Let us conclude this chapter with a statement about the faith in mathematics as a tool capable of describing the observable universe, and the basis for this close relationship. Einstein had this to say on the subject:

> How can it be that mathematics, being after all a product of human thought which is independent of experience, is so admirably appropriate to the objects of reality? Is human reason, then, without experience, merely by taking thought, able to fathom the properties of real things?[154]

In this one statement, Einstein was pondering on the separation between the mind and reality, and on how mathematics appears to bridge between the two. His presumption that mathematics is independent of experience clashes with the views presented here; we have argued that mathematics is a system of symbolic logic that is underpinned by our perception of a binary true/false, and that many of its branches are conceptualised using the same elements of our experience that they were designed to model (e.g. numbers, space, and dimensions).

This faith in mathematics relates to its applicability to the measurable world (as defined in §5), and with the implication that nothing (including relations) can exist in that world that would not be susceptible to mathematical description. This is not the same as saying that nothing can exist at all that is not describable mathematically; only that this is so within the measurable world. This premise appears to be the case, and so it is not unreasonable to assume that the objective reality adheres to some related paradigm in a stricter way, and that our measurements are merely benefitting from that. The measurable world is effectively the window from our subjective reality onto the objective reality, and so it is bound to be imperfect. For instance, properties may not be accurately measurable because certain aspects may be inaccessible to us, or because of the 'observer effect'; or a system may not be predictable because it exhibits chaotic behaviour, or because we have convinced ourselves that stochastic descriptions are fundamentally significant (as with *quantum mechanics*). Supporting this, though, may be a much more rigid pattern of change that is deterministic in the mathematical sense, and which would constitute the ultimate target for fundamental physics. This is not something that we can ever prove, but we can try to formalise the idea.

Note that the objective reality being a static pattern nicely explains why mathematics is so apt a tool for describing it, but there are many more mathematically consistent models with no relevance to the objective reality. This is just a roundabout way of saying that reality and mathematics are different things, as explained earlier in this chapter, and that the objective reality exists independently of any attempt to describe it. Mathematics can eliminate models that are inconsistent, but the most appropriate model — the one that we deem to describe the objective reality most perfectly — cannot be deduced from mathematics alone; we have to make some basic assumptions.

For our *block universe* model of the objective reality, where we have something akin to dependent and independent variables, we will express this more clearly as a **Determinate Pattern Conjecture (DPC): that the pattern of changes over time in the block universe can be fully modelled by sets of consistent mathematical structures and axioms that are finite,**

deterministic, and continuous. By implication, if anything cannot be modelled within these constraints then it cannot be part of the measurable world since it can have no direct relation to the *block universe*. Let us look at the implications of those limits for our subjective reality:

- *Finitism*: Mathematics has the concept of infinity, but you cannot do any arithmetic with it. If the measurable world is finite then infinity has no practical application, and it exists solely as a mathematical concept. Note that an infinite magnitude is distinct from the concept of an infinite series of ever-decreasing terms that yields a finite result, and from the concept of infinitesimal subdivisions.
- *Determinism*: Anything that is truly random has no underlying pattern, and hence no predictability. Even if not fully known, if there is some guiding influence then observations will not be truly random, and so statistics and probability will be applicable predictive tools. This suggests that the *block universe* is mathematically deterministic, and particularly that the state at one time can be described in terms of the state either side of it.
- *Continuity*: The continuity of all change, and the associated 'persistence of form' (§2.1), observed in our subjective reality suggest that the *block universe* is similarly continuous, with no singularities or step-changes.

The DPC is a form of *mathematicism* — the belief that everything can be described ultimately in mathematical terms, or that the universe is fundamentally mathematical — that tries to explain why mathematics is so appropriate to a description of the measurable world, and to put limits on which branches of mathematics might be applicable to the *block universe*. We have previously postulated that the objective reality is a *block universe* because that affords a dimensioned description of the objective reality, and so would be susceptible to measurement and mathematics (§5.4). If the objective reality is other than this then it presents a huge obstacle to further study, although §11.5 does try to imagine one such scenario.

Let us take a closer look at the nature of infinity since mathematics has the concept but it is not really a number; you cannot see it on a numeric scale and you cannot do any arithmetic with it. So does it exist anywhere in the universe? Well, probably not. Physicists have tried to imagine the universe as 'finite and unbounded' — in other words, no brick walls but no infinities either (see Chapter 11). Since the prediction of an infinite value would be at odds with the notion of a measurable world then it is usually taken as an indication of an error in the associated theory.

In 1925, Hilbert remarked "... the infinite is nowhere to be found in reality. It neither exists in nature nor provides a legitimate basis for rational thought ... The role that remains for the infinite to play is solely that of an idea ...".[155] Around the same time (1924), Hilbert explained how an infinite number of anything leads to counter-intuitive consequences. In his 'paradox of the Grand Hotel', a hotel has an infinite number of rooms, all of which are occupied. However, when a new guest arrives then space can always be made by moving existing residents up one room: room 1 to room 2, 2 to 3, etc. Since there is no limit to the number of rooms then every resident in a room n can be moved next door to $n+1$, and this could even use coarser movements (e.g. n to $n+10$, or $2n$) to accommodate any number of new guests. Note that there are still an infinite number of occupied rooms, and even when the residents begin to check out then there will always be an infinite number of rooms still occupied. In effect, the concepts of infinite and finite values do not mix well: whether you have an infinite number of unoccupied rooms and a finite number of guests check in, or an infinite number of occupied rooms and a finite number of guests check in or out, then the concepts of *all* and *infinite* cannot mean the same thing.

In the bullet list above, we mentioned randomness in conjunction with probability, but this needs some clarification because probability is not about randomness[156]; it is about unknowns. Furthermore, probability as a forecasting tool has no place in a *block universe*, so what is its fundamental nature?

We might define probability as the relative number of ways that a given event can happen compared with the ways it cannot happen, given certain initial conditions, and it is represented by a value between zero and one (or 0% and 100%). Those initial conditions may involve a range of values for one or more explicit variables (e.g. pressure and temperature), with all other conditions being as similar as possible. The fact that each set of initial conditions cannot involve the exact same starting points in space and time reflects an assumption that the laws of physics are the same for all such points (see spatio-temporal translation symmetries, §8). When there are no explicit parameters (e.g. the shaking of dice) then the different outcomes are deemed to be the result of 'hidden variables', which are either unknown or are too complex to include. When the events are categorised or factored according to certain explicit variables, whether they be initial conditions or outcomes (such as the position on a detector screen, or the sum of the face values on two dice), then the results constitute a probability distribution.

Probability distributions are invariably described in terms of randomness, but — given that there is no such thing in the underlying *block universe* — how is it implicated? Consider an event where there are a discrete number of outcomes (e.g. the throwing of a dice, or the tossing of a coin), but where the initial conditions involve 'hidden variables', and hence cannot be specified fully. We can give the probability of each outcome if we know their relative likelihoods, e.g. our dice has an even probability of 1/6 for each outcome, and our coin 1/2. But there can only be one outcome for each set of initial conditions; it is just that we do not have enough information to make a precise determination of it. If we correlate multiple similar events then the outcomes will be independent of each other, and so may not be the same since the set of initial conditions will differ while still being consistent with a general class (i.e. we would strive to make those conditions as similar as possible within practical limits). The same probabilities would therefore apply in each instance, but when we correlate all the results then there are different patterns that may emerge representing how they match or differ, e.g. H, H, T, H, T, T, ... for a series of coin tosses. Whether these are deemed to be successive events in the same trial or spatially separated trials is irrelevant; they are all different instances in space-time. We can assign overall probabilities to these different patterns, e.g. for all H, all but one H, ... even numbers of H/T, ... all but one T, all T. This forms a bell-shaped curve, called a *normal* or *Gaussian distribution*, where the mean value is for even numbers of H/T, and the mean becomes more of a sharp peak as the count of correlated cases increases. In other words, a probability distribution describes the relative ways that a collected set of results can occur rather than a specific one. This explanation applies to continuous outcomes (such as the detector screen of Chapter 7) as much as it does to discrete outcomes, and when the distribution varies over a region of space then we can describe it by a probability density. What this explanation does not entertain is any notion of randomness, chance, or choice.

There is another interpretation of probability. The standard interpretation, described above, is called *frequentist probability*, and constitutes a measure of the frequency or chance of something happening. The other major interpretation of probability is called *Bayesian probability*, after the Rev. Thomas Bayes, an English mathematician and theologian who first provided a theorem to express how a subjective degree of belief should change to account for new evidence. Essentially, a *Bayesian probability* represents a state of knowledge about something, such as a degree of confidence. This gets philosophically interesting because some people (the objectivists) consider it to be a natural extension of traditional Boolean logic to handle concepts that cannot be represented by a precise true or false. Other people (the subjectivists) consider it to be simply an attempt to quantify personal belief in something. Either way, *Bayesian probability* is clearly an assessment of potential outcomes where the classes of endpoint conditions have been reduced (becoming more stringent), but equating those classes with a state of knowledge (or belief) cannot be relevant to the objective reality. Everything in the static *block universe* of the objective reality must be an absolute true or false, but is that consistent with *frequentist probability*? Note that we are ignoring the prevailing probabilistic interpretation of *quantum mechanics* here, which we dismissed in §7.6.

The implication of the above definition of *frequentist probability* is that if something is predictable, even within the bounds of some distribution, then there is a causal reason for it. This sounds the same as Einstein's stance, except he considered there to be just one reality, and that we could both measure and understand it. We are now separating the objective reality from our subjective one, and arguing that no subjective assessment of the former is possible. The application of *frequentist probability* generally relates to future events that are yet to be observed, and so it presumes not only the existence of subjective time but also of conscious observers, thus making it irrelevant to the objective reality. In other words, both the application and the interpretation of probability is relevant only within our subjective reality, and we need an alternative view for a *block universe*, as presented in §7.6.

Furthermore, the belief that the possible outcomes of future events are meaningful, predictable, and comparable, even if they never occur, is underpinned by several assumptions:

- *Counterfactual definiteness*: That even if the outcomes never occur then it is still meaningful to consider their possible observation or measurement.
- *Continuous symmetries*: Basically that the laws of physics are the same at all points in space-time (§8).

- *Principle of relativity*: that the outcomes are independent of the observer's frame of reference.
- *Causality*: It is probably not quite accurate to say that probabilistic forecasting presumes causal relations, but it certainly presumes that there are predictable correlations between prior and future events.

But the above definition of probability is not quite correct. Rather than it being specific to the outcomes of future events, it is really about the transition from one configuration to another, as described by some process or rule, when either the initial or the final configuration is not fully determined. To illustrate this, consider a pair of dice being thrown. We can say that there is a 1/12 probability of the total of the face values being 4 (i.e. 3 face combinations out of 36 possible), but if we know that the result is 4 then we can alternatively say that there is a 1/3 probability that one of the contributing dice showed a face value of 2. In this example, the dice are actually irrelevant and we could equally use computer-generated numbers (i.e. no dice), or even use algorithmic transitions between two configurations. Hence, it should be no surprise that neither subjective time nor causation is involved in this example.

We are describing the endpoint conditions as classes of circumstances because we are never in a position to define them uniquely and fully in the physical case, otherwise the endpoint events of some change would be fully correlated by *mathematical determinism*. We are being careful with our wording here as we cannot make meaningful reference to prior, future, or causation. Effectively, a probability is ambivalent about describing events where either of the endpoints is not fully specified. It comes down to our knowledge of those endpoints and since we cannot amass knowledge of events that we deem to have not happened then we employ probability as a forecasting tool. In a *block universe*, though, probability can be considered to be a density of possibilities given two classes of circumstances representing the endpoint events, and this is much more similar to the mathematical view given in the preceding paragraph. Note the similarity of this interpretation and that of *quantum amplitude* in §7.6.

We currently have no idea why certain things happen at the subatomic level, such as a radioactive nucleus emitting an alpha or beta particle, or the spontaneous emission of a photon when an electron transitions from one energy state to a lower one (which in turn is responsible for the effects called luminescence, fluorescence, and phosphorescence). But the fact that they are stochastically predictable suggests there is an underlying mechanism there (as maintained by Einstein), but we know of no observable parameters that we can utilise in order to make them deterministic. This raises the question of whether certain things will always be inherently non-deterministic due to the hidden nature of that further information, and whether our measurement process may be too blunt and only capable of accessing selected information. This would have repercussions for fundamental physics, but we will return to this in Chapter 12. The essential point here is that a stochastic description of something is not the same as it being random.

The stochastic description of some radioactive sample that apparently decays randomly is fairly straightforward: the quantity of items (e.g. atoms) remaining after a time t is given by:

$$N(t) = N_0 e^{-\lambda t} = N_0\, e^{-t/\tau}$$

where N_0 is the initial sample ($N(0)$), λ is a constant called the decay rate, and τ is another constant called the mean lifetime. Hence, $\tau = 1/\lambda$. But we usually describe such decay via a half-life, $t_{1/2}$, which is the period after which half of any given sample has decayed. Hence, $t_{1/2}$ is given by:

$$N(t) = (1/2)^{\frac{t}{t_{1/2}}}$$

which means that $t_{1/2} = \tau \log_e 2$.

However, if the decay events were truly random then there would be no predictability. Not only do we have constants that characterise such decay rates, but those constants are the same for samples of a similar ilk (i.e. for the same atoms or particles), they are independent of the location or time of the measurement, and they are independent of the observer (given appropriate transformations from one frame to another). If a single event was observed then we could say that the outcome was random, meaning that there was no obvious mechanism making it predictable, but with a large sample then such constants indicate a type of correlation.

Looking at the static network of the associated world-lines in a *block universe*, we could say that there was an average length of the world-lines, or that there was an average density of the decay events over the timeline of the world-lines.

But it is also possible that these events are 'just there' in that world-line network, and are inherently unpredictable (in violation of our DPC). In other words, that the timeline is regularly punctuated by such indeterministic events, but they are not individually related to the states either side along the time dimension.

The DPC wording of 'fully modelled' is deliberate because we have already identified phenomena that are not totally part of the measurable world, and so cannot be fully modelled mathematically — the implication being that they cannot be part of the objective reality. For instance:

- *Qualia*: Instances of subjective conscious sensation.
- *Emotions*: Subjective assessment of such things as qualia, recollections, and mental states.
- *Subjective time*: Mathematical physics has no basis for the concept of 'now', and no way of accurately expressing the perceived flow of time.
- *Causality*: The chain of cause and effect can be described mathematically, but the specific mechanism at each node cannot. We overlay something extra onto certain correlations that we have witnessed.
- *Motion*: The path of an object can be described mathematically, but not the dynamical aspect that we observe.
- *Change*: Mathematics cannot fully describe the experience of any dynamical change.
- *Chance*: The notion that things may happen in one of several ways, and by implication the concept of probability as a measure of this. That fortuitousness has some random and undetermined nature.
- *Choice*: The notion that we can consciously select one of several possibilities, leading then to the notion of free will.

Each of these examples involves conscious experience: qualia and emotion are entirely within the mind and so immune to measurement, and the remainder form part of our subjective reality, which is the product of the conscious mind's cognition of our environment. The DPC eliminates these as potential components of the objective reality, and consequently requires that our fundamental theories do not presume them or otherwise incorporate them.

On the other hand, the illusions of causality and predictability, in the face of both variant parameters and space-time starting positions, strongly support the presence of an underlying deterministic pattern in the objective reality.

— 11 —

Space-Time and Gravitation

Is the space-time of this objective reality genuinely real?
Where to next?

Apart from a few brief mentions, Einstein's theory of *general relativity* is conspicuous by its absence in this book. The reason is that it is widely known to be separate from *quantum theory*, with the former describing large-scale phenomena and the latter describing small-scale phenomena, but a major issue between them (ignoring their different mathematical frameworks) is the way that space-time is treated.

Although this chapter reaches no conclusive statement about the nature of space-time, it expresses a deep unease with the fact that such a fundamental concept is so poorly understood. Either we take space-time, and more often the separate space and time components, for granted because we think we know them so well, or we assign to them properties that are far beyond what we observe.

We have so far considered an objective reality that involves the 'flat' *Minkowski space-time* of *special relativity*. This chapter will try to look beyond this view of the objective reality, and so should not be considered a fundamental contribution to the book's arguments. Those arguments acknowledge the prevailing notion that space-time is a passive stage upon which the protagonists of the universe (the objects, forces, fields, etc.) conduct their reality. Our equations model the universe in terms of these protagonists, distributed throughout a three-dimensional space (and often more than three), and evolving in the direction of time that we observe as past-to-future. But what is this space-time? Is it nothingness or 'somethingness'?

In our everyday lives, and most of physics, space is just the separation between different objects, and time the separation between different events. The notion of the *luminiferous aether* was proved false by the experiments of Michelson and Morley in 1887 and so space must, then, be a simple empty vacuum. But space and time still 'exist', and are measurable, which may be a problem for materialist philosophies. In fact, space-time plays a crucial part in the nature of measurement (§5.4), thus underpinning all of science as undertaken through our subjective realities (i.e. everything that is not purely theoretical), despite itself being measurable only by the comparison of relative extents.

In popular culture, a 'dimension' may be synonymous with a separate reality or universe, as in 'alternate dimension' or 'parallel dimension', but this is an abuse of the term. A dimension is really just a measurable extent in a particular direction. Hence, a brick has three dimensions: its length, breadth, and height. When we talk about spaces then their dimensionality indicates the minimum number of coordinates needed to specify any given location. In our real space (as distinct from mathematical ones) then this would be three. It does not matter whether these coordinates are simply some x, y, and z values relative to three orthogonal axes, or a longitude, latitude, and distance from the centre of our Earth; there will always be three required.

The *Minkowski space-time* that we have thus far assumed to be at the heart of the *block universe* is passive and truly empty in the absence of matter, but is that realistic? To say that space and time are defined by the separation of objects and events misses the point that we need at least two objects. If we consider a space-time devoid of everything except one stable particle then we would lose at least the following, and hence all chance of physical description:

- *Location:* It would be impossible to specify a location in either space or time because there would be nothing to relate to.
- *Velocity and momentum:* Neither their magnitude nor direction could be defined.
- *Energy:* The concept of energy (kinetic, potential, etc.) would no longer make any sense because location and velocity are undefined.
- *Handedness and chirality:* There would be no up/down, left/right, front/back, and no concept of 'incongruent counterparts'.
- *Rotation:* Rotation could not be defined, although we will mention rotational inertia later in this chapter.
- *Rotational direction:* Clockwise and anticlockwise would have no meaning, and could not be differentiated.
- *Scale:* There would be no such thing as bigger, smaller, etc., and no concept of measure.

Although usually described as four-dimensional, *Minkowski space-time* is really of 3+1 dimensions because we cannot hide certain differences. Its time dimension involves imaginary (in the mathematical sense) coordinates, although this is just a geometrical property that arises from the relativity of inertial observers, and especially the fact that they must all measure the speed of light to be the same. There must be some fundamental significance to this because the mathematics of *special relativity* (see Appendix A) is very symmetrical and elegant in its four-dimensional form, but what other differences exist between the dimensions?

With only one spatial dimension then time and space would appear similar: a world-line would have a projection through both dimensions, and its coordinates on either dimension could be related to unique coordinates on the other, i.e. either $x = f(t)$ or $t = f(x)$. With two spatial dimensions then we start to see the beginnings of what we observe in everyday life: we are free to move in space, but not in time. The world-line has a projection through the single time, meaning there are no degrees of freedom in that dimension, but it also has a projection through the 'block' of spatial dimensions. A world-line can then be expressed in terms of the common time dimension: $x = f(t)$ and $y = f(t)$, or more generally $x_i = f(t)$, which is why time is usually considered an independent variable in physics. The spatial dimensions therefore comprise an irreducible set of indistinguishable components. Every point in such an n-dimension space would require n coordinates, but there would be no preferred frame of reference and so each dimension (or associated coordinate) would have no independent meaning. We could map a spatial 'block' using any number of coordinate systems (not always Cartesian), and using arbitrary orientations of those systems, but we would always need n coordinates (three in our particular case) to specify any particular spatial location.

If world-lines had some innate temporal direction (§8) then we could say that they must form a *directed acyclic graph* (DAG) since we have no evidence of any temporal loops, such as a particle interacting with itself. This is an unlikely proposition since nothing in the future has been observed to affect anything in the past, and no conscious entity has ever demonstrated genuine prescience; otherwise it would destroy our illusion of causality. We are here saying that the world-lines have an indelible extent through time, but the spatial extents mean nothing in the absence of other world-lines, i.e. they are about separation rather than position.

Modern physics views space-time as some pliable substance that may be bent or distorted by mass and energy, admitting gravitational waves originating from accelerated masses, and possibly even admitting 'wormholes' connecting widely separated space-time locations. This concept seriously undermines our concept of measurement with some circularity. In §5.4, we saw that all of our measurements are based upon comparison of changes (movements, displacements, etc.) in space-time, but if the geometry of space-time is distorted in the presence of massive objects then how can we assess such a configuration in order to determine the modified geometry?

Space-time is also considered to be a seething mass of changes and oscillations, variously known as *quantum foam*, *quantum fluctuations*, *vacuum energy*, or *zero-point energy* — a view derived from an application of Werner Heisenberg's *uncertainty principle* to empty space (see §7.2 and §7.3 for a different view).[157] This overrunning of mathematics into a space-time absent of matter was also the source of the 'ghost waves' associated with *de Broglie–Bohm theory* (§7.6). Some theorists even consider that space-time may be quantised or granular, rather than continuous, at very tiny scales below the so-called *Planck length* of 1.6×10^{-35} m. This notion arises through an attempt to unify *general relativity* and *quantum theory* (together: 'quantum gravity') that avoids infinities, but it then causes problems for *special relativity*. If space-time has a fundamental unit of size then it must be a universal constant, but then it would not transform correctly from one inertial frame to another (i.e. it would not be *Lorentz invariant*).

11.1 Gravity

Isaac Newton believed that space and time were absolute entities, but although his theory of gravitation was very successful at explaining observed phenomena, he was also critical of it. It provided no indication of the mediator by which one body could influence another that was separated from it, and it implied an instantaneous 'action at a distance'.

> It is inconceivable that inanimate Matter should, without the
> Mediation of something else, which is not material, operate upon,
> and affect other matter without mutual Contact ... That Gravity
> should be innate, inherent and essential to Matter, so that one body
> may act upon another at a distance thro' a Vacuum, without the
> Mediation of any thing else, by and through which their Action and

Force may be conveyed from one to another, is to me so great an Absurdity that I believe no Man who has in philosophical Matters a competent Faculty of thinking can ever fall into it. Gravity must be caused by an Agent acting constantly according to certain laws; but whether this Agent be material or immaterial, I have left to the Consideration of my readers.[158]

His well-known equation showed that the attractive force was dependent upon the two gravitational masses.

$$F = \frac{G\,M\,m}{r^2}$$

Galileo had shown that the acceleration due to gravity, at the Earth's surface, was the same for all objects — effectively $a = F/m = G\,M/r^2$, meaning that the acceleration of the falling body (m) was dependent only upon the Earth's mass (M) and the distance from its centre (G being a constant) — and so demonstrated what was later to become the *equivalence principle*, that gravitational masses and inertial masses are the same.[159] In other words, that the 'mass' responsible for generating the gravitational force was the very same 'mass' that would be used in the equations of motion to determine the effect of that force. Einstein formalised this principle and used it to create a geometrical theory of gravitation (the main part of *general relativity*) in which objects were simply following a preferred (or natural) path: a *geodesic*, that was the equivalent of the straight line in a 'flat' Euclidean space.[160] From this point of view, free fall is just inertial motion in that modified geometry, and so no acceleration is felt — strangely, this is not emphasised enough at school. You would feel yourself thrown into your seat when accelerating in your car, but not if accelerating to the ground in free fall; you would only feel the air resistance.

Along with this theory came the pervasive notion that space-time has a 'fabric' that can be distorted, or admit holes (so-called 'wormholes') linking one location to another. It is worth taking a moment, though, to consider what Einstein's equations really said. The majority of texts talk about his theory in terms of mass (and energy) causing space-time to 'curve' — an image reinforced by the rubber sheets, or potential-well graphics, used to illustrate it — but the equations do not specifically say that space-time is curved, merely that the geometry is no longer Euclidean. An example of a curved space would be the surface of a globe, where the angles of a triangle do not add up to the usual 180 degrees. This two-dimensional surface is 'curved' through a third dimension (the radius direction), but Einstein's equations do not mandate extra dimensions. Whether space-time is curved in this way, or distorted in some other way (stretched, condensed, etc.), or even whether this is purely a geometrical description of something quite different, is a separate issue.

Ignoring the so-called *cosmological constant*, Einstein's equations may be expressed as follows:

$$G_{uv} = \frac{8\pi G}{c^4} T_{uv}$$

where G_{uv} is the *Einstein tensor* [161] — related to *the Ricci curvature tensor* and the *metric tensor* — and T_{uv} is the stress-energy-momentum *tensor*. In other words, the equation merely expresses a relationship between a space-time geometry (via a metric) and a distribution of stress, energy, and momentum, but like all such equations it does not indicate a causal relationship; it does not say that the presence of mass, etc., changes the local space-time, or that they are part of the same thing, or that space-time itself is a consequence of mass.

Newton's equation turns out to be a close approximation that may be derived from Einstein's equation, but there is an obvious difference: Newton's equation requires at least two masses, and it makes no sense to talk about the gravitational force of a single body. Einstein's equation, however, suggests that there is a permanent distortion of space-time geometry associated with all masses, even in isolation.

In 1915, the same year as *general relativity* was published, German physicist and astronomer Karl Schwarzschild (pronounced 'shvartz-sheeld') solved the equations for a single non-rotating spherical mass, and published his solution early in 1916. The interesting thing about his solution is that it involves a singularity close to the centre, called the *Schwarzschild radius*, within which the geometry is undefined. This radius is given by $r_s = 2\,G\,M\,/\,c^2$, and would be about 9mm for the Earth's mass. This value was already known from Newton's equation as it represents the *event horizon* beyond which light cannot escape the gravity, a concept that would eventually become known as a 'black hole' in the 1960s. However, the concept of a singularity or discontinuity in the geometry of space-time goes against our DPC, so is it a realistic solution? It was later shown that this was a coordinate singularity rather than a real spatial one. What this means is that the mathematical space inside the *Schwarzschild radius* does not really exist, but the coordinate system used was not capable of expressing this, and so leaves an apparent 'hole'. By choosing a different coordinate system then the singularity can be made to go away, thus illustrating that it is not a physical discontinuity. There is evidence that 'black holes' exist, but their internals will not be described by this solution of an unrealistic scenario that also ignores *quantum mechanics*.

So what is the significance of this 'curvature' of space-time? Are we saying that it is not real? Well, we do observe that the motions of both particles and macroscopic objects may be either straight lines or curves, but there are different ways of accounting for this. Newton's laws stated that the natural paths were straight lines, and that other paths result from the action of forces (classical mechanics). More modern treatments use *Hamilton's principle* and the *calculus of variations* to identify natural paths as those for which a quantity known as the 'action' is a minimum (or, more generally, has a stationary value). Richard Feynman's *path integrals* is another approach demonstrating that the natural paths are the ones for which the 'phase arrows' cancel least. Yet another example is the *de Broglie–Bohm theory* where particle paths are influenced by some type of non-local 'pilot wave'. Fuelled by the *equivalence principle* — that gravitational mass is equivalent to inertial mass, and hence that inertial-mass × acceleration = gravitation-mass × intensity-of-gravitation-field — Einstein sought an explanation where the natural paths were determined by a modified geometry (see note 160). So it stands as a means of describing and predicting paths, but that is not the same as space-time actually having a curvature, or a malleable 'fabric'.

11.2   Quantum Gravity

General relativity — which is actually a generalisation of *special relativity* that includes all non-inertial observers (e.g. accelerating, rotating), but is generally taken as synonymous with the geometrical theory of gravity — has been tested with great accuracy in our macroscopic world. This includes the already-known advance of Mercury's perihelion (the closest point of its orbit), the deflection of starlight around the Sun (observed during an eclipse), gravitational 'red shift', and gravitational *time dilation*. *Quantum mechanics* (or, more specifically, *quantum electrodynamics*) has also been tested to incredible accuracy at the subatomic level. Unfortunately, though, it has been impossible (to date) to combine *general relativity* and *quantum mechanics* (together: 'quantum gravity') using a single mathematical framework. Until we have a single theory, rather than two, then we cannot confidently address situations where gravitational and quantum effects are both manifest, and due to their vastly different scales then these situations boil down to so-called 'black holes' and the 'big bang'.

One of the major issues is that *general relativity* is crucially dependent upon space-time, and being able to attribute geometric properties to space-time, whereas space-time does not play much of a role in *quantum mechanics*. In particular, Einstein's equations relate the geometry of space-time to the distribution of energy-momentum — both expressed in *tensor* form — and although *quantum mechanics* would represent energy-momentum using operators, it has no precedent for representing space-time in that way. There is a 'semi-classical gravity' approximation in which only the energy-momentum terms are given a quantum representation, but it is considered inelegant, and breaks down under certain conditions.

When *quantum mechanics* was initially applied to fields[162] rather than to particles (cf. *quantum field theory*), it ran into problems with infinite results being calculated. This was resolved using a technique (one bordering on trickery) called 'renormalisation' that got the infinities to cancel out. Although a hypothetical particle called the graviton has been proposed as the mediator of the gravitation field for 'quantum gravity', just as the photon is the mediator of the electromagnetic field, this renormalisation technique fails when applied to it. The metric describing the geometry of a gravitational field is a field in the mathematical sense, but it is not quantisable in the sense of *quantum field theory*.

Another perceived issue with combining these two theories is the principle of *quantum superposition*: that alternative states of a system can be added, or superposed, to describe a new state that is also a solution of the linear wave equations. If such states are real, as viewed by many physicists, rather than mere mathematical contrivances (§7.6), then it creates problems for 'quantum gravity' since Einstein's equations are non-linear (§5.5), and so the identical principle cannot apply.

There are also observed differences of the gravitation force that make it stand apart from the other fundamental forces:

- Gravity is incredibly weak when compared to the other forces. At the scale of a proton, gravity is about 10^{-36} the strength of the electromagnetic force. This means that we have no available experiments where gravitational and quantum effects can be observed together.
- The source of gravitation (i.e. mass) is not quantised as is electric charge, for instance. The quantity of mass may be any value, possibly down to that of elementary particles.
- Gravity is always attractive. No one is quite sure whether antimatter would attract or repel matter because (a) we do not have enough antimatter, (b) we do not have a good enough theory to predict the effect, and (c) if you ever brought them together in sufficient quantities then all and sundry around it would be destroyed.
- There is no equivalent of a neutral charge. As far as we know, all mass is attractive. Having said that, because gravity is so weak, it may be the case that elementary particles do not have a gravitation force in the way that large masses do, but we will come back to this again soon.

For simplicity, we have described 'quantum gravity' as a unified description of gravity (specifically *general relativity*) with *quantum mechanics* (specifically *quantum field theory*), but the taxonomy of unification theories is a little more complicated, and it is worth laying out some of it. Of the four fundamental forces — gravity, electromagnetism, and the two nuclear forces (strong and weak) — a unified description of only electromagnetism and the weak nuclear force has so far been achieved, called the *electroweak force*. The *standard model* of particle physics describes the individual electromagnetic and the nuclear forces, and also classifies all the elementary particles currently known, but a 'grand unified theory' (GUT) is an attempt to find a unified description of these three forces (not gravity) as a single one. A 'theory of everything' (TOE) is some theory that would account for all observed phenomena in the universe, but is usually taken to mean just the fundamental interactions. Hence, since 'quantum gravity' would provide a unified description of all four fundamental forces then it is considered a sufficient basis for a TOE, implicitly relying on a picture based upon *physicalism* and *reductionism*. Although subjects such as consciousness, free will, and time are usually excluded from a TOE, and are delegated to the field of philosophy, they certainly should be included as they are part of the same universe; not including them is an implicit admission of failure.

11.3   More Dimensions

Rather than trying to quantise gravity, what about trying to geometricise the other fundamental forces: electromagnetism, strong nuclear force, and weak nuclear force? Other classical potentials can be given a geometric interpretation and so can this be done at the subatomic level?

Adding extra dimensions, beyond the four for which we have direct evidence, is a popular route, and in 'string theory' there may be as many as 10 or 11 proposed. In a mathematical sense, this approach may be viewed as simply adding extra degrees of freedom, and so could be used to explain almost anything, but it could also imply extra degrees of freedom in a movement sense and we do not want that. As noted above, we are free to move around in the block of three spatial dimensions, but we are not aware of any others. In order to overcome this, such theories make those extra dimensions small, or tightly wrapped. For instance, if you take a two-dimensional piece of paper and roll it tightly in one direction then you only have the remaining one — the length of the roll — to move freely within; the other dimension then has a finite extent, and this is usually made incredibly small (in the order of the *Planck length*) in order to explain why we are not aware of it. As with *general relativity*, though, these higher-dimensional spaces are not Euclidean ('flat') and we are back to assuming that space-time has a 'fabric'.

It has been shown that we cannot have more than one temporal dimension that behaves like our subjective time, but it is unclear whether this applies to the objective time of a *block universe*. This dimension behaves mathematically like our spatial ones, rather than like our subjective time with its past-to-future progression, and is different in that we, and our constituents, have an extent in that direction, and hence no freedom to move in that direction (in those models, that is, that accommodate some notion of movement).

One early example of a higher-dimensional theory was the *Kaluza–Klein theory* which employed a fifth dimension in order to unify the theories of gravity and electromagnetism. It was originally proposed by German mathematician and physicist Theodor F. E. Kaluza as an extension of *general relativity*, and was presented to Einstein in 1919. It provided a neat way of incorporating the electromagnetic four-potential (magnetic vector potential plus electric scalar potential) into a space-time metric. It was not immediately popular because there was no observational evidence for this fifth dimension, illustrating a clear departure of modern mathematical physics where 'string theory' easily gets into double figures with extra dimensions. However, it demonstrated a symmetry between the two forces that hinted at some fundamental significance, somewhere. In 1926, it was modified in accordance with the burgeoning *quantum theory* by Swedish theoretical physicist Oskar B. Klein, who also proposed that this fifth dimension was somehow rolled up, or 'compactified'. At the time, the *tensor* representation was considered very complex in five dimensions, and various constraints were imposed on it in order to restrict the degrees of freedom. Although Einstein was initially impressed, and eventually presented Kaluza's paper to the Prussian Academy in 1921, his interest waned because it gave no hint as to the origin of elementary particles such as the electron.[163] In 1979, the electromagnetic force and the weak nuclear force were unified in a non-geometrical manner (*Weinberg–Salam theory*) and so interest in the *Kaluza–Klein theory* faded further.

There is, in fact, a major sticking point with a geometrical description of electromagnetism: gravity applies to mass, and to all mass as far as we know, but electromagnetism applies only to charged particles. So consider, for a moment, a single positively charged particle such as a proton. As an electron gets close to it then it will be attracted due to its opposite charge, and we can imagine a geometrical interpretation of this similar to that of gravitational attraction. But now imagine that a neutral particle, such as a neutron, is also in the vicinity. If space-time is really curved then both the electron and the neutron should be affected, but since only the electron is affected then we are forced to conclude that this curved space-time is merely a mathematical device for describing a given path taken, and not some absolute property of space-time. In other words, we should expect all particles to share the same space-time, and so be subject to the same geometrical properties of that space-time.

11.4   Big Bang

The 'big bang'[164] is one of the most misunderstood and abused concepts of modern physics. Much of this is a result of popular science media perpetuating the same description and the same questions, such as 'what was there before the big bang?' So let us take a look at the history of the concept.

In 1912, American astronomer Vesto Slipher was the first to observe a 'red shift' in the spectral lines of light from faraway galaxies. The 'red shift' is a form of the *Doppler effect*. With sound, if you listen to a vehicle approaching you at speed, the noise it makes is of a higher pitch than when it is travelling away from you because the sound waves get bunched up or stretched out. With light, the effect involves a similar change of the wavelength, and hence of the colour. One interpretation of a shift to the red end of the spectrum (i.e. a lengthening of the waves) is that those galaxies are moving away from us.

In 1929, American astronomer Edwin P. Hubble discovered that the distances to such galaxies were generally proportional to their 'red shifts'. His interpretation was that the further away they are, the higher their apparent velocity relative to us. In conjunction with American astronomer Milton L. Humason, Hubble formulated *Hubble's law* to describe this observed effect. However, unbeknown to Hubble, this observation had been made already by Belgian priest, mathematician, and astronomer Georges Lemaître in 1927, but he had further considered the implications by extrapolating backwards and proposing his theory of the 'primeval atom' — later to become known as the 'big bang'.

English astronomer Sir Fred Hoyle is credited with coining the actual term 'big bang' during the BBC Radio's *Third Programme*, broadcast on 28 March 1949, although not as a serious description. Hoyle believed in 'continuous creation' and remarked that "… on scientific grounds this big bang hypothesis is much less palatable …", and that "… cannot see any good reason for preferring the big bang idea …" since it was " … distinctly weak".[165] Unfortunately, the term has stuck! It is unfortunate because it is a misnomer: there would have been no bang (nor any noise at all) and it would not have been big (it would have been infinitesimally small). There would not even have been an explosion. With an explosion, particles are thrown outward into pre-existing space, but in the case of the universe, it is space that appears to be expanding between the particles, and this is usually described as a 'metric expansion of space'.

There is no place we can point to and say that is where the expansion started. The observed expansion is uniform in all directions (i.e. isotropic) and would be observed to be the same from all galaxies (homogeneous). What we can deduce is that space was smaller the further back in time we consider. The point at which the size would be zero is called the origin and is estimated to have been about 13.7 billion years ago.[166] The associated mathematical model describes this as a singularity since it would entail mass having been infinitely dense and the gravitational intensity being infinitely great, but this is unrealistic and based upon insufficient knowledge.

One of the most asked questions is 'what was before the big bang?' but the question does not mean anything as there was no time before the origin. Stephen Hawking compared this to asking what lies south of the South Pole, remarking that "… there is nothing south of the South Pole".[167] The mental model he was using here was that of a one-dimensional closed (i.e. no spatial boundary) universe that was expanding (south-to-north), and possibly contracting later. The analogy between lines of latitude on a sphere and space (i.e. the 'parallels') results in the absence of spatial boundaries, but the analogy between lines of longitude and time (i.e. the 'meridians'), rather than a straight line joining the poles, also results in an absence of temporal boundaries.

> These histories [of the universe] may be pictured as being like
> the surface of the Earth, with the distance from the North Pole
> representing imaginary time and the size of a circle of constant
> distance from the North Pole representing the spatial size of the
> universe. The universe starts at the North Pole as a single point. As
> one moves south, the circles of latitude at constant distance from the
> North Pole get bigger, corresponding to the universe expanding with
> imaginary time (Fig. 8.1). The universe would reach a maximum size
> at the equator and would contract with increasing imaginary time to
> a single point at the South Pole.[168]

Neither pole would be a singularity in the geometrical sense since the analogy involves a closed surface, so the same physical laws would apply, and with the implication that the origin of the universe would also not constitute a geometrical singularity. In fact, talk of it being a singularity is always in the mathematical sense, and mostly results from an extrapolation of *general relativity* back to that instant; few believe in a true physical singularity as that would imply we cannot have laws of physics that are continuously applicable, and even our DPC (see Glossary) would exclude such a condition.

There is other evidence for an historical origin (e.g. *cosmic microwave background*, or CMB, and the relative abundance of different elements) but it is of the kind supporting an expanding model rather than being direct evidence for such an expansion. Other mechanisms have been proposed for the observed 'red shift', such as 'tired light', but none are now mainstream. The constant of proportionality[169] in *Hubble's law* — effectively the measure of how fast physicists think the universe is expanding — has proved hard to pin down, and current research is yielding quite different values depending upon the methods used.[170] In 1998, two independent research projects suggested that the rate of expansion was actually accelerating, and a Nobel Prize was awarded accordingly,[171] but very recent evidence may now bring this into question.[172] As nice and elegant as our favourite model may be, we have to remember that nature does not care about our mathematics, and at some point we may have to consider a radical alternative rather than trying to patch it up yet again.

So is the universe spatially or temporally infinite? If it were spatially infinite (which, again, would be excluded by our DPC) then how could it be expanding? There is no difficulty expressing such a combination mathematically, but from an intuitive point of view then it feels wrong that an infinite amount of space could expand, and somehow become 'more infinite'. A more common view is that space is finite and unbounded, meaning that there is only a certain amount of it, but that there are no boundaries; no 'brick walls'. This is easiest to appreciate by extrapolating from the image a circle (representing a one-dimension, finite, unbounded universe), to the surface of a sphere (a two-dimensional example), and beyond to instances that cannot be envisaged but can be described mathematically. Having a finite, unbounded universe removes the problem with the infinites, and also allows us to calculate a finite average density of matter — otherwise, we would be forced to divide infinity by infinity. The issue here with such models is that, again, they suggest that space-time has a 'fabric' that can be distorted or curved.

A well-known analogy for an expanding finite unbounded universe is the inflating balloon proposed by Sir Arthur Eddington. The surface of a balloon may be imagined to be a two-dimensional universe that is undergoing an expansion in another direction, corresponding to time.

> For a model of the universe let us represent spherical space by
> a rubber balloon. Our three dimensions of length, breadth, and
> thickness ought all to lie in the skin of the balloon; but there is only
> room for two, so the model will have to sacrifice one of them. That
> does not matter very seriously. Imagine the galaxies to be embedded
> in the rubber. Now let the balloon be steadily inflated. That's the
> expanding universe.[173]

This expanding membrane is a fair analogy for space expanding as a function of measured time. If you were to draw a couple of dots on the surface then their separation increases as the radius of the balloon increases. Not only that, though, the increased separation is greater for two dots that were initially further apart, simply because there is more membrane expanding between them.

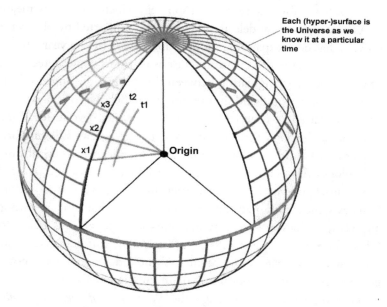

Each (hyper-)surface is the Universe as we know it at a particular time

Fig. 11-1, Simple model of an expanding universe.

In this diagram, the separation of x_1 and x_3 has increased more than that of x_1 to x_2 between the two times t_1 and t_2. If the separation is expressed as:

$$x = a\theta t$$

where a is a constant and θ is an expression of the angular separation from the origin, then the speed of separation would be given by $dx/dt = a\theta$. In other words, the speed is greater for points with a greater angular separation, but there is no actual acceleration; the speed does not increase as the spatial separation increases for two points with a fixed angular separation. It would seem that the apparently accelerating expansion of the universe could be described as a purely geometrical effect.

The equivalent of this analogy for *a block universe* might be the shells of an onion, where each shell represents the spatial part of the universe at a given time, but the whole universe is the sum total of all these shells. A true expansion could not occur since nothing would be moving, but the shells would have increasingly large sizes as we looked further from the origin. A better equivalent to the question of what was there before the 'big bang' might then be 'what lies before the centre of a sphere?', which is similarly meaningless.

As nice as these models are, they are not supported by observation. If the universe has been expanding for only about 13.7 billion years then we should be able to measure this curvature, just as mariners could detect the curvature of the globe by triangulating between three ships: the angles of a triangle in such situations would add up to more than 180^0. Unfortunately, all evidence suggests that space-time is 'flat' at that scale, i.e. beyond local gravitational influences, although very recent CMB evidence may still support a curved universe[174]. In order to get around this, American theoretical physicist and cosmologist Alan H. Guth proposed, in 1981, the idea of *cosmic inflation*: an exponential growth of the universe within the first 10^{-32} seconds (or even less) of its existence. Although there is no known mechanism accounting for such an event, it does not prevent mathematical descriptions being formulated (cf. *inflaton* particle and field). Unfortunately, this explanation looks quite unattractive in a *block universe* since it would demand bizarre 'non-flat' static geometries giving the appearance of an inflation across time.

So is time infinite? Although the *second law of thermodynamics* is time-symmetric (Chapter 3), it should still result in *thermodynamic equilibrium* (maximum entropy) after enough time. Although the law is defined within an *isolated system*, it is usually taken to predict the 'heat death' of the entire universe, where everything ends in equilibrium and in a state of maximum entropy. But this is not the case at the moment since we still see changes in the overall state, and so the universe can only have been around for a finite time, which then implies that it had an origin (or at least a point of lowest entropy) some finite time from now. If this origin is equated with the finite extent of a primordial universe then it must have a similarly finite extent now. Nothing can transition between finite and infinite within a finite interval — not without a major discontinuity — and so we have to conclude that the spatial extent is also finite in the current epoch, a finite time from the origin. This would pin down one end of time, just as with the radius in Fig. 11-1, but not the other end. Hawking's one-dimensional analogy does this for both ends, though it implies an apparent expansion followed by a contraction (sometimes called the 'big crunch') if it could be observed from the perspective of a subjective time. If this structure were the case then it is not clear what effect the eventual transition would have on the nature of consciousness. A problem with both views, however, is that those temporal endpoints would constitute absolute instants, relative to which (in principle) we could define an absolute clock and absolute simultaneity.

NB: when these arguments refer to objective time, including the space-time of a *block universe*, then they try to avoid using the terms *before* or *after* in order to prevent the presumption of a preferred direction.

11.5   Emergence

It was stated that this chapter expresses an uneasiness and suspicion over the way that physics overloads the notion of space-time with all manner of properties when it is still fundamentally intangible to us and non-absolute. Although *general relativity* is widely considered to be unshakeable, there are phenomena that it has yet to explain, and one of these — inertia — is an important omission that is rarely mentioned these days.

In classical mechanics, in order to make something deviate from its natural (inertial) path, a force must be applied because there will be a resistance. This resistance is known as inertia, but we are not really sure what causes it. Newton's laws of motion apply to inertial reference frames (i.e. those not subject to a net force) and in order to make them apply to non-inertial ones — such as ones accelerating, decelerating, or rotating — then a correction factor is required: a fictitious force, known as an inertial force. For instance, when a force makes a car accelerate, someone in the car feels as though a reverse force is pushing them into the seat. A bucket full of water being spun at the end of a rope has a real force keeping it from flying away (the centripetal force applied via the rope) but the water appears to be thrown outward via a centrifugal inertial force, and would even show a concaved surface.

The *Coriolis force* is a slightly more complicated inertial force associated with rotating frames. Imagine something moving from the centre of a rotating turntable to a fixed point beyond the circumference (and not touching the turntable). To an inertial observer off the turntable, the path would be a straight line, but to a non-inertial observer on the rotating turntable, the path would be a curve that may be attributed to this inertial force. Although it is sometimes explained as a consequence of the conservation of angular momentum, the dependency is really the other way around.

In the eighteenth century, Bishop Berkeley attributed inertia to the fixed stars. Because he believed that all motion was relative, he considered the case of a single globe in the absence of all else in the universe. It would then be impossible not only to imagine that it was moving but also that it was rotating. It is not possible to say it has a particular angular momentum, and to introduce something capable of testing (or stopping) any rotation changes the circumstances by defining a frame of reference. He then considered a pair of isolated globes, pointing out that it would still be impossible to imagine them rotating about their common centre of mass, although rotation relative to each other would be obvious. But with a backdrop of the so-called fixed stars then both of these rotational scenarios could be imagined. In 1872, Austrian physicist and philosopher Ernst Mach improved upon this line of reasoning by suggesting that an object rotating relative to the fixed stars is geometrically identical to the fixed stars rotating around the object, and so any law of inertia must respect that symmetry.[175] His implication that inertial frames are those not accelerating (or rotating) relative to the fixed stars greatly influenced Einstein during his development of *general relativity*, and he referred to it as 'Mach's principle'.

Unfortunately, 'Mach's principle' was never incorporated into *general relativity*, so the origin of inertia is as much a mystery now as before, although routinely ignored as not requiring explanation. Instead, Einstein's *equivalence principle* equated the gravitational force with certain inertial effects. A man in a closed box, located on the Earth, and holding two spheres, would see them fall if he let go (Fig. 11-2(a) and (b)). But similarly, if that box was in outer space and being accelerated then he would see the same result, due to an inertial force that is equal and opposite to the accelerating one. Note that this equivalence only holds within a localised region, otherwise he would notice that the path of the spheres would not be truly parallel in the gravitational case.

Fig. 11-2, Equivalence principle.

In the earthbound case, the floor is exerting a real force upward (preventing free fall) and the spheres still appear to fall due to an inertial force. Putting it another way, free fall in a gravitational field is technically an inertial motion (i.e. one following a *geodesic*), although that term is sometimes used specifically for steady motion away from fields of force. Putting it yet another way, if the whole box was allowed to free fall, then the man would experience weightlessness, and <u>not</u> experience the ordeal illustrated in Fig. 11-2(c).

So why is inertia so important? Well, physicists and philosophers have known for a long time that all motion is measurable only relative to something else, and that space-time locations themselves are similarly measurable only as a separation from something else, so why should inertia be exempt from our description of reality? Why should it be possible to measure acceleration in an absolute fashion? To describe gravitational effects as a generalisation of rectilinear inertial motion, and to simply take inertia itself as a given (detected when an object moves away from a *geodesic* path), places the foundations of *general relativity* into some doubt. Several predictions of *general relativity* have been tested to a very precise level, but the equations are still challenged on the basis of their foundation, their complexity, and their applicability to other situations.[176]

The usual (inertial) mass of an object is effectively a measure of its inertia, while the gravitational mass (as used in Newton's equation) is a measure of the intensity of the associated gravitational force. Einstein's *equivalence principle* equates these,[177] and the realisation that gravitational and inertial forces both induce the same acceleration in different bodies, dependent only upon their inertial mass, led Einstein to his geometrical interpretation. However, it is not inconceivable that both forces are real and related.

The fixed stars may be a colossal distance away, but they also comprise a colossal mass in total. The amount of this mass is proportional to the distance squared, so if there was an inertial interaction that was inversely proportional to the distance (rather than the usual inverse-square law) then it would be more significant locally than the equivalent contribution from neighbouring masses.

English physicist Dennis W. Sciama (pronounced 'sharma') looked at the viability of this idea,[178] and confirmed that an inertial interaction could exert an acceleration-dependent force $F \propto (m_1 m_2 / r) \, \alpha$, and possibly a static (or not acceleration-dependent) force $F \propto m_1 m_2 / r^2$, which he equated with gravity.[179] Ideally, these would appear as series terms in the expansion of a more general theory. It might be possible that a new geometrical version of this idea could be constructed, but such a revision of Newtonian dynamics would have consequences for *general relativity* as it stands.

There is also observational evidence for something being not quite right in our understanding of gravity. The rotational speeds of stars in large spiral galaxies, and of galaxies in galactic clusters, are faster than to be expected from *general relativity*. Based upon the predicted gravitational force then the outer limits should be flying away, but they are not. There are two main attempts to explain this: 'modified gravity' and 'dark matter'. With 'modified gravity', either an alternative to *general relativity* is sought (such as MOND: 'modified Newtonian dynamics'), or tweaks are made to it. 'Dark matter' was first proposed by the Swiss astronomer Fritz Zwicky in 1933 as a mechanism for explaining the anomalies in terms of hidden gravitational sources, i.e. some completely unknown form of matter that is not luminous in any frequency range, and which does not form macroscopic structures (otherwise we could detect specific gravitational effects on luminous structures such as neighbouring stars).

These anomalous scenarios are all characterised by having large-scale distributions of matter: much more of it, and scattered over a vastly larger area, than for a mere solar system. Now it may be that the calculations are inaccurate since the equations for *general relativity* are complex and non-linear (§5.5), requiring approximations to be used in non-trivial cases, and these may be breaking down under those conditions. Or, it may be that the original premise of *general relativity* was incorrect.

Remember that we suggested, earlier, that masses at the scale of elementary particles might not exhibit gravitational forces, and so implying that gravity is an ensemble effect that is only observable when there are enough components. Well, there is a concept called 'emergent gravity', or 'entropic gravity', developed by Dutch theoretical physicist Erik P. Verlinde, where the force is claimed to be a statistical effect rather than a fundamental interaction (i.e. a so-called 'entropic force').[180] In the framework of a type of 'emergent space-time', it claims to explain the entropic origin of inertia itself. He later extended the work to present a type of MOND, which also posits an acceleration-dependent effect that falls off with an inverse-linear relationship.

Before leaving this chapter, we must look at a particularly extreme possibility, one that will not go away but is acutely uncomfortable to consider: fully 'emergent space-time'. This is hard to imagine — even more so than 'curved space-time' — because our notions of space and time are so heavily entrenched, and originating from our direct perception. But they are still intangible and non-absolute, suggesting that they are only evident as a result of something else, and that our explanations involving non-Euclidean geometries, extra dimensions, and an expanding space-time, are simply trying to keep that entrenched viewpoint alive. Since this approach would move the concept of space-time from the *block universe* of the objective reality into our subjective reality, then what different part of the objective reality would underpin it?

We believe space-time has a particular structure everywhere, but we cannot observe it all. Every observer — in fact, every fundamental particle — has two 'light cones' that encompass any causal connections: one pointing to the future that embraces every subsequent event that they can directly influence from the current instant, and one pointing to the past that embraces every prior event that could influence them at the current instant. They are called 'light cones' because their sides embrace connections that can propagate at light-speed; ones at less than light-speed being within the cones. We extrapolate from these to consider the intersection of all such 'light cones' and deduce a universal space-time that is shared by all objects. But our stance, here, of trying to reject both a space-time with any explicit properties (including a malleable geometry) and a space-time of infinite extent leads us inexorably to this concept of a fully 'emergent space-time'.

Imagine, for a moment, a solitary particle, and remember that in a *block universe* this would be a static world-line rather than a traversed path. We could not say anything about the endpoints other than the scalar length of their separation, and we could not say anything about its shape because there is nothing to relate it to (unless it looped back on itself). In effect, the dimensionality of the hosting space-time would be irrelevant, so let us discard it; we will then refer to our line as a 'thread' in order to emphasise the difference from the world-line concept. If we extend this to two threads then it is tempting to think of their separation — increasing, decreasing, or twisting as it might be — as dictated by some laws of physics, but then this would presuppose that they have some separation from each other that is still this space-time 'stuff'. All we would really have are two sets of endpoints but still nothing to relate them to since we have dropped the surrounding space-time framework. In our universe, the world-lines corresponding to such threads would almost certainly not begin or end in nothingness because of our conservation laws; the endpoint events would correspond to what we know of as interactions, and these must be either direct (e.g. collision, absorption, emission, annihilation, or decay) or mediated by another type of force-carrying particle (which must have its own world-line). Thus we do not need to consider frames of reference, or space-time geometries; only this scalar value that we think of as a separation between those interactions.

The whole of our perceived space and time might be underpinned by such a dimensionless network of threads, and the constancy of the separation values, and their additive properties, would be related to the invariance of space-time intervals in a *block universe*. It would be meaningless to ask whether those separations are physically real, or to ask whether they could be subdivided rather than simply being scalar quantities since that would require an intermediate interaction to probe the difference. In fact, the question of whether space-time is quantised (or granular) would go away if it was emergent in this way. Our perceived three dimensions of space just happen to be the minimum number in which world-lines would not have to cross, and our time dimension would be related to the thread extents, i.e. the separation between their endpoints.[181]

So is this not a variation of 'string theory', with its one-dimensional vibrating strings? This is unlikely. As well as a huge difference in scale (strings are at the level of the *Planck length*), strings still exist within a dimensioned space-time (possibly with a high number of such dimensions), whereas these threads are not hosted in any type of dimensioned space; they are part of a dimensionless network defined by their individual endpoints, and space-time is emergent from them. Actually, to be accurate, we could not even refer to their endpoints (we did that just to bridge the gap to observable world-lines) since to visualise them as having any type of length is again presuming a dimensioned framework; all we would have is a scalar magnitude for each thread, but then the concept of any 'connection' between them is difficult to imagine in the absence of a dimensioned framework.

This is all conjecture, of course. If space-time was emergent then it would put a very different slant on all views that presumed it had a 'fabric' or other real properties, including *general relativity*, inertia, the expanding universe, *quantum fluctuations*, etc. But it would also mean that the use of fields in mathematical physics could no longer be fundamental. The alternative to an expanding (or contracting) universe is a static universe, but this is generally treated as synonymous with an infinite steady-state universe. Notwithstanding the fact that a *block universe* is absolutely static, it is possible to imagine a universe of 'emergent space-time' that is finite in all respects, and which does not demand an origin or a geometrical expansion. The problem is then one of deducing associated patterns and constraints that would emerge as *Minkowski space-time*, *Riemannian space-time*, or an expanding universe.

— 12 —

Conclusions

So what does reality mean and how much can we expect to understand through science? What are the limits of mathematics and metaphysics?

The development of science has involved an acceptance that we do not occupy a privileged position in the universe (e.g. the Earth is not the centre of the universe), and that we are just another component of it. Essentially, we — the observer — must be described by the same theories that we seek to describe the observed. Hence, previous chapters have examined topics such as consciousness, free will, intelligence, aesthetics, and the very nature of measurement.

We have identified two levels of reality: subjective and objective, with one of the core distinguishing features being a flowing subjective time versus a static objective time. Our subjective reality is formed from our perceptions of the things around us, sliced up into spatial snapshots in the temporal direction, but the objective reality is independent of any observation. There is obviously a dependency between the two but we have no direct access to the latter, and so it must be inferred. We have equated the objective reality with the long-standing concept of a timeless *block universe* since it provides a clear mapping for our perceived space and time, and for our notion of measurement. Motion cannot exist without subjective time and so cannot be part of the objective reality, but neither can any form of dynamical change, choice, potentiality, probability, causality, or rationale. All of these must be part of our subjective reality, and yet they somehow depend upon the objective reality. Without understanding this dependency then we cannot include a description of ourselves within a consistent theory of reality, and we cannot see how distorted the viewpoint from our subjective reality really is.

So is the *block universe* concept not the same as saying that the future is all planned out, and so making the case for fate/destiny? No, these are quite different concepts on a number of levels. To suggest that the future is pre-planned implies some rationale for it, and hence some form of design. Fate and destiny both refer to subsequent events that are set to occur in a specific way, with destiny usually relating to events in a future scenario rather than starting from the present one. *Fatalism* is the view that future events are out of our control and that we have no other choice, whereas *predeterminism* is the view that future events are already decided or are already known, and usually the result of some supernatural agent. *Determinism* is more often the view that future events are determined by prior events through the phenomenon known as causality, but this is better described as *causal determinism* to distinguish it from *mathematical determinism*. The apparent conflict with free will, which was addressed in §6.4, leads to fallacious arguments such as the so-called 'idle argument': why should we make any effort to direct our future if it is already determined? *Superdeterminism* is usually equated with the view that everything is causally determined by prior events going right back to the origin of the universe, but there is a different type of *superdeterminism* that is applicable to a *block universe*: one that is based upon *mathematical determinism* rather than *causal determinism*. *Superdeterminism* in general may be equated with *logical determinism*, the view that all propositions about the future are either true or false (not indeterminate or unknown), and so are not fundamentally different from those about the past or the present.

The point being made here is that each of our familiar terms has experiential baggage that prevents them from accurately conveying the notion of a *block universe*. We cannot even describe a *block universe* as some type of stasis since stasis implies lack of movement or activity, which then implies that movement is the natural state of things, which further implies that movement has some fundamental significance.

So does the perspective of our subjective reality really distort things so much? Our scope has been necessarily large since our consciousness — the origin of our subjective reality — also allows for emotion and a sense of beauty in things. Science takes it for granted that these are entirely subjective, if not fanciful, yet they are employed in our creative processes and our judgement of theories about the universe. Further subjective contributions to our cognitive abilities include the recognition of identity, the very act of measurement or observation, and the assignment of meaning to thoughts and observations. None of these concepts exist in the objective reality; they have no basis there, and are all baggage associated only with our subjectiveness. This may seem hard to accept as it would seem to *pull the rug* from beneath the feet of scientific endeavour. If true then we need a clearer picture of the goals of such endeavour, and of our own lives and creative efforts.

Consider the main phenomenological issues that we have encountered thus far:

- *Physicality*: The notion that everything that is real has a physicality (either a material presence, or a direct effect upon material presences), and that everything else — possibly with space and time aside — must be imaginary. This notion leads us to struggle with the concept of consciousness, and even to suggest that there is something mystical about it, or outside of the laws of physics. We have made the case that the mind is an emergent non-physical entity, meaning that its existence supervenes upon some physical substrate (the brain in this case) but it cannot be reduced to the specific mechanical, chemical, or biological workings of that substrate. Yet it is real in that it can influence, and be influenced by, the physical world.

- *Dynamism*: The notion that things can move in the physical sense, or that things can change from one instant to another. Chapter 2 highlighted that mathematics can only describe a rate of change relative to some variable, or to some axis of a graph, but it cannot fully describe any of the changes we experience relative to time; the mathematics of change and the experience of change are fundamentally different.

- *Causality*: The notion that every effect has a prior cause, which in turn has a cause of its own. In §8.2, we equated this concept at the physical level with the capacity for apparent change against the statistical progression to equilibrium, and energy is the term we give to this capacity. But it was also noted that this interpretation stemmed from our experience of causal entities rather than of discrete events.

- *Measurement*: The notion that we can observe or measure all things, at least in principle. Notwithstanding the fact that there must be fundamental limits to what our equipment can detect or record, we are also limited to observing changes in the causal present; we can calculate or infer what may have occurred in the past, and we can predict what may occur in the future, but these are not direct observations. All changes will leave evidence in the form of knock-on effects, artefacts, or even deliberate recordings, but our direct observation of them (including of measurement apparatus) can only occur over the limited periods of time where we are causally connected to them. At very small scales then the 'observer effect' becomes an issue as the equipment must be part of the system where a measurement is deemed to be taking place. We also have phenomena that are not measurable, such as qualia, emotion, etc.

• *Arrow of time*: The notion that the universe evolves from past to future, that its changes are the result of causal interactions, and that events ahead of us are unknown and can only be predicted. Such predictions are based upon prior measurements and the laws by which we expect things to evolve, but the measurements themselves are also based upon predictable correlations (i.e. laws) between causes and effects (§5.4). In other words, there is a fundamental connection between these cases, and both are reliant upon smooth, finite, and deterministic changes over time. A more subtle aspect of the arrow is that we believe we can steer the progression of events leading into the future, and that we have total freedom of choice when configuring apparatus for some scientific investigation.

Our subjective reality therefore appears to consist of a three-dimensional space encompassing objects that move and change from instant to instant. The sequence of changes is smooth and shows some regularity that makes it predictable. When these changes are observed in the order dictated by our consciousness, their smoothness and predictability suggest to us that they are determined by prior changes, constituting a continuous chain of cause and effect. But the choice of causal agency (large or small) depends upon our perspective, and what type of explanation makes the most sense there. The notions that nothing happens without a reason ('principle of sufficient reason') and that each effect has a single unique cause ('causal exclusion principle') are based upon an empirical assessment of events around us, and not upon any specific laws of physics. Whether we say that someone was deliberately pushed over a cliff, or that the pressure of someone's arm moved their centre of gravity over the edge and the force of gravity then pulled them down, could both be correct; it is a matter of expediency rather than fundamentality. Mental causation is just such a case that naturally leads to the impression of there a being choice of future outcomes, and ultimately to the notion of free will.

While trying to assess the impact of this insular perspective, below, we will frequently draw upon quotations from Albert Einstein. Not because he was always correct, but because he clearly thought deeply about such issues and made public many of his personal opinions.

Having argued that the objective reality is essentially a static pattern that could be addressed using mathematics (if we had sufficient details), we have constructed our DPC to impose constraints upon the possible nature of this pattern. This effectively acts as a philosophical razor by eliminating possibilities that would violate the limits implied by that conjecture, in a similar manner to 'Occam's razor' (paraphrased as 'the simplest solution is most likely the right one') being used to eliminate overly complex explanations. This constrains the types of mathematics that we need, it limits the nature of corresponding observables in our subjective reality, and it assists in our judgement of candidate theories to explain our reality.

But we have a problem: the two goals of physics stated in §1.3 were predictability and understanding, but understanding is an entirely subjective aspiration; it has no meaning in the absence of conscious entities. This then implies that you cannot ask philosophical questions, and particularly metaphysical ones, about the objective reality because they would necessarily involve dynamical and causal relationships (the *how* and *why*). The *scientific method* may imply objectivity (§1.2), but that is clearly not possible given the usage, here, of the terms objective and subjective since the acts of measurement and observation are necessarily subjective in their interpretation; and yet it remains a guiding principle in the study of the laws of nature, including their reproducibility in similar circumstances and predictability in related circumstances. In contrast, mathematics is entirely objective, but how can it be rated as a significant description of some phenomenon in the absence of an understanding? If different mathematical frameworks deliver the same results when applied to physics then how can we say one is more significant than another without considering the theories through which the mathematics was derived and interpreted?[182] Would economy and symmetry alone be sufficient?

The whole world of experience (for us and for other conscious species) involves the recognition of patterns in the world around us. It is easy to imagine an evolutionary advantage to this because it gives such entities options in how to proceed — what to do, and what not to do — but we are not perfect. There are a couple of relevant concepts in the psychological field of pattern recognition: *apophenia* (perceiving connections or patterns between things where there are none) and *pareidolia* (perception of images, or sounds, in random or unconnected data, e.g. optical illusions). The fact that we can misconstrue images, sounds, correlations, and meaningful connections in our everyday life suggests that the patterns we observe in physics might not be significant — whatever that word actually means here. A physicist might interpret the word as meaning noteworthy or indicative of something requiring explanation, as opposed to noise or coincidence, but a deeper interpretation would be that it has some meaning relevant to the underlying reality.

Taking a wider viewpoint (with more observations and measurements), and representing it mathematically with the simplest of possible schemes, sounds like a way to capture the pattern rather than any explanation, but we are still hamstrung by the phenomenological issues mentioned at the beginning of this section. What this is trying to convey is that virtually every physical theory will make reference to those issues, and the few that do not will be entirely mathematical, but which can we accept as a significant description of reality? It would seem that there are no other options but mathematics, but that would only satisfy one of our goals: predictability rather than understanding.

So what are the repercussions for physics? Well, for most of physics — those parts that seek to predict and explain observable phenomena of our subjective reality — little or none, but for fundamental physics, some rather deep ones. We must accept that a consistent, and yet economical, mathematical model is the best that we can expect for fundamental physics because of the static nature of the objective reality. We must also accept that there is no context deserving of our faithful notions such as subjective time, motion, dynamical change, causality, and probability, and hence that devising theories that presume them at this level is doomed to failure. Finally, we must also accept that elements of our core being, such as consciousness, thought, emotion, rationale, and free will, do not require anything special in the objective reality in order to explain them, that they are perfectly 'real' within our subjective reality, and they play a causal role there despite their non-physical status. In other words, that both levels of reality are important but they are surprisingly different.

Our approach to physics rightly employs mathematics as we probe the fundamental levels, but in trying to determine that pattern of change in the objective reality, we attribute space-time with abstract notions — such as modified geometry, *wave functions*, fields, 'pilot waves' — that somehow control or direct the motions that we observe, and we then try to interpret these as explanations that can be visualised with some degree of physicality. But after removing change and causality from the objective reality, we should be able to see the bias that we have injected into our thinking.

A particularly worrying consequence, as far as fundamental physics is concerned, relates to falsifiability (§1.3). Modern science requires theories to be falsifiable rather than verifiable, but although this remains possible within our subjective reality, it is not so in the object reality since we have no direct access to it; we can only observe or measure corresponding phenomenon in our subjective reality, and these are significantly skewed as a result of the aforementioned list of phenomenological issues. Measurement, for instance, is simply a correlation between some phenomenon and an observable change over space and time (§5.4) that is based upon repeatable correlations of a similar type having been observed, and this is not the same as saying that the measured quantity is a fundamental property of the reality. This is just another perspective on the fact that understanding (that other goal of physics) is inapplicable to the objective reality, and so we cannot contrive theories with the goal of an ultimate understanding. The only applicable tool we can use there is mathematics, but this cannot — on its own, and without recourse to causal interpretation — *explain* any change.

When we say something is real, what do we really mean? Reality is simply the totality of all things deemed to be real within a system, and this then implies that the objective and subjective realities have different flavours of 'real'. Mathematics can model shapes, patterns, and other relationships, and so would be appropriate for modelling the objective reality, which is why it seems to be ideally suited to describing observable changes in the measurable world. But it cannot handle any aspects of experience; it cannot describe qualia or emotion because they are not part of the measurable world, and so are not quantifiable. General physics employs mathematics to make sense of our subjective reality, and hence it must presuppose the fundamentality of dynamical change and causality because we perceive interdependent changes occurring relative to time.

Fig. 5-1 depicts a hierarchy of these realities in conjunction with the mind and the various 'world' terms that we have used here. The hierarchy is of interfaces between these elements (e.g. the measurable world being our window onto the *block universe*), but everything within the depicted objective reality can be viewed as emergent, beginning with the mind; if there were no conscious minds then there would only be the objective reality in that figure. That this emergence is possible at all is wondrous, but each of these elements has its own context for what is real. Surely, you might say, the material world is not dependent upon conscious minds. Well, you have to consider what you mean by 'material'. If it is tangible, occupies volume, moves in space as a function of time, and has chemical or physical properties, then that is a subjective assessment; we cannot know its true nature in the objective reality.

Reassessing our concept of reality may not only change which questions we can meaningfully ask in a particular context, but it may also change the criteria by which we judge new theories. A case in point concerns the *Wheeler–Feynman absorber theory*, which, although a very elegant time-symmetric theory, was criticised partly because it could not be reconciled with causality. Judging a description of the objective reality by imposing experiential and phenomenal constraints is upside-down.

Einstein clearly expressed his belief in an accessible reality as follows during a Herbert Spencer lecture, delivered at Oxford on 10 June 1933.

> If, then, it is true that this axiomatic basis of theoretical physics cannot be extracted from experience but must be freely invented, can we ever hope to find the right way? Nay more, has this right way any existence outside our illusions? Can we hope to be guided in the right way by experience when there exist theories (such as classical mechanics) which to a large extent do justice to experience, without getting to the root of the matter? I answer without hesitation that there is, in my opinion, a right way, and that we are capable of finding it. Our experience hitherto justifies us in believing that nature is the realization of the simplest conceivable mathematical ideas. I am convinced that we can discover by means of purely mathematical constructions the concepts and the laws connecting them with each other, which furnish the key to the understanding of natural phenomena. Experience may suggest the appropriate mathematical concepts, but they most certainly cannot be deduced from it. Experience remains, of course, the sole criterion of the physical utility of a mathematical construction. But the creative principle resides in mathematics. In a certain sense, therefore, I hold it true that pure thought can grasp reality, as the ancients dreamed.[183]

Einstein was putting great emphasis upon experience, not as a source of mathematical inspiration but as a goal that our mathematical creations could describe unambiguously, and in doing so furnish an understanding of reality. He was, therefore, implicitly referring to our subjective reality, but this particular extract does not consider that the objective reality might be much further removed — despite his *special relativity* often being taken as a basis for a *block universe* model.

In stark contrast, in a letter from 1950, Einstein suggested that our experience profoundly distorted our perspective as we are effectively prisoners within our subjective reality, and so unable to perceive "the whole" as some super-observer.

> A human being is a part of the whole, called by us 'Universe', a part
> limited in time and space. He experiences himself, his thoughts
> and feelings as something separate from the rest—a kind of optical
> delusion of his consciousness.[184]

But although conscious entities are endowed with a capacity for recognising patterns, or correlations, we appear to be unique on this planet in our aspirations to understand those patterns. Analysing a bend in the road is one thing, but to ask why it is that shape is quite another. There may be explanations that satisfy our curiosity (e.g. land ownership in the case of the road) but they all presuppose the fundamental nature of causality, and hence of things having a dependency upon past events. We have said that a *block universe* is *superdeterministic*, but the correlation between its events extends into both the past and the future, so what does that mean for our notions of explanation and rationale? Is our quest only justifiable within our subjective realities?

For no clear reason, we want to find answers, and a reason for our existence. To learn that the ultimate reality is one to which such questions do not apply is extremely hard to accept. We may never know for sure if any other species on this planet shares even a shadow of such musings. When an ape looks at the Moon, does it wonder what it is, and why it appears with some regularity, or simply recognise those patterns and use them to guide its activities? Yet we are so endowed, and without an obvious evolutionary advantage. Yes, finding answers may increase our technological achievements, but those achievements may yet curtail our evolution, and so be a distinct disadvantage to our species. Our deepest quests are simply not inspired by technological application.

In 1939, while making a case for the parallel rather than competing co-existence of science and religion based upon their "strong reciprocal relationships and dependencies", Einstein wrote:

> One can have the clearest and most complete knowledge of what *is*,
> and yet not be able to deduct from that what should be the goal of our
> human aspirations. ... our existence and our activity acquire meaning
> only by the setting up of such a goal and of the corresponding values.[185]

The cited material, which also included later work from 1941, involved notions beyond the realm of science, such as mankind's goals, aspirations, valuations, and meaning of its existence. We accept their importance as part of our reality, despite their ethereal non-physical nature, but attributing responsibility for them to religion clashes with the definition of religion set out in §1.2. This is uncomfortably close to the historical view that religious teachings were necessary in order to distinguish right from wrong, or good from evil, or to endow any type of moral compass, and that it was inconceivable that these aspirations and judgements could emerge naturally, or be adopted voluntarily, rather than in fear of divine retribution. If such a view were true then it would imply that all atheists must be immoral folk.

Nevertheless, it is true that conscious entities require a personal or social imperative. Many species share basic goals of survival and procreation, but humans have adopted further imaginative goals that cannot be reconciled with any such advantage to their survival. Whether it is creative expression through the arts or engineering, or intellectual expression through the sciences or mathematics, it is unclear where these goals originate from. Are they a natural consequence of a certain complexity of consciousness, or of intelligence? It is a related goal that we should be interested in knowing about the objective reality, and yet our subjective reality is more important, and more accessible to us. We casually remarked in Chapter 6 that many people see only their immediate subjective reality, but this misses the fact that they may still have a belief system that provides them with answers to deeper questions, such as a rationale for why we are here, what our purpose is here, or what happens next.

Physicists may baulk at the thought of dogmatic teachings (although it still happens in more subtle ways within science), yet they possess their own faith in things that they must take as given. In their case, it is at least the fact that we can describe the measurable world by mathematics. This cannot be proved in any way, although it is beautifully evident. It is unsurprising that in this application of mathematics we must abandon any attempt to present meaningful metaphysical questions, but we still try — this is how we have evolved, or how we were made (if that is your belief).

So is the scope of scientific explanation limited by the fact that mathematics (and hence also physics) does not apply to certain elements of our reality? This is a good question, but it may be dismissed by physicists who harbour physicalist beliefs, and who would therefore deny that emergent non-physical phenomena (such as the mind, or semantic information) are, in any way, real. Having argued that such things do exist, and that the mind is rather important as both a causally connected entity and one from which our whole viewpoint is centred, then we have to accept that we cannot have theories that fully include ourselves (or any conscious entities) without admitting such phenomena as real. But as they are not part of the measurable world, and so cannot be described through mathematics, then they cannot be addressed through physics — we need different tools!

During one of her frequent visits to Einstein during his stomach illness of 1917, Frau Hedwig Born, wife of Max Born, once asked him "Do you believe that absolutely everything can be expressed scientifically?" "Yes," he replied, "it would be possible, but it would make no sense. It would be description without meaning—as if you described a Beethoven symphony as a variation of wave pressure".[186] Although Einstein was right in citing an art form, as he did, he was less correct about scientific description. In his mind, describing the physicality of something (e.g. the variation in pitch, amplitude, and harmonic interference of sound waves) was enough to define everything about it, but he did emphasise that 'meaning' is apart from that description. Meaning is relevant to conscious entities seeking to explain the apparent causal progression of their environment, but also to sentient entities who have the capacity for emotional assessment of that environment (§6.1). Although implicitly mentioning this, he had missed an example of something (the emotional assessment) that cannot be described scientifically.

It seems we are forming the conclusion that our subjective reality is not just an incredible product of the conscious mind, which by its nature observes a temporal progression of change in a tangible and measurable world, but that the objective reality (whatever its true nature) somehow conspires to enable its emergence as a shared phenomenon. Immanuel Kant expressed a similar perspective in 1755 as "God put a secret art into the forces of Nature so as to enable it to fashion itself out of chaos into a perfect world system".[187] We should resist any temptation to grasp at metaphysical answers that make us feel good, but the gulf between a subjective reality that cannot be fully addressed by mathematics and an objective reality which can only be addressed by mathematics is stark.

There is a philosophical concept called the *anthropic principle*, which relates the conditions of the universe to its capacity for supporting conscious entities able to observe it. There are two forms of this: the *strong anthropic principle* (SAP), which states that the universe must be capable of supporting conscious entities at some point because of the way it is, and the *weak anthropic principle* (WAP), which states that the conditions in our vicinity must support life because we are obviously here pondering the issue. Note that these versions of the principle are distinct from the *temporal anthropic principle* (TAP) defined in this book, although related by virtue of the implications for conscious life.[188] The SAP is often misunderstood as an argument for God, but English cosmologist and theoretical physicist John D. Barrow describes it as follows:

> ... because there appear to exist a large number of remarkable and apparently disconnected 'coincidences' which conspire to allow life to be possible in the Universe, the Universe *must* give rise to observers at some stage in its history.[189]

Another way of looking at the SAP is that we somehow 'cause' the universe to be as it is, or to 'bring it into being'. If there is such a thing as a 'multiverse' (or any of the related concepts) then the universe we see can only be the one we are in, in which case the SAP is not unlike the WAP. This all sounds a little like the 'consciousness-causes-collapse interpretation' of *quantum mechanics*, which we dismissed in §7.6, but it is true that we create our subjective reality. SAP is by far the more contentious of the two forms of this principle; the WAP, by comparison, is almost taken as obvious. Sabine Hossenfelder makes the case that the WAP is not useless conjecture, and that it can put valid constraints upon the laws of physics, citing the example of Fred Hoyle's prediction of a specific isotope of carbon based upon life being impossible otherwise.[190]

The underlying problem is that the fundamental constants of nature appear to be finely tuned to a very high degree to support life as we know it, and this raises questions such as 'is it just coincidence?', 'are we just in the sweet-spot of a spectrum of possible values?', or 'was it designed that way?'. In essence, even a small variation could preclude the existence of the stable elementary particles, the fundamental forces, stable atoms, molecules, DNA, and of life itself. Implicit in this is the belief that with the correct chemical soup, life would just happen through *abiogenesis*, and would eventually evolve to conscious entities such as us — a belief that is not challenged here but is worth noting.

Our physics is not really good enough to know how independent of each other those fundamental constants are (or indeed whether they are constant at all), what the probabilities are of potentially different combinations, and hence what the probability is that we are here thinking about it. If we assume a flat distribution then we still have to select arbitrary values for the range of the distribution, and this leads to circular arguments.[191] If we ignore the 'intelligent design' view, which has strong scientific arguments against it, and we ignore the possibility of coincidence (which would also have interpretational issues in a *block universe*) then science is left with few possibilities: (a) those constants vary across the universe and that we just happen to be in a favourable location, (b) we are in one of the many causally linked bubble-like worlds of an *eternal inflation* 'multiverse', or (c) we are in one of many causally disjoint universes of a bigger 'multiverse'.

The constants themselves are not predicted by any of our theories, and would appear arbitrary if it were not for the fact that they appear to support conscious life. There is a view, termed 'naturalness', that certain dimensionless ratios of these constants (i.e. ones that do not depend upon our choice of units, and so would be significant everywhere) should be of the order of unity rather than, say, 10^{-38} or 10^{76}. But this does not appear to be the case, and why should it be so anyway? To our subjective assessment then 'naturalness' may appear simpler, neater, more balanced, or just more beautiful, but what cares nature of our opinions? Does a relative magnitude even have any objective significance given that §5.4 and §10.1 both make the case that measurement, and even counting, is an entirely subjective assessment?

But there are issues bigger than just an apparent fine-tuning of these fundamental constants: certain structural properties of the universe are coincident with our subjective reality, and without which we could not be here. If gravity is an emergent phenomenon, rather than a fundamental force, then that is a pretty big coincidence as it forms such a critical part of our environment. Then there is space-time; there are sound reasons proposed for why our space has just three dimensions, including that world-lines could not pass without touching if there were fewer, and that the inverse square law would be inappropriate if there were more, thus seriously impacting forces such as gravity and electromagnetism. There are even arguments for why an even number could not work. As for why the time dimension is different, and appears in our equations as an imaginary quantity in conjunction with space, the reason is unclear. It certainly plays a role in the illusion of causality since it results in a limiting speed, and the concept of *causal horizons* (see Appendix A).

Having relegated *subjective time*, and the so-called psychological 'arrow of time', to the qualia of conscious entities then it is all the more astounding that conscious entities can share a subjective reality, or that this affords them an opportunity to peel back the layers and ask questions. The fact that we cannot ask meaningful metaphysical questions about the underlying *block universe* — ones that do not presume causality, rationale, or the evolution of a dynamical system — does not detract from the fact that it supports our subjective reality. In a whimsical way, it is almost like the characters in a filmstrip suddenly becoming alert and aware of their progressive existence, but at the same time wanting to comprehend the nature of a filmstrip.

Removing causality from the objective reality removes the metaphysical problems of 'infinite regress', and also of Aristotle's 'cosmological argument' and 'first cause', but at some considerable cost. It also addresses the final remark in §1.1 about finding a final answer that does not lead to further questions, albeit in an unexpected way. It is, then, a serious consequence, amounting to a showstopper, that any question involving a 'why?', 'how?', or even 'when?' has no objective meaning, and so we are unable to frame any meaningful question about the objective reality.

Reaching the conclusion that the objective reality is a static pattern with deterministic relations over time will lead inexorably to futile attempts at deeper questions. We are almost incapable of accepting such an explanation, even when it makes total sense within mathematical physics, where such a pattern could be wholly addressed using mathematics, but we stubbornly want to know more. How can something just be, without an origin or dependency upon some prior circumstance or rationale? If the objective reality has somehow allowed the emergence of such incredible features as consciousness, and a shared subjective reality, then how can that level of detail or coincidence have just come about by itself? But these are all idle questions because they cannot be applied to the objective reality.

In 1781, Kant wrote "Our reason (Vernunft) has this peculiar fate that, with reference to one class of its knowledge, it is always troubled with questions which cannot be ignored, because they spring from the very nature of reason, and which cannot be answered, because they transcend the powers of human reason".[192] You may retreat into a view that there might be some super-time, with associated super-causality and super-consciousness, but this is not a viable solution as it takes us right back to where we were with our own subjective time. Like it or not, we are incapable of imagining any radically different alternatives to our own experience.

On a personal note, as a lifelong atheist, I find it disturbing that the components of the objective reality have conspired to support a shared subjective reality, and the emergence of conscious entities endowed with the capability for art, literature, love, pain, empathy, and the quest for what underpins their own existence. This appears to be far more than cosmic fine-tuning, and yet I am equally aware that I am guilty of the same misguided questions that I outline above. To experience a sense that there is something more that you cannot observe, or ask about, or seek in any rational and objective fashion, is acutely uncomfortable.

Mysteries are what keeps science in an active state of progression, but what happens if we cannot categorise the next step in our research as a mystery: something that is difficult or impossible to understand or explain? Einstein believed mystery to be an essential ingredient in our creativity and learning:

> The most beautiful thing we can experience is the mysterious. It is
> the source of all true art and science. He to whom this emotion is
> a stranger, who can no longer pause to wonder and stand rapt in awe,
> is as good as dead: his eyes are closed.[193]

But this presupposes that all mysteries have explanations, even if we have insufficient knowledge or intelligence to form them. If it turns out that explanation and cognition are inappropriate at that next step then technically they no longer constitute true mysteries.

What, then, is the goal of fundamental physics? Has physics run its course, as proposed by John Horgan (§1), or have we lost sight of its true course due to a line of reasoning immured by subjective experience? If the objective reality is a static acausal *block universe* then our expectations of finding reason and understanding, rather than simply predictability (§1.3), do not make any sense. In §1 and §5.1, we lamented times gone by when physics and metaphysics were more balanced in the pursuit of knowledge, yet there is a growing modern ethic of 'shut up and calculate' which simply applies the mathematics that seems to work, and disregards the possibility of any deeper questions — would this not seem more appropriate for the objective reality?

What of that long-running debate between Einstein and Bohr? Einstein not only believed in an objective reality — one that exists independently of us — but that we uncover that reality through observation and measurement. Bohr believed that there was no reality until those observations or measurements occurred, and so that operation (which corresponds mathematically to the *wave-function collapse*) effectively creates the reality. Furthermore, that it only makes sense to describe the universe in terms of its observables, implying that there is no underlying reality, and no 'hidden variables'. The views presented in this book would mean that neither Einstein nor Bohr were entirely wrong, or entirely correct. There is an objective reality, but it is not directly accessible to us, and our conscious observations and measurements effectively do create our subjective reality: an animated version of the former.

But here is the stinger: it is not a binary choice, and we cannot pursue one reality without an acknowledgement of the other. The reductionist approach of physics (and science in general) is always beset by phenomenological issues, and can have only one ultimate outcome: the realisation that the underlying reality is static, acausal, and can only be addressed by mathematics. In a *block universe* (excusing the recursion) 'meaning' is meaningless, thus suggesting that metaphysics — and, indeed, any set of anthropocentric questions and musings — is meaningless at that level. Accepting this limit as the only significant goal for physics would not only be useless to our everyday lives, but would be unattainable without inferences derived from the study of our subjective reality. When focusing on our subjective reality, though, then those phenomenological issues are intrinsic and unavoidable, which necessitates that we understand the relationship between consciousness and the world around us. That this has not happened within physics is a consequence of the nature of consciousness being inaccessible to mathematics, and so we need a methodical study that somehow embraces both perspectives.

One way to consider an Existence that embraces the different realities on an equal footing, and hence including everything that we deem to exist and be real within both of those realities, is to imagine a notional qualitative 'dimension' that separates the subjective from the objective. All things may be part of the pattern of the objective reality, but their true nature will be fundamentally alien and inaccessible to any form of perception. This separation would not, therefore, be a simple physical versus non-physical one. Collapsing that notional dimension would leave us with an objective reality consisting of the *block universe*, with its objective nature corresponding to the fact that that we have eliminated all subjectiveness, and hence all emergent entities, behaviours, and properties. In other words, it would have removed all conscious entities and all things that they deem to exist in their lives.

And so, at the most objective end of this 'dimension', we have only the *block universe* and the world-lines representing particles and quanta, the full nature of which admittedly remains vague. As we move along from there to consider different degrees of subjectiveness then we must include the basic structures formed by the 'cohesive influences'. The view that these are all separate with properties of their own, possibly including distinctness and identity, is entirely subjective. These structures appear to follow rules, according to our perceptions, that include motion, dynamical change, and causality. Weak emergence is a subjective perception that can be deconstructed into the properties and behaviours of smaller structures, whereas strong emergence passes a threshold into things that only have significance to conscious minds, and so cannot be deconstructed physically. This latter group includes the notion of consciousness itself, its constituent faculties, and semantic information. At the furthest end of the 'dimension' are specific instances of our mental concepts and phenomenal experience, as opposed to the general faculties, and states thereof, within which these instances are formed.

The best we can hope for with the objective reality is to get a sense of the structure of the *block universe*, including the variation of the world-lines and their properties over time, and the relationships between those variations — limited, obviously, by the constraints of our measurable world (§5). But any expectation of rationale or insight would be fruitless. We can expect those variations — what we have hitherto called the 'shape of change' — to demonstrate symmetries and other patterns, but the mathematics that we choose to model our findings can only be judged upon how it addresses those features, its scope (embracing all of them), predictive scope (addressing newly discovered features), and economy of form (compact framework with as few independent concepts as possible). Whether these can be construed as 'beauty' says more about our sense of beauty than it does about the nature of reality.

Our subjective reality, however it originates, is still of tremendous importance to us and to our everyday lives, and so metaphysics remains important in differentiating those elements of our phenomenal experience that are entirely subjective from observations that are backed by an objective consensus in order to reveal a 'glimpse' of the objective reality. Knowing the point at which our questions cease to be meaningful helps avoid the temptation to extrapolate them downwards.

For, with evident rhyme but illusive reason, the Universe is what it is!

Epilogue

The poetry of loss and change.

You may feel that the rational analysis and observation presented in this book does not satisfy your innermost hopes, fears, or yearning for answers. Having relegated time and causality to subjective illusion, and explained that we cannot, therefore, ask meaningful questions about the nature or origin of the universe, then you may feel that it paints a very bleak picture of our existence and role.

In philosophy, *absurdism* refers to the exploration of the conflict between our tendency to seek meaning and purpose in life, and our inability to find any in a universe that exists independently of us. As Chapter 12 explains, though, it is still a case of astonishing mystery and wonderment that the elements of the objective reality have allowed the emergence of entities such as ourselves that seek to understand.

Adding such poetry to a book of this nature is admittedly unusual, but, as the preface explains, the pieces give a clearer glimpse into the mind of the author than any logical presentation ever could.

The Great Wave

An ode to loss and change from a rational mind coming to terms with the fleeting nature of history. Its words try to express a deep sadness for the loss of the past, our poor attempts to capture or retain it, and nature's apparent indifference. It uses a motif of water (waves, surf, and tide) as a metaphor for time, as in 'time and tide wait for no one'. First published 4 April 2016 at https://parallax-viewpoint.blogspot.com/2016/04/the-great-wave.html.

259

Fixed grey faces gaze silently through their glaze, evoking memories of a
time gone by and of lives that were,
But where is yesterday? When was tomorrow? An eternity of fleeting
moments lost to the seething surf,
Lives beyond capture by any tree-lined garden of descent, graven on some
far-distant tablet beyond the sight of man, save the muse of Parmenides,
For lifeless and textureless is the world beyond the *duir*, daubed in
questionable hue from the palette of want.

Lain waste, their legacies of stone; the First Ones, long passed into shadow as
though but a dream, bequeathing debt immortal,
Fading, failing, falling into darkness, unto dissolution, decay and dust,
fettered by the illimitable dice,
Events and stories forsaken by the relentless arrow to lie fallow in their
starless stasis betwixt the pages of every passing instant,
Celestial progenies cast adrift and abandoned by nature's unmindful *Doxa*,
unworthy of all remembrance.

From mankind, whose words be louder than its thoughts, writ in blackest
quill, the dogma that serves the meek through the mighty,
While sages patiently strive to learn the magical music by which all things
dance, but finding only purest melody and no tempo,
A world of adamantine illusion, wishfully tamed and told through the
balancing runes,
A lost chord stripped of all harmony, and the *myste* with two faces poised in
suspended masquerade.

So great the gift of time — the giver of Life, the æon of being, the conjurer of
cause, and yet the arrow by which we fall,
Weep not for the past, nor for the lost moments, parting kisses, or stolen
memories,
The price we pay for *life* is change — is wax and wane — is loss and gain,
but the thief of days wields an arrow fashioned and shaped by conscious
minds,
Taking the coin from our mouths, the thief knowingly smiles back with our
own faces.

To the end of days, when all our suns have set on the crimson tide of life's
blood,
When all our whispers have fallen silent on the Bible-black firmament, and
their echoes have all flown their paper prisons and coulomb cages,
From the last glimmers of life, dream-dashed and robbed of love and hope,
still clinging to its rock,
One final desperate cry will be heard afore The Great Wave:

...There can be no *rhyme* for there was no *reason*!

The Jester and the Conjuror

The jester and the conjuror are performers in a dialogue poem — tarot counterparts being the fool and the magician — representing mankind's naïve questions and some fanciful authority figure dismissing those questions until the jester realises that he is asking the wrong ones, at which point the conjuror acknowledges a kindred connection. First published 3 May 2017 at https://parallax-viewpoint.blogspot.com/2017/05/the-jester-and-conjuror.html.

What are we but weak warm flesh, and blood in its hold;
ashes and dust in a tick, or the blink of a soul.

Foolish son of Adam —
Your fickle dust is shared. You are not your physicality:
mere silhouettes dancing on the face of reality.
Mountain, sea, and tempest share not your dreams of ebb and flow.
For them no time, and beauty none in song, love, or rainbow.

Are we lost in the vastness of infinity,
forgotten in the silence of eternity?

Foolish son of man —
No rule nor law can lay siege to such a far-distant wall.
Beyond number only are falsehoods by which you trip and fall.
Though celerity and brilliance be weighed and measured,
missed is the glister of your gift, and of life so treasured.

Why am I given free will to steer the fateless,
but so little time to illume the fathomless?

Foolish son of Jof —
Your will is held fast in its gyves by time's pattern aslope,
bound between the weight of memory and the wings of hope.
Causation is the illusion that affords you your thought,
but seeking root and reason by chasing change will yield nought.

So all the myriad waning moons and mourning suns
witness not the passing lives, nor of what becomes?

Learned son reflected —
Now is the seat and palpable throne of the conscious mind,
extending dominion over qualia and their kind.
Unbowed by the measurable world, unconquered by rune,
for this is your fate; this is your legacy; this is You!

Eskaton

Thoughts on the loss of civilisation. Eskaton (Greek: ἔσχατον) literally means lastly, or most recently, but is sometimes loosely translated as 'dawning of a new day'. Whether its end-of-days theme is historical or prophetic reflects the cyclical nature of events. First published 18 January 2019 at https://parallax-viewpoint.blogspot.com/2019/01/eskaton.html.

On cold icy countenance did Heaven's hammer fall,
and tumult and turmoil did summon the ocean tall
For all that was, and then,
repaid in myriad gem
Given by the great hand but taken by the small.

For Aion smote the cheek of Gaia, so cool and white
Her mantle of Aegean blue loosed in silent flight
Yet innocent of all crime
The iterant chaos of time
Her fate seduced by blow celeste from indelible night.

Under legion trumpet her children wept, though mused and wise,
as fire, brimstone, and scoria burned their Eden and their eyes
Safe haven in cavern deep
Sanctuary on silver seed
To wait, to slumber, to heal, and like phoenix arise.

Appendix A:
Special Relativity Mathematics

*A mathematical treatment of special relativity
demonstrating its simplicity and symmetry.*

This appendix includes a brief mathematical tour of *special relativity* designed to show, to the mathematically inclined, the simplicity and orthogonality of Minkowski's four-dimensional representation, and hence of the concept of a space-time continuum. Although Minkowski's reformulation added nothing fundamental to Einstein's original work — no new predictions or changes to existing predictions — it demonstrated a symmetry that suggested space and time were intimately connected, and could be treated in an orthogonal way. This symmetry also revealed itself in a connection between momentum and energy, suggesting a significance that was not revealed by classical mechanics. This tour therefore serves as an illustration of how setting the goal of mathematical symmetry might yield a deeper insight into the underlying patterns of the objective reality.

In pre-relativity physics, translating the coordinates from one inertial frame of reference (S) to another one having parallel axes (S') involved an equation of the form:

$$x'_i = x_i - (a_i + v_i\, t)$$
$$t' = t - b$$

This is called the *Galilean transformation.* The quantities x_1 to x_3 are the normal three spatial coordinates. The terms a_i and b represent the difference in origins between the two frames and can be ignored if they have the same origin. The terms v_i are the relative velocities of the two frames in the three spatial directions.

Note that our Latin subscripts here range from 1 to 3, but will soon range from 1 to 4 as we introduce the four-dimensional space-time representation.

There are other conventions used in proper *tensor calculus*, such as subscript/ superscript for covariant/contravariant quantities, but some use Latin indices for 1-to-3 and Greek for 1-to-4, some use zero-based indices (e.g. 0-to-3 rather than 1-to-4), and some simply use Latin and Greek indices to distinguish different coordinate systems.

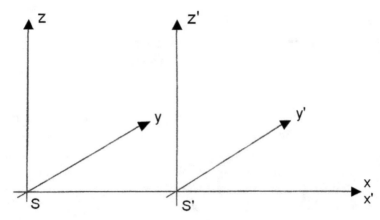

Fig. A-1, Relative inertial frames of reference.

A more familiar form of this transformation, using traditional x, y, z, and t, that represents a relative velocity along the x-axis only is:

$$x' = x - v t \tag{A.1}$$
$$y' = y$$
$$z' = z$$
$$t' = t \tag{A.2}$$

The *Galilean transformation* makes two important assumptions: (i) time is absolute and so the time of an event is the same in both frames, and (ii) length is absolute and so the distance between two points is the same in both frames. In other words, using Pythagoras, that $\sum(x'_i - x_i)^2$ is invariant.

The transformation works fine for Newtonian physics but causes a problem for equations such as Maxwell's since it implied that the speed of light (c) depends on the speed of the observer relative to the source of the light. For instance, if S' sent a light signal to S then S would measure the speed as $(c - v)$ because S' is travelling away from S; c would not be a universal constant.

If all inertial frames are to agree that light travels the same distance in the same time interval (t_0 to t) then the following must always be true:

$$(x - x_0)^2 + (y - y_0)^2 + (z - z_0)^2 = c^2(t - t_0)^2$$

We can replace this equation with the following much simpler one if we substitute a fourth coordinate, x_4, for ict, where i represents the square root of minus one.

$$\sum (x_i - x_{i0})^2 = 0$$

The value of the subscript i now ranges from 1 to 4 so that $x_1 = x$, $x_2 = y$, $x_3 = z$, and $x_4 = ict$.

What this has done is to treat time and space coordinates in the same consistent way to yield a single space-time interval that is the same for all inertial observers. The fact that it is zero is convenient since it avoids introducing an arbitrary constant. The square root of -1 is unfortunately referred to as an *imaginary number* since $(-1)^2 = (+1)^2 = +1$ implying that -1 has no square root. There is nothing supernatural about it, though, and it occurs in many mathematical situations.

Now that we have a four-dimensional space-time continuum (known as *Minkowski space-time*) to play with, let us consider a rotation of one inertial frame relative to another. This is known as the *special Lorentz transformation.*

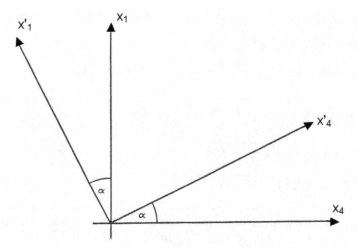

Fig. A-2, Relative velocity represented by rotation of frames of reference.

We are leaving out x_2 and x_3 here for simplicity. The standard equation for a rotation of Cartesian coordinates in the (x_1, x_4) plane yields:

$$x'_1 = x_1 \cos \alpha + x_4 \sin \alpha$$
$$x'_2 = x_2$$
$$x'_3 = x_3$$
$$x'_4 = -x_1 \sin \alpha + x_4 \cos \alpha$$

Reverting back to x and t representations, this becomes:

$$x' = x \cos \alpha + ict \sin \alpha \qquad (A.3)$$
$$ict' = -x \sin \alpha + ict \cos \alpha \qquad (A.4)$$

The rotation actually describes one inertial frame (S') moving at a constant velocity relative to the other (S). So what is the difference between this diagram and a traditional 'travel graph' that we may have used at school? Well, it is true that the axis x'_4 represents a body moving in the coordinate system of S. However, that is not the same as being able to transform to-and-fro between the two coordinate systems as we are doing here. The essential difference is that we have a single set of space-time coordinates that can be interrelated — space and time are no longer independent of each other.

If v is the conventional velocity, x/t, then:

$$\tan \alpha = iv / c \qquad (A.5)$$

$$\cos \alpha = 1 / \sqrt{1 - v^2/c^2}$$

$$\sin \alpha = (iv/c) / \sqrt{1 - v^2/c^2}$$

Substituting these into Eqs. (A.3) and (A.4) gives:

$$x' = (x - vt) / \sqrt{1 - v^2/c^2} \qquad (A.6)$$

$$t' = (t - vx/c^2) / \sqrt{1 - v^2/c^2} \qquad (A.7)$$

If v is much less than c — that is, we are nowhere near the speed of light — then these equations are approximately the same as the *Galilean transformation*: Eqs. (A.1) and (A.2). However, the new transformation now means equations such as Maxwell's are then true for all inertial observers. Note that v must always be less than c or the equations result in infinities and imaginary numbers. Also, if we solved for equations transforming S' to S, rather than S to S', then they would have an identical form except that the sign of v would be reversed. In other words, the predicted effects of *special relativity* are completely reciprocated between S and S'. They are the result of a different perspective of the observer — not a physical change in the frame being observed.

Let us look at a spatial interval $(x' - x'_0)$ in S'. How would S see this at a given instant in time of t? Well, subtracting Eq. (A.6) from itself for the two ends of the interval gives:

$$(x - x_0) = (x' - x'_0)\sqrt{1 - v^2/c^2}$$

S would see the interval reduced by the factor $\sqrt{1 - v^2/c^2}$ which is always less than or equal to 1. This is called the *Lorentz–FitzGerald contraction* although no physical contraction occurs. S' sees the length correctly, and also measures a similar contraction for a spatial interval in S. It is simply a matter of perspective between the two inertial frames.

Now let us look at a time interval $(t' - t'_0)$ in S' measured at a given location x'. If we use the inverse form of Eq. (A.7) to map S' to S then we have:

$$(t - t_0) = (t' - t'_0)/\sqrt{1 - v^2/c^2}$$

S sees the same time interval as being longer. This is called *time dilation*[194] although time has not increased or slowed down. S' measures the time interval correctly, and also measures a similar dilation for a time interval in S.

Note that we had to use the inverse of the *Lorentz transformation* Eq. (A.7) to calculate this. The reason is that though the two events were at the same location in S' (i.e. x'), S would not see them at the same location.

In general, if S had two simultaneous events at (t, x_0) and (t, x) then S' would see them separated by the following time interval:

$$(t' - t'_0) = (v/c^2)(x - x_0)/\sqrt{1 - v^2/c^2}$$

Note that $t' \neq t'_0$ unless $x = x_0$ and so there is no such thing as absolute simultaneity.

Let us briefly go back to the suggestion earlier that the speed of light is always the same — no matter whether the source is moving towards you or away from you. In pre-relativity physics, the closing speed of two objects is simply the sum, $w = (v + u)$, but that is different now. Eq. (A.5) relates the velocity to the angle of rotation in *Minkowski space-time* so let us use it to calculate the closing velocity, w, of v and u by considering two successive rotations by angles of α and β.

$$iw \, / \, c \; = \; tan \, (\alpha + \beta) \; = \; (tan \, \alpha + tan \, \beta) \, / \, (1 - tan \, \alpha \, tan \, \beta)$$
$$= \; (iv/c + iu/c) \, / \, (1 - (iv/c)(iu/c))$$

Hence:

$$w \; = \; (v + u) \, / \, (1 + vu/c^2)$$

Note that even if $v = c$ and $u = c$ then w is still only c, not $2c$.

An interesting corollary to all this is that although the concept of simultaneity has now gone, the ordering of events is preserved. Two observers will both see events A and B in the same order, no matter what their relative velocities are; the measure of the separation is changed, but its sign is never flipped. This is crucial for the illusion of causality to work.

Mass-Energy Equivalence

Einstein's famous equation of mass-energy equivalence ($E = mc^2$) can be derived from the transformations so far obtained for *special relativity*. We first need to look at how velocities transform between S and S' and that will involve some calculus.

Special relativity defines a special time-like interval called the 'proper time' (τ) that is an invariant, i.e. the same for all inertial observers. S and S' will have different coordinates for two events (x, y, z, t) and (x_0, y_0, z_0, t_0) but they will both agree on the value of the following:

$$\tau^2 \; = \; (t - t_0)^2 - ((x - x_0)^2 + (y - y_0)^2 + (z - z_0)^2)/c^2$$

Note that this is 0 for events along the path of a ray of light. Also, for events at a fixed location (i.e. $x=x_0$ etc.) then it is just the normal local time interval.

Consider successive positions of a point moving relative to S. Let ds be the distance travelled between times t and $t+dt$, and let v be the speed ds/dt. Then:

$$d\tau = \sqrt{dt^2 - ds^2/c^2} = \sqrt{1 - v^2/c^2}\ dt$$

A velocity would normally be defined like $v_x = dx/dt$ but this would not transform as a vector in space-time using the *Lorentz transformation*. Instead, we will start with the $x_i = (x, y, z, ict)$ that we used before, and differentiate it using the 'proper time' to get a new vector.

$$V_i = dx_i/d\tau = (dx_i/dt)\,(dt/d\tau) = (dx_i/dt)\,/\sqrt{1 - v^2/c^2}$$

$$= (v_x, v_y, v_z, ic)\,/\sqrt{1 - v^2/c^2} \tag{A.8}$$

The vector V_i is called the 4-velocity because it has four components rather than the usual three.

So if S' is moving at velocity u relative to S in the x_1 direction, where $u = -ic\ tan\ \alpha$, then we have:

$$V'_1 = V_1\ cos\ \alpha + V_4\ sin\ \alpha$$
$$V'_2 = V_2$$
$$V'_3 = V_3$$
$$V'_4 = -V_1\ sin\ \alpha + V_4\ cos\ \alpha$$

To simplify things here, let γ be a function defined by $\gamma(v) = 1/\sqrt{1 - v^2/c^2}$. Using the trigonometric relations:

$$sin\ \alpha = tan\ \alpha\,/\sqrt{1 + tan^2\ \alpha} = -(u/ic)\,\gamma(u)$$
$$cos\ \alpha = 1\,/\sqrt{1 + tan^2\ \alpha} = \gamma(u)$$

By using Eq. (A.8), then we can rewrite the 4-velocity transformations as:

$$v'_x\,\gamma(v') = (v_x\,\gamma(u) + ic\,(-u/ic)\,\gamma(u))\,\gamma(v)$$
$$v'_y\,\gamma(v') = v_y\,\gamma(v)$$
$$v'_z\,\gamma(v') = v_z\,\gamma(v)$$
$$ic\,\gamma(v') = (-v_x\,(-u/ic)\,\gamma(u) + ic\,\gamma(u))\,\gamma(v)$$

Rearranging these gives:

$$v'_x = (v_x - u)\, \gamma(u)\, \gamma(v)\, /\, \gamma(v')$$
$$v'_y = v_y\, \gamma(v)\, /\, \gamma(v')$$
$$v'_z = v_z\, \gamma(v)\, /\, \gamma(v')$$
$$1 = (1 - uv_x/c^2)\, \gamma(u)\, \gamma(v)\, /\, \gamma(v')$$

By dividing the first three equations by the fourth then we have:

$$v'_x = (v_x - u)\, /\, (1 - uv_x/c^2)$$
$$v'_y = v_y\, \sqrt{1 - u^2/c^2}\, /\, (1 - uv_x/c^2)$$
$$v'_z = v_z\, \sqrt{1 - u^2/c^2}\, /\, (1 - uv_x/c^2)$$

If all velocities are much less than c then this approximates to simply:

$$v'_x = (v_x - u), \qquad v'_y = v_y, \qquad v'_z = v_z$$

If we multiply our 4-velocity by the mass of an object to create a 4-momentum vector, how does that affect the law of conservation of momentum? Well, the quantity being conserved is then:

$$P_i = m\, V_i = m\, (v_x, v_y, v_z, ic)\, /\, \sqrt{1 - v^2/c^2}$$

We can see that the first three components are not quite the same as the classical values for momentum as they are increased by a factor of $1/\sqrt{1 - v^2/c^2}$. The fourth component, as we shall see later, is related to the conservation of mass -energy. In other words, the four-component form will embrace both of the conservation laws for momentum and mass-energy.

Einstein initially modified the definition of mass to incorporate this square root term — also known as the *Lorentz factor*.

$$P_i = (m_0\, /\, \sqrt{1 - v^2/c^2})\, (v_x, v_y, v_z, ic)$$

m_0 is termed the 'rest mass' of the object. The fact that the effective 'relativistic mass' is measured as being greater for a moving object should not be confused with it 'getting heavier', or even bigger. Weight is only applicable when a mass is affected by a gravitational field, whereas mass is really a measure of the inertia of an object.

The 4-force vector is defined as:

$$F_i = dP_i/d\tau = m_0 \, (dV_i/d\tau)$$

The 4-force can be expressed in terms of the classical force vector as follows:

$$
\begin{aligned}
F_i &= (d/d\tau) \, (p_x, p_y, p_z, imc) \\
&= (d/dt) \, (p_x, p_y, p_z, imc) \, (dt/d\tau) \\
&= (f_x, f_y, f_z, ic \, dm/dt) \, / \sqrt{1 - v^2/c^2}
\end{aligned}
$$

The *inner product* (or 'dot product') of the V_i vector with itself $(V_i \cdot V_i)$ is just $(-c^2)$ so if we differentiate with respect to the proper time then we have:

$$V_i \cdot (dV_i \, / \, d\tau) \implies V_i \cdot F_i = 0$$

In other words, F and V are orthogonal. Expanding on F and V then gives:

$$(v_x, v_y, v_z, ic) \cdot (f_x, f_y, f_z, ic \, dm/dt) \, / \sqrt{1 - v^2/c^2} = 0$$

The work done by the force (i.e. the energy expended) is found by integrating the rate at which work is done (i.e. $(v_x, v_y, v_z) \cdot (f_x, f_y, f_z)$) over a given period of time (t_1, t_2).

$$\int_{t1}^{t2} c^2 \, dm/dt \, dt = m_2 \, c^2 - m_1 \, c^2$$

Since the 'work done' is simply the increase in kinetic energy of the body then the kinetic energy must, therefore, be given by:

$$T = mc^2 + C$$

where C is a constant. When $v = 0$ then $T = 0$ so this sets the value of C at $(- m_0 c^2)$. Hence:

$$T = mc^2 - m_0c^2 = m_0c^2 / \sqrt{1 - v^2/c^2} - m_0c^2$$

If v is much less than c then this approximates to $\frac{1}{2} m_0v^2$, which is the classical value for the kinetic energy. In effect, this is saying that the measured increase in the mass of a moving body is equivalent to the increase in its kinetic energy, and that the relation between them is given by the famous $E = mc^2$.

We mentioned, above, that Einstein initially opted to merge the *Lorentz factor* into the mass, simply referring to it as the relativistic mass, m, but he soon backed off on this. It was energy that was conserved rather than mass, although the two concepts are now considered as a single conservation law of mass-energy. He believed that energy increased the inertia of an object, and thus that the inertial mass would be measured differently. The associated myth of mass being 'converted' to energy was discussed in §5.5. Still, his mistake did leave the world with a simple iconic equation that everyone could recite.

There is another representation of this relationship, known as the *relativistic dispersion relation*, which physicists prefer because it is independent of the frame of reference. We will start with the inner product of the 4-momentum, which is *Lorentz invariant*, but for simplicity we will assume that we only have one spatial dimension to worry about.

$$P_i \cdot P_i = \sum_i P_i P_i = p^2 - (mc)^2$$

Multiplying by $-c^2$ gives:

$$E^2 - p^2c^2 = m^2c^4 - m^2v^2c^2$$
$$= (m_0\gamma(v)c^2)^2 (1 - v^2/c^2) = (m_0c^2)^2$$

In other words, $E^2 - (pc)^2 = (m_0c^2)^2$. Since the rest mass, and hence the rest energy, are invariant then this relationship between the relativistic energy and relativistic momentum holds for all frames of reference. Notice that for massless particles, such as the photon, then it means that $E = pc$, or energy and momentum are effectively the same thing (related by a fundamental constant). We already saw this in Eqs. (7.1) and (7.2).

Twin Paradox

There is a famous paradox in *special relativity* that has confused many students at one time or another — including this author. In this thought experiment, an identical twin makes a high-speed journey into space, and on returning to Earth finds that he has aged less than his twin who stayed behind.

The apparent paradox is because the effects of *special relativity* are symmetrical and reciprocated between two inertial observers, as we have already explained. Hence, since the earthbound twin can be considered moving relative to the astronaut twin then neither should see a difference when they meet again.

The argument is further complicated by the popular view that time slows down when you are moving close to the speed of light — which it does not.

The explanation of the effect — verified by experiment — is that the astronaut twin is distinguished by undergoing a deceleration and acceleration during the about-turn. It does not matter whether you consider that the Earth was initially at rest or moving since the effects of acceleration and deceleration would be indistinguishable from each other to the astronaut twin. However, whereas all inertial motion is relative, acceleration and deceleration are absolute, and only one twin would have experienced them. It is not the acceleration or deceleration itself that causes the ageing difference. It is the fact that the returning twin changes from one inertial frame to another during that about-turn. Before the about-turn, both twins see the other's clock as recording time more slowly, just as we have explained already for two inertial frames of reference. After the about-turn, though, the astronaut twin has a different inertial frame of reference. The relative simultaneity between the new frame and the Earth frame is then different and the astronaut sees a sudden change in the age of his earthbound twin.

In summary, the effect is not due to either twin simply travelling close to the speed of light, or due to one of them experiencing forces during the about-turn. It is due to there being three inertial frames involved rather than two. The two frames for the travelling twin are inclined differently to the Earth frame in *Minkowski space-time*, and jumping from one to the other changes the relative simultaneity of the two twins.

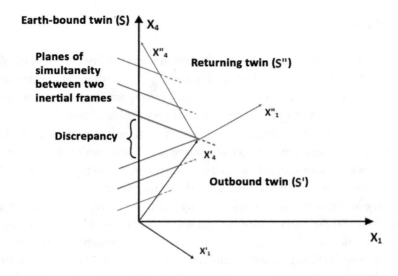

Fig. A-3, Change of inertial frame of reference in the 'twin paradox'.

In this diagram, the 'planes of simultaneity' are lines in the Earth frame (S) corresponding to a constant time t' in the astronaut frame (S'). The equation relating t' to S is:

$$t - vx/c2 = constant$$

In other words, the equivalent simultaneity in S depends on the location.

Notes

PREFACE

1 Part of the end-of-life monologue, rewritten by actor Rutger Hauer, and delivered by his character, Roy Batty, in Ridley Scott's classic 1982 movie, *Blade Runner* (https://en.wikipedia.org/wiki/Tears_in_rain_monologue : accessed 21 September 2020).

CHAPTER 1

2 John Horgan, "The Delusion of Scientific Omniscience", *Scientific American* (4 September 2019).

3 There is no single definitive list of philosophical branches. These five have a traditional standing, but there may be additional ones noted elsewhere such as political philosophy or axiology (value theory). The application of philosophy to other fields of study (some of which are analysed independently in later chapters) may also be considered branches, including science, mathematics (Ch. 10), mind (Ch. 6), language, education, law, and so on. Many fields of study actually span more than one of the cited branches, such as perception, i.e. as a part of cognition (epistemology), as a means to appreciating art (aesthetics), and whether it means anything in relation to reality (metaphysics).

4 This viewpoint, and our distinction of physics from metaphysics, may have shifted over time since many questions that were once considered metaphysical — beyond the reach of physics — are now considered to be part of fundamental physics. For instance, in 1893, French theoretical physicist Pierre M. M. Duhem, while responding to a criticism of his views on physical theories by a Catholic civil engineer, equated physics with the first of our goals (predictability) and metaphysics with the second (understanding). Source: Pierre Duhem, author, Roger Ariew and Peter Barker, transl. and eds., *Essays in the History and Philosophy of Science* (Hackett Publishing Co., 1996), p.31.

5 This is the original, static interpretation of eternalism. There is a more recent interpretation that may be described as dynamic eternalism, and is associated with a 'growing block universe', but that is wholly rejected here on the grounds that it is merely propping up the psychological perspective of reality.

6 Albert Henrichs, *Harvard Studies in Classical Philology*, vol. 103 (Harvard University Press, 2008), p.69.

CHAPTER 2

7 Sir Arthur S. Eddington, *Space, Time and Gravitation: An Outline of the General Relativity Theory* (1920; reprint Cambridge University Press, 1987), p.51.

8 Hermann Weyl, author, Olaf Helmer, transl., *Philosophy of Mathematics and Natural Science* (1949; reprint Princeton University Press, 2009), p.116.

9   William Faulkner, *Requiem for a Nun* (1951, reprinted London: Vintage, 1996), p. 85; in the original context, Temple Drake states to Gavin Stevens, defence lawyer for her domestic servant Nancy Mannigoe, 'Template Drake is dead', and he responds with the quoted line, implying that she cannot escape her scandalous past and that it is a part of everything she does.

10 Although the concept of world-lines arose as a description of the path traced by a particle in a four-dimensional continuum, it is often used to describe the complete history of a particle as a continuous sequence of space-time events. In this *block universe* context, however, it *is* the particle; particles are no longer moving point objects, but have a static extent through the time dimension. This view is sometimes known as *perdurantism*, a four-dimensional view of persistence that differs from three-dimensional *endurantism*, where an object is wholly present at each instant of its existence. We will occasionally use the term to describe the extent of macroscopic objects over time.

11 Freeman Dyson, *Disturbing the Universe* (New York: Basic Books, 1979), p.193.

12 Research in the 1950s revealed that 98% of the atoms in the human body are replaced every single year — source: "Science: The Fleeting Flesh", time.com, *TIME* (http://content.time.com/time/magazine/article/0,9171,936455,00.html : accessed 14 July 2020); reprinted from *Time Magazine*, 11 October 1954. It has been concluded that 100% of our atoms are replaced every five years — source: u/sciencethrowaway2, "Are 98% of the atoms in the human body replaced every year?", *Reddit*, Q&A forum: r/askscience, posted 18 March 2011 (https://www.nytimes.com/2005/08/02/science/your-body-is-younger-than-you-think.html : accessed 14 July 2020). There is a widely quoted figure of 7–10 years, but this is apparently related to the replacement of cellular tissue rather than the underlying atoms — source: Nicholas Wade, "Your Body Is Younger Than You Think", *New York Times*, 2 August 2005, online archive (https://www.nytimes.com/2005/08/02/science/your-body-is-younger-than-you-think.html : accessed 14 July 2020).

13 "Heroes and Villains", *Only Fools and Horses*, BBC sitcom, s.8, ep.1 (1996); story recounted by the character Trigger, played by Roger Lloyd-Pack. This issue of identity is properly known as Theseus' Ship Paradox. Comedy fans may be aware of an earlier sitcom, also starring David Jason, containing a similar skit. In "Laundry Blues", *Open All Hours*, BBC sitcom, s.2, ep.1 (1981), there is the following exchange between Granville (David Jason) and Arkwright (Ronnie Barker). Granville: We need a new brush. Arkwright: Nonsense! That's a marvellous old brush, that! I've had that for fourteen years. It's only had two new heads and three new handles.

14 If you imagine that such spheres might be given L (left) and R (right) identities then viewing them from the other side would be an entirely indistinguishable view, but with the L and R interchanged. There is no frame of reference in which their positions can be distinguished. The situation changes for three or more spheres if their separations are not all identical since it would then be possible to define certain positional relations relative to the pair with, say, the minimum separation, but still insufficient. You can define a Cartesian frame of reference in n dimensions using n+1 points (one centre and n fixing the axes) but this assumes that you have unique identities for these points, otherwise all axes are symmetrical, and each has a +/- symmetry of its own. In effect, you can only differentiate object positions relative to some separate local significantly asymmetric structure.

CHAPTER 3

15 Two important terms, here, need to be distinguished: in a *closed system*, the matter within the system is constant, but energy is allowed in and out; in an *isolated system*, neither matter nor energy is allowed in or out.

16 The symbol ε is Hilbert's epsilon operator, and the symbol $\gg$ is used here to represent a generic transition from one state to another, either an observable one (connected by time, but without implying causation or any particular mechanism), or an abstract one (connected by algorithmic steps).

17 We are using the term algorithm to describe sequences of definable steps — ones that may be 'scripted' and 'enacted' (see Chapter 9) — but we may later refer to the *second law of thermodynamics* as having a mathematical foundation rather than a physical one, so what is the difference? Mathematics involves a manipulation of symbols that may represent concepts that include (but are not limited to) numbers, but an algorithm is a procedural mechanism that manipulates decisions (selections based on distinct criteria) and actions. Those actions may be mathematical, but an algorithm is the more general concept as it may be unrelated to calculation or to any acknowledged branch of mathematics. Our interchangeable usage reflects a belief that they are really two sides of the same coin. More on this in §10.2.

18 Cristian Farías, Victor A. Pinto, and Pablo S. Moya, "What is the temperature of a moving body?", *Scientific Reports*, vol.7, article 17657 (15 December 2015); DOI: 10.1038/s41598-017-17526-4 .

CHAPTER 4

19 Steven Weinberg, *Dreams of a Final Theory* (London: Vintage, 1993), p.137.

20 There are some naïve claims that we travel at the speed of light through time. This is based on the definition of an interval within the space-time of *special relativity* (App. A): $ds^2 = dx^2 + dy^2 + dz^2 - c^2\, dt^2$. If you were motionless then dx, etc., would be 0, and so dividing through by dt gives $ds/dt = -c$, which looks like a velocity. The negative sign is not significant, and is a result of the particular convention used for defining that interval. However, the algebraic manipulation is also meaningless: although the constant c is referred to as the 'speed of light' it is actually a universal constant, and used here as a constant of proportionality to place spatial and temporal variables on an equal footing. The final derivative is telling us no more than the conventions we adopted in defining that interval.

21 Stephen Hawking, *A Brief History of Time: From the Big Bang to Black Holes* (London: Bantam Press, 1988), p.147.

22 This quote has been attributed to many people, but the earliest verified source is probably: Ray Cummings, "The Time Professor", short story in *Argosy All-Story Weekly*, 8 January 1921 (Frank A. Munsey, 1921). In particular, it is attributed to John Wheeler by Brian Greene (*The Fabric of the Cosmos: Space, Time, and the Texture of Reality* (Vintage Books, February 2005), p.226), but Wheeler admitted that his phrase, "Time is nature's way to keep everything from happening all at once", was "Discovered among the graffiti in the men's room of the Pecan Street Cafe, Austin, Texas" — source: John Archibald Wheeler, author, Wojciech H. Zurek, ed., "Information, Physics, Quantum: The Search for Links",

Complexity, Entropy and the Physics of Information (Addison-Wesley, 1990), p.10; the proceedings of the 1988 workshop on complexity, entropy, and the physics of information held May-June, 1989, in Santa Fe, New Mexico.

23 Richard Taylor, *Metaphysics* (1963; reprint Prentice-Hall Inc., 1992), p.36.

24 Martin Heidegger, author, Michael Heim, transl., *The Metaphysical Foundations of Logic* (Indiana University Press, 1984), pp.114–115.

25 Gottfried Wilhelm Leibniz, author, George Martin Duncan, transl., "The Principles of Nature and Grace. 1714", *Philosophical Works of Leibniz* (New Haven: Tuttle, Moorehouse, and Taylor, 1890), article 7, p.212; translated from the original French of 1714; book hereinafter cited as *Leibniz-Philosophical-Works*.

26 *Leibniz-Philosophical-Works*, "The Monadalogy. 1714", article 32, p.222.

27 David Hume, author, L.A. Selby-Bigge, ed., "Of the inference from the impression to the idea", *A Treatise of Human Nature* (1739; reprint Oxford: Clarendon Press, 1896), p.87.

28 Ibid. p.93.

29 Immanuel Kant, author, F. Max Müller, transl., "The Analogies of Experience: Second Analogy: Principle of Production", *Critique of Pure Reason*, 2nd rev. ed. (New York: Macmillan, 1922), p.158; originally published in German 1781, and revised 1787; translated to English in 1881; book hereinafter cited as *Kant-Critique-Pure-Reason*.

30 Max Black, "Why Cannot an Effect Precede its Cause?", *Analysis*, vol. 16, issue 3 (January 1956), pp.49–58; DOI 10.1093/analys/16.3.49 .

31 David Williams, *Weighing the Odds: A Course in Probability and Statistics* (Cambridge University Press, 2 August 2001), p.498.

32 Miles-per-hour (mph) figures from: Rhett Herman, "How fast is the earth moving?", *Scientific American* (26 October 1998).

CHAPTER 5

33 J.B.S Haldane. *Possible Worlds, and Other Essays* (1927, reprint London: Chatto & Windus, 1932), p.286; emphasis in the original; quote mistakenly associated with Eddington, Werner, and Priestly. Book also published as: *Possible Worlds and Other Papers* (New York: Harper & Brothers, 1928).

34 Immanuel Kant, author, Ernest Belfort Bax, transl., *Prolegomena and Metaphysical Foundations of Natural Science*, 2nd rev. ed. (London: George Bell and Sons, 1891), § 32, p.62; originally published in German 1783. Book hereinafter cited as *Kant-Prolegomena*.

35 Ibid., § 13 p.33.

36 Ibid., § 32 p.62.

37 *Kant-Critique-Pure-Reason*, p.203.

38 Ibid., p.206.

39 Ibid., p.207.

40 Ibid., p.211.

41 Ibid., p.235.

42 Ibid., p.802.

43 Amie Thomasson, author, Edward N. Zalta, ed., "Categories", *Stanford Encyclopedia of Philosophy* (3 June 2004, revised 7 March 2018), online (https://plato.stanford.edu/archives/sum2019/entries/categories/ : accessed 23 May 2019).

44 *Kant-Critique-Pure-Reason*, "First Section of the Transcendental Aesthetic: Of Space", pp.18–19.

45 Paul Guyer and Jonathan Nelson, *The Cambridge Companion to Kant and Modern Philosophy* (Cambridge University Press, 2006).

46 *Kant-Prolegomena*, § 13, p.32.

47 The view that the laws of nature are what really happens, while the laws of science are what we think happens (and inaccurately so), can be traced back to a paper delivered by English-born Australian philosopher Michael J. Scriven at the 1959 annual meeting of the American Association for the Advancement of Sciences. See: Michael Scriven, "The Key Property of Physical Laws: Inaccuracy", H. Feigl and G. Maxwell (eds.), *Current Issues in the Philosophy of Science* (New York: Holt, Rinehart & Winston, 1961), pp.91–101.

48 *Leibniz-Philosophical-Works*, "The Principles of Nature and Grace. 1714", article 7, p.213.

49 It will be hard for readers to appreciate the full force of these statements that counting is not fundamental since everything that we can cite from the measurable world is framed by space and time, and so will exhibit aspects of distinctness. It is not just a matter that a super-observer cannot physically count 1, 2, 3, ... (because they would have no subjective time), but that countability itself has no meaning without accessible distinctness. One approach to understanding might be to consider things that do not exist in our physical world, and so have no representation within it; it would then be impossible to conceive or visualise them and so they would not be countable.

50 This is the 'butterfly effect', as described by American mathematician and meteorologist Edward N. Lorenz in the 1960s.

51 John Gribbin and Mary Gribbin, *Richard Feynman: A Life in Science* (Viking, 1997), pp.266–267. See also: Richard P. Feynman, Fernando B. Morinigo, William G. Wagner, *Feynman Lectures on Gravitation* (Addison-Wesley, 1995), pp.9–10.

52 Edward P. Tryon, "Is the Universe a Vacuum Fluctuation?", *Nature*, vol.246 (14 December 1973): p.396.

53 A. Einstein, author, Anna Beck, transl., "Does the Inertia of a Body Depend Upon its Energy-Content?", *Volume 2: The Swiss Years: Writings, 1900-1909 (English translation supplement)*, *The Digital Einstein Papers*, an open-access site for published volumes (https://einsteinpapers.press.princeton.edu/vol2-trans/188 : accessed 1 February 2020), p.174; Einstein, *The Collected Papers of Albert Einstein*, vol.2 (Princeton University Press, 21 February 1990); article originally published in *Annalen der Physik*, issue 18 (21 September 1905), pp.639–641.

54 A. Einstein, author, Anna Beck, transl., "On the Inertia of Energy Required by the Relativity Principle", *The Digital Einstein Papers*, vol.2 (English) (https://einsteinpapers.press.princeton.edu/vol2-trans/252 : accessed 1 February 2020), p.238; Einstein, *The Collected Papers of Albert Einstein*, vol.2 (Princeton University Press, 21 February 1990); article originally published *Annalen der Physik*, issue 23 (13 June 1907), pp.371–384.

55 We are here using the term matter to mean anything that occupies space, and so has volume. The term is also used for anything that has rest mass, and so includes elementary particles and atoms, but space and volume are only weakly meaningful at that level, and the current argument relates to our perception of the macroscopic world.

CHAPTER 6

56 Allison Eck, "What Birdsong Can Teach Us About Creativity", *NOVA website* (https://www.pbs.org/wgbh/nova/article/what-birdsong-can-teach-us-about-creativity/ : 9 April 2014, accessed 8 June 2020).

57 Torin Alter and Sven Walter, eds., *Phenomenal Concepts and Phenomenal Knowledge: New Essays on Consciousness and Physicalism* (Oxford University Press, 2007), introduction by the editors.

58 Ibid.

59 Jeffrey Goldstein, "Emergence as a Construct: History and Issues", *Emergence*, issue 1, vol.1 (1 March 1999): pp.49–72; DOI: 10.1207/s15327000em0101_4 .

60 J. Tomberlin, ed., *Philosophical Perspectives: Mind, Causation, and World*, vol.11 (Malden, MA: Blackwell, 1997), pp.375–399; online article http://people.reed.edu/~mab/papers/weak.emergence.pdf (accessed 6 April 2020).

61 David J. Chalmers, "Facing up to the problem of consciousness", *Journal of Consciousness Studies*, vol.2, issue 3 (1995), pp.200–219.

62 Ian Sample, "Scientists find genetic mutation that makes woman feel no pain", *The Guardian*, international edition (28 March 2019); online (https://www.theguardian.com/science/2019/mar/28/scientists-find-genetic-mutation-that-makes-woman-feel-no-pain : accessed 10 February 2020).

63 Frank Wilczek, interviewed by Sabine Hossenfelder, *Lost in Math: How Beauty Leads Physics Astray* (New York: Basic Books, 2018), p.151.

64 *Kant-Critique-Pure-Reason*, "First Section of the Transcendental Aesthetic: Of Space", p.18.

65 *Kant-Critique-Pure-Reason*, "Second Section of the Transcendental Aesthetic: Of Time", p.24.

66 John Cottingham, author, Ray Monk and Frederic Raphael, eds., "Descartes' Philosophy of Mind", *The Great Philosophers* (London: Phoenix, 2001), p.107.

67 Ibid., p.97.

68 Ibid., p.129.

69 Gilbert Ryle, *The Concept of Mind* (London: Hutchinson's University Library, 1949), p.17.

70 A property A is said to supervene on a property B if any change in A necessarily implies a change in B.

71 In people who have a severed *corpus callosum* ('split-brain' patients), one side of the brain might perceive an object, but the other side with language cannot say what it is. Whether this constitutes, or could develop into, a true instance of 'dual consciousness' is still debated.

72 *Kant-Critique-Pure-Reason*, "Third Conflict of the Transcendental Ideas", p.362.

73 Ibid., p.363.

74 Jaegwon Kim, *Physicalism, Or Something Near Enough* (Princeton University Press, 2005), p.42.

CHAPTER 7

75 Einstein did not use the term photon. This was used later, having been adapted from a slightly different usage by American physical chemist Gilbert N. Lewis in 1926. For a fuller account, see: Helge Kragh, "Photon: New light on an old name", *arXiv.org*, Cornell University eprint (https://arxiv.org/abs/1401.0293v3, 1 January 2014, revised 28 February 2014).

76 It surprises many that Einstein never received a Nobel Prize for his theories of relativity, but there are purported to be several reasons. The disagreement with Henri Bergson obviously had an effect because Svante Arrhenius, who chaired the prize committee for physics, mentioned that "the famous philosopher Bergson in Paris has challenged this theory, while other philosophers have acclaimed it wholeheartedly". But although Einstein had been repeatedly nominated since 1910, there were strong anti-Semitic views in Germany during that time, which targeted prominent Jews such as Einstein and Minkowski. The so-called 'Study Group of German Natural Philosophers' (or, as Einstein called it, the "Antirelativity Company"), led by engineer Paul Weyland, and including scientists Philipp Lenard and Ernst Gehrcke, tried to disparage the theories of relativity using any means possible, including racial slurs. The committee initially claimed that mere theories did not meet the requirements that Alfred Nobel had laid out, and that these theories were also unproven. But even when proof started to emerge, the committee still hesitated because they were so controversial — and their understanding of them was limited. They eventually weaselled out by selecting his work on the photoelectric effect, something that would eventually lead into *quantum theory*. Source: Albrecht Fölsing, *Albert Einstein* (Penguin Group, 1997), pp.536+; and Ronald William Clark, *Einstein: The Life and Times* (Harper Paperbacks, 2011, originally published 1971), pp.316+.

77 Peter Rodgers, PDF document, "The double-slit experiment", *physicsworld.com* (https://www.physics.umd.edu/courses/Phys401/appeli/EXTRAS/double-slitexperiment.pdf : created 1 September 2002, accessed 25 June 2019); extended version of "A brief history of the double-slit experiment" appearing in the September 2002 issue of *Physics World*, p.15.

78 Feynman, Leighton, Sands, *The Feynman Lectures on Physics: Definitive Edition*, vol.1 (Addison-Wesley, 2006), p.37–2.

79 Rafi Letzter, "Giant Molecules Exist in Two Places at Once in Unprecedented Quantum Experiment", *Scientific American* (8 October 2019).

80 Felix Bloch, "Reminiscences of Heisenberg and the early days of quantum mechanics", *Physics Today* (December 1976): p.23.

81 Walter J. Moore, *A Life of Erwin Schrödinger* (Cambridge University Press, 1994), p.140.

82 Actually $c_1\phi_1 + c_2\phi_2$ would be a solution, where the coefficients are complex-valued. These have the net effect of changing the amplitude and phase of the *wave functions*, but these are only relative properties and have no absolute significance. In fact, the amplitude is usually scaled so that the probabilistic interpretation yields a total of 1 when all of the alternatives are considered.

83 In case your mathematics is a little rusty, imagine a complex number $z = x + iy$, where $i = \sqrt{-1}$. The complex conjugate is defined by $z^* = x - iy$, and the absolute square, $|z|^2 = z\,z^* = x^2 + y^2$.

84 Albert Einstein, author, K. Przibram, ed., *Letters on Wave Mechanics: Correspondence with H. A. Lorentz, Max Planck, and Erwin Schrödinger* (NY: Philosophical Library, 1963), p.48; letter from Lorentz to Schrödinger, dated 27 May 1926.

85 The *wave function* can be represented in a configuration space of positional coordinates ($\psi(x,t)$), also called q-space, or of momenta coordinates ($\psi(p,t)$), also called p-space. These are two ways of looking at the same system, and they are related by a *Fourier transform*. When Schrödinger referred to a q-space of "… more than three coordinates" then he was considering an N-body problem, where there would be three spatial dimensions per body in the configuration space.

86 Ibid., pp.61–63; letter from Schrödinger to Lorentz, dated 8 June 1926.

87 Irene Born, transl., *The Born–Einstein Letters: Correspondence between Albert Einstein and Max and Hedwig Born from 1916 to 1955 with commentaries by Max Born* (Macmillan Press, 1971), p.91; book hereinafter cited as *Born-Einstein-Letters*.

88 Jeremy Bernstein, *Quantum Profiles* (Princeton University Press, 1991), p.42.

89 *Born-Einstein-Letters*, p.164; marginal comments on a Born manuscript, dated 18 March 1948.

90 Max Jammer, *The Philosophy of Quantum Mechanics: The Interpretations of QM in historical perspective* (John Wiley and Sons, 1974), p.61.

91 The *group velocity* is the velocity that would keep pace with a constant amplitude, whereas the *phase velocity* is the velocity that would keep pace with a constant phase.

92 P. A. M. Dirac, "The Lagrangian in Quantum Mechanics", *Physikalische Zeitschrift der Sowjetunion* [Physical Journal of the Soviet Union], vol.3, no.1 (1933, received November 1932): pp.64–72.

93 Again, in case your mathematics is rusty: *complex numbers* can be represented in a two-dimensional complex plane (an *Argand diagram*) with real components on one axis and imaginary on the other. Switching from Cartesian coordinates to polar ones allows complex values to be represented alternately as $z = x + iy = r(\cos\theta + i\sin\theta) = re^{i\theta}$.

Then, $z^* = re^{-i\theta}$ and so $|z|^2 = z\,z^* = r^2 = x^2 + y^2$. This is why multiplying ψ by a constant phase $(e^{i\theta})$ has no effect on $|\psi|^2$, and why multiplying by a general complex constant only scales its amplitude.

94 Richard P. Feynman, *QED: The Strange Theory of Light and Matter* (Penguin Books, 1990), p.43.

95 H. D. Zeh, "On the interpretation of measurement in quantum theory", *Foundations of Physics*, vol.1, issue 1 (March 1970), pp.69–76; DOI: 10.1007/BF00708656 .

96 Stephen L. Adler, "Why Decoherence has not Solved the Measurement Problem: A Response to P. W. Anderson", *arXiv.org*, Cornell University eprint (https://arxiv.org/abs/quant-ph/0112095, 17 December 2001); DOI: 10.1016/S1355-2198(02)00086-2 .

97 A. Einstein, B. Podolsky, and N. Rosen, "Can Quantum-Mechanical Description of Physical Reality Be Considered Complete?", *Physical Review*, vol.47 (15 May 1935): p.777; DOI: 10.1103/PhysRev.47.777 .

98 Manjit Kumar, *Quantum: Einstein, Bohr and the Great Debate About the Nature of Reality* (2009; reprint London: Icon Books, 2010), p.313.

99 N. Bohr, "Can Quantum-Mechanical Description of Physical Reality Be Considered Complete?", *Physical Review*, vol.48 (15 October 1935): p.696; DOI: 10.1103/PhysRev.48.696 .

100 *Born-Einstein-Letters*, p.158.

101 C. L. Herzenberg, "Grete Hermann: An early contributor to quantum theory", *arXiv.org*, Cornell University eprint (https://arxiv.org/abs/0812.3986, 20 December 2008).

102 J. S. Bell, "On the Einstein Podolsky Rosen paradox", *Physics Physique Fizika*, vol.1, no.3 (November 1964): pp.195–200; DOI: 10.1103/PhysicsPhysiqueFizika.1.195 .

103 Ibid., §VI, "Conclusion".

104 Henry Pierce Stapp. "S-Matrix Interpretation of Quantum Theory", *Physical Review*, vol.3, issue 6 (15 March 1971): p.1303; DOI: 10.1103/PhysRevD.3.1303 .

105 Alain Aspect, "Bell's inequality test: more ideal than ever", *Nature*, vol.398 (18 March 1999): p.189.

106 Often attributed to Einstein, but a similar modern usage can be found at: David Lindley, *Where Does The Weirdness Go?: Why Quantum Mechanics Is Strange, But Not As Strange As You Think* (Basic Books, 20 March 1997), pp.3–8.

107 J. S. Bell, "Bertlmann's Socks and the Nature of Reality", *Journal de Physique Colloques*, vol.32, no.C2 (March 1981); DOI: 10.1051/jphyscol:1981202 .

108 Another type of experiment relies on entangled spins of two spin-½ particles. The spins must be opposite for each pair (i.e. one up and one down), and so the different correlation conditions occur at different detection angles: correlated at 180°, anti-correlated at 0° and 360°, and uncorrelated at 90° and 270°. The *quantum correlation* is then $C = -cos(\theta)$ rather than $C = cos(2\theta)$.

109   Kumar, *Quantum: Einstein, Bohr and the Great Debate About the Nature of Reality*, p.327; after Einstein's death, Bohr imagined debating with him over new issues he was working on.

110   As well as generalised coordinates (e.g. position and momentum) for each particle, this abstract space usually replicates these for each particle in the system, and so can involve many dimensions for a complex system. In modern *quantum mechanics*, the classical *configuration space* is replaced by a complex-valued vector space (called a *Hilbert space*) for representing states, and this may have an infinite number of (mathematical) dimensions.

111   N. F. Mott, "The wave mechanics of α-Ray tracks", *Proceedings of the Royal Society*, vol.126, issue 800 (2 December 1929): pp.79–84; DOI 10.1098/rspa.1929.0205 .

112   Roger Penrose, *The Road to Reality: A Complete Guide to the Laws of The Universe* (Vintage, 2005), p.819.

113   C. L. Herzenberg, "Grete Hermann: An early contributor to quantum theory", *arXiv.org*, Cornell University eprint (https://arxiv.org/abs/0812.3986, 20 December 2008), p.12.

114   Actually, the wave equation is fully deterministic in being able to calculate the *wave function* from any point in time, and in either temporal direction. But the *wave function* is not an observable quantity, and its interpretation as a probability yields the indeterminism. In other words, *quantum mechanics* cannot accurately predict what our measurement systems will record.

115   David Bohm, "A Suggested Interpretation of the Quantum Theory in Terms of 'Hidden' Variables", *Physical Review*, vol.85, Issue 2 (January 1952): pp.166–179.

116   P. C. W. Davies and J. R. Brown, *The Ghost in the Atom: A Discussion of the Mysteries of Quantum Physics* (1986; reprint Cambridge University Press, 1989), pp.127–128; interview with David Bohm.

117   Ibid., p.128.

118   David Bohm, *Wholeness and the Implicate Order* (1980; reprint Routledge Classics, 2002), §7, pp.102+. See also: Jeremy Bernstein, *Quantum Profiles* (Princeton University Press, 1991), pp.64–65.

119   *Born-Einstein-Letters*, p.192.

120   Jean Bricmont, *Quantum Sense and Nonsense* (Springer, 27 Oct 2017), p.203.

121   J. S. Bell: *Speakable and unspeakable in quantum mechanics* (Cambridge University Press, 1987), p.115.

122   A metric defines distance between a pair of points, infinitesimally close in a curved space, in terms of the differential variations on each of the space's dimensions. Technically speaking, rather than for a general topological space, this is for a manifold: a smooth space that locally resembles a Euclidean space. The metric may be line-integrated to find the length of a path between two points separated by a finite distance. A geodesic is a path for which the length is a minimum.

123   This folding of the spatial dimensions of the configuration space may be a controversial notion, but it is partly justified by the presumption of a *block universe*. While the spatial locations of interacting particles in an N-body problem will not be independent, the use of a configuration space presumes that all combinations of their separate locations

might be possible under the dynamics of different configurations. But within a *block universe*, there are no dynamics — only static configurations, and they exist in a single 3+1 dimensional space-time.

124 Murray Gell-Mann, *The Quark and the Jaguar: Adventures in the Simple and the Complex* (1995; reprint Abacus, 2001), p.147.

125 Davies and Brown, *The Ghost in the Atom*, p.47; interview with John Bell.

126 Ibid.

127 George Musser, "Does Some Deeper Level of Physics Underlie Quantum Mechanics? An Interview with Nobelist Gerard 't Hooft: Is the notorious randomness of quantum mechanics just a front?", spookyactionbook.com, *Spooky Action at a Distance*, posted 7 October 2013 (https://spookyactionbook.com/2013/10/07/does-some-deeper-level-of-physics-underlie-quantum-mechanics-an-interview-with-nobelist-gerard-t-hooft/ : accessed 18 December 2019); abridged transcript of lunchtime interview at the EmQM13 conference on Emergent Quantum Mechanics, 3–6 October 2013, Vienna; also published on the blog of *Scientific American*, same date.

128 David Bohm and Basil J. Hiley, *The Undivided Universe: An Ontological Interpretation of Quantum Theory* (1993; reprint Routledge, 2006), p.2.

129 So is this variation of *superdeterminism* a local or non-local theory? It is clearly deterministic and acausal, so if we use the interpretation of *locality* as meaning local causality then this cannot be so. But all the connections by which we infer the notion of causality are local in the relativistic sense (separated by time-like intervals), which would imply a local theory. However, it is the interference between the paths taken and not taken (effectively properties across space-time) that actually qualifies it as a non-local theory.

CHAPTER 8

130 Very recent research has confirmed that actual atoms of anti-hydrogen behave identically to normal hydrogen, including the *Lamb shift*: a very fine split in the energy levels. Source: The ALPHA Collaboration, "Investigation of the fine structure of antihydrogen", *Nature*, vol.578 (20 February 2020): pp.375–380; DOI: 10.1038/s41586-020-2006-5 .

131 "Emmy Noether: Professor Einstein Writes in Appreciation of a Fellow-Mathematician", "Letters to the Editor", *New York Times* (4 May 1935); obituary to Noether who had died 14 April 1935; relevant sentence "In the judgment of the most competent living mathematicians, Fräulein Noether was the most significant creative mathematical genius thus far produced since the higher education of women began".

132 Feynman, Leighton, Sands, *The Feynman Lectures on Physics: Definitive Edition*, vol.1, pp.52–53.

133 These terms come from spatial transformations in analytic geometry. In an active, or alibi, transformation, points or objects are moved within some space ('alibi' meaning elsewhere). In a passive, or alias, transformation, only a change to the coordinate system is made ('alias' meaning under another name).

134   Frank Arntzenius and Hilary Greaves, "Time Reversal in Classical Electromagnetism", *The British Journal for the Philosophy of Science*, vol.60, issue 3 (September 2009): pp.557–584; DOI: 10.1093/bjps/axp015 .

135   Feynman, *QED: The Strange Theory of Light and Matter*, p.98.

136   David Z. Albert, *Time and Chance* (2000; reprint Harvard University Press, 2003), p.18.

137   Ibid., p.19.

138   David B. Malament, "On the time reversal invariance of classical electromagnetic theory", *Studies in History and Philosophy of Modern Physics*, vol.35, issue 2 (2004): pp.295–315; DOI: 10.1016/j.shpsb.2003.09.006 .

139   Craig Callender, "Is Time 'Handed' in a Quantum World?", *Proceedings of the Aristotelian Society*, vol.100, issue 1 (2000), pp.247–269, quotation in footnote 4; DOI: 10.1111/j.0066-7372.2003.00015.x .

140   Bryan W. Roberts, "Time Reversal", *PhilSci-Archive*, eprint (2019); URI: http://philsci-archive.pitt.edu/id/eprint/15033 .

141   B. F. Skinner, "'Superstition' in the pigeon", *Journal of Experimental Psychology*, vol.38, issue 2 (1948): pp.168–172.

142   Latham Boyle, Kieran Finn, and Neil Turok, "CPT-Symmetric Universe", *Physical Review Letters*, vol.121, issue 25 (21 December 2018); DOI: 10.1103/PhysRevLett.121.251301 .

143   Steven Carlip, "Viewpoint: Arrow of Time Emerges in a Gravitational System", *Physics*, vol.7 (https://physics.aps.org/articles/v7/111 : accessed 17 January 2020, published 29 October 2014), pp.111–113; free online magazine from *the American Physical Society*; citing Julian Barbour, Tim Koslowski, and Flavio Mercati, "Identification of a Gravitational Arrow of Time", *Physical Review Letters*, vol.113, issue 18 (31 October 2014): DOI: 10.1103/PhysRevLett.113.181101 .

144   Free energy is usually a synonym in thermodynamics for usable energy. We are here distinguishing between free energy that has been lost to the environment (some of which we may never see again) and that which has been trapped or captured and could be released to do work.

145   Looking for bigger explanations (upscaling of causality) seems to be the prerogative of people going about their daily lives, and contrasts sharply with the *reductionism* inherent in scientific analysis. We live in a world where *holism* (treating things as wholes) is predominant, and we rarely think in terms of the constituents of those wholes. Returning to the storm example, it is natural to talk of the storm as a thing in its own right, and being causally responsible for damage, etc. We might look for bigger explanations in terms of cyclical weather patterns, the effects of the Moon, etc., but not the constituent molecules or their relative motions. When this route of upscaling appears to have run its course, then we may invent even bigger explanations, including conspiracy theories, supernatural elements, horoscopes, and even deities.

146   A noteworthy fact that leads to the appearance of this distribution, rather than all molecules ending up with the same identical speed, is that the three components of the momentum for two colliding particles (p_x, p_y, p_z) are independently conserved. Although the particles may depart from each other in any direction, these components are independent of each

other, which means that no part of p_x can be converted to a change in p_y, etc. Their kinetic energy (which is also conserved) is a scalar that depends on their directionless speed (as opposed to velocity), but the three vector components of momentum provide for degrees of freedom within which the speeds of all colliding pairs can vary. The distribution is therefore strongly related to the number of spatial dimensions.

CHAPTER 9

147   Richard P. Feynman, *What Do You Care What Other People Think? Further Adventures of a Curious Character* (New York: W. W. Norton & Co., 2001), p.58; as told to Ralph Leighton.

148   Such systems are more precisely referred to as 'expert systems', and they are technically part of the field of AI, although they are still delivering answers by applying some combination of rules and a knowledge base that have been predefined. They may have come a long way since the early 1970s versions, but they are still not intelligent.

149   Andrew Hodges, author, Ray Monk and Frederic Raphael, eds., "Turing: A Natural Philosopher", *The Great Philosophers* (London: Phoenix, 2001), p.529.

150   Ibid., p.538.

CHAPTER 10

151   Contemporary platonism is the view that there exist abstract objects — ones that are non-physical and non-mental — but since this is probably a deviation from the original views of Plato then it is written here with a lowercase 'p'. Source: Mark Balaguer, author, Edward N. Zalta, ed., "Platonism in Metaphysics", *The Stanford Encyclopedia of Philosophy* (12 May 2004, revised 9 March 2016), online (https://plato.stanford.edu/archives/spr2016/ entries/platonism/ : accessed 15 September 2020).

152   The set of natural numbers is actually termed a *countably infinite* set, as is the set of integers, or the set of even integers, or the set of rational numbers. The set of real numbers is termed an *uncountable infinite* set, as is the set of irrational numbers.

153   A proposition is any statement that can be said to be true or false, and propositional logic manipulates such statements in an algebraic way. Boolean logic (or Boolean algebra) is a model for propositional logic that uses operators of AND, OR, and NOT on sets of objects matching specific assertions. Predicate logic (or first-order logic) is more general than this and allows a similar manipulation of statements about the properties of objects, and relations between such properties. For instance, by using the notion of *quantifiers* that generalise a statement about an object having some property to a number or range of objects (or *quantity* of) having that property. Examples of formal quantifiers include "∀" (meaning "for all") and "∃" (meaning "there exists").

154   Albert Einstein , author, G. B. Jeffery and W. Perrett, transl., "Geometry and Experience", *Sidelights on Relativity* (1922; reprint Dover Publications Inc., October 1983), p.28; translated from German to English; expanded from an address of the same title given by Einstein to the Prussian Academy of Science, in Berlin on 27 January 1921.

155   David Hilbert, author, Paul Benacerraf and Hilary Putnam, eds., "On the Infinite", *Philosophy of Mathematics: Selected Readings*, 2nd ed. (Cambridge University Press, 1983), p.201.

156   Our usage of the term randomness may need some clarification, too, because it is so etched into our world of experience. A dictionary might define it as something occurring without method or conscious decision. A clearer definition might be something that lacks any pattern or predictability, but it should not be confused with indeterminism. Indeterminism specifically relates to events that are not determined (either causally or mathematically) by prior events, whereas random is a general lack of pattern or coherence. For instance, a randomised deck of cards is one where there is no general relationship between successive cards, and hence no pattern. Supporters of indeterminism usually hold that causes are *necessary* but not *sufficient*, and so do not constrain things to a single specific future.

CHAPTER 11 ...

157   One research team claims to have captured virtual photons from a vacuum and converted them to real ones. Source: Chalmers University of Technology, "Scientists create light from vacuum", *Phys.org* (https://phys.org/news/2011-11-scientists-vacuum.html : created 17 November 2011, accessed 27 March 2020).

158   Isaac Newton, unpublished letter to Richard Bentley dated 25 February 1692/3 [dual dating], quoted in I. Bernard Cohen, *Introduction to Newton's 'Principia'* (Harvard University Press, 1978), pp.302–303.

159   This was the meaning employed in the theory of *general relativity*; however, the *equivalence principle* now has weak and strong variations. The strong principle states all the laws of nature are the same in a uniform static gravitational field and the equivalent non-inertial (accelerated) reference frames. The weak principle states all the laws of motion for freely falling objects are the same as in an inertial (unaccelerated) reference frame. These principles apply to a localised region where, for instance, it would be impossible to tell that the neighbouring paths of gravitational attraction are radial (to the centre of the attracting body) rather than parallel.

160   In flat space-time, the preferred path is one of shortest distance, and even in a curved space such as the surface of a sphere this shortest-distance principle holds (i.e. the great circles). But in the space-time of *general relativity* it is (rather surprisingly) one of maximal *proper time* (i.e. as measured by a clock in free fall) because the predominant curvature in a gravitational field is that of time rather than space. This led John A. Wheeler to introduce the 'principle of maximal aging' as a way of explaining it.

161   A tensor is a multidimensional mathematical entity, and may be viewed here as a multidimensional array for simplicity. You can think of it as a generalisation of a scalar (0-dimensional) and vector (1-dimensional). When a tensor describes a quantity that has a value at each location over a region of some space then it is technically a 'tensor field', but they are so important that they are regularly called just tensors. In physics, their importance lies in the fact that they can represent quantities independently of the chosen coordinate frames. For instance, whether something was represented by Cartesian or polar coordinates would not change the basic form of an equation.

162 In physics, a field is a quantity or property that has a value at each point in space-time. Although there are observable phenomena that deserve the field description, such as magnetic fields and gravitational fields, it is more often a mathematical abstraction, and especially in *quantum field theory*. It is so common, now, to define fields — including photon fields, electron fields, proton fields, gluon fields, Higgs field, inflaton field, and even 'super quantum potential' (*de Broglie–Bohm theory*) — that physicists may be forgiven for thinking that they all have some substance in reality.

163 Albrecht Fölsing, author, Ewald Osers, transl., *Albert Einstein: A Biography* (Viking Penguin, 1997), p.557.

164 We are discussing this model here in the broadest terms. The current 'standard model of cosmology', known as *lambda-CDM*, is a version of the expanding universe expressed via a solution of Einstein's *general relativity* equations, and including their *cosmological constant* (usually equated with 'dark energy'), cold 'dark matter' (CDM), the *cosmological principle* (that the large-scale spatial distribution of matter in the universe is homogeneous and isotropic), and sometimes *cosmic inflation.*

165 Simon Mitton, *Fred Hoyle: A Life in Science* (Cambridge University Press, 2011), p.129.

166 Although this is the widely accepted value, recent evidence suggests that the universe could be as much as two billion years younger. Source: Seth Borenstein, "Study finds the universe might be 2 billion years younger", *Phys.org* (https://phys.org/news/2019-09-universe-billion-years-younger.html : created 12 September 2019, accessed 25 November 2019).

167 Stephen W. Hawking and Leonard Mlodinow, *The Grand Design* (Bantam Books, 2010), pp.172–173.

168 Hawking, *A Brief History of Time*, pp.137–138.

169 The so-called *Hubble constant* (H_0) is only constant across all spatial observations at a particular time. The *Hubble parameter* (H), on the other hand, is a generalisation that is accepted to vary over time, and H_0 is simply the current value of H.

170 Leila Sloman, "Hubble Tension Headache: Clashing Measurements Make the Universe's Expansion a Lingering Mystery", *Scientific American* (29 July 2019).

171 Jason Palmer, "Nobel physics prize honours accelerating Universe find", *BBC News* (4 October 2011); online (https://www.bbc.com/news/science-environment-15165371 : accessed 23 September 2020).

172 Jacques Colin, Roya Mohayaee, Mohamed Rameez, Subir Sarkar, "Evidence for anisotropy of cosmic acceleration", *Astronomy & Astrophysics*, vol. 631 (November 2019), article no. L13; DOI: 10.1051/0004-6361/201936373 .

173 Sir Arthur Eddington, *The Expanding Universe* (Penguin Books, 1940), p.67.

174 Rafi Letzter, "Is the Universe a Giant Loop?", *Scientific American* (5 Nov 2019), online (https://www.scientificamerican.com/article/is-the-universe-a-giant-loop/ : accessed 1 March 2020).

175 Ernst Mach, author, Philip Edward Bertrand Jourdain, transl., *History and Root of the Principle of the Conservation of Energy* (Open Court Publishing Company, 1910).

176   One comprehensive analysis may be found at: Myron W. Evans, Stephen J. Crothers, Horst Eckardt, Kerry Pendergast, "Criticisms of the Einstein Field Equation: The End of 20th Century Physics", *Academia.edu* (https://www.academia.edu/6882112/CRITICISMS_ OF_THE_EINSTEIN_FIELD_EQUATION : published 21 March 21 2010, accessed 5 November 2020); collection of papers questioning the fact that Einstein ignored the Riemann torsion tensor when applying his mathematics to *general relativity* — citing work by Alpha Institute for Advanced Studies (AIAS) — questioning the prediction of gravitational waves, implications for the conservation of energy-momentum, and the existence of infinitely dense point masses.

177   Meaning equated in the empirical sense. In principle, there could be a constant of proportionality, but it is easier to equate them numerically and simply absorb that constant into the equations describing gravitational attraction.

178   In order to avoid infinite results then it cannot be true that the universe is infinite, and homogenous, and not expanding; at least one has to give. Sciama considered the universe to be expanding.

179   D. W. Sciama, *The Physical Foundations of General Relativity* (Heinemann Educational Books, 1972), p.34.

180   Erik P. Verlinde, "On the Origin of Gravity and the Laws of Newton", *arXiv.org*, Cornell University eprint (https://arxiv.org/abs/1001.0785, 6 January 2010); DOI: 10.1007/ JHEP04(2011)029 .

181   This particular type of network geometry is also related to the field of 'distance geometry'. There must be constraints on the degrees of freedom in such a dimensionless network, but it is unclear how they might facilitate a description employing a four-dimensional framework, or at what point the resulting emergent space would appear Riemannian rather than Euclidean or Minkowskian. Some related research may be found at: James R. Clough and Tim S. Evans, "Embedding graphs in Lorentzian spacetime", *PLoS ONE* (https:// journals.plos.org/plosone/article/file?id=10.1371/journal.pone.0187301&type=printable : published 6 November 2017, accessed 15 January 2020); DOI: 10.1371/journal. pone.0187301 . A cheaper approach might be to presume that each thread has a real length and exhibiting properties along that length from which spatial and phase relations might emerge (i.e. that space is emergent but not time), and even accounting for the difference between space-like and time-like intervals.

CHAPTER 12 ...

182   Clearly, new observations might differentiate two frameworks if they no longer give the same answers in alternative circumstances, but we are here more interested in whether one can be deemed more *significant* than the other. Most readers will be aware of the different frameworks describing gravity from Newton and Einstein, but before them planetary motions were described in terms of deferents and epicycles rather than heliocentric ellipses. Newer frameworks are increasingly abstract, and reliant upon invisible properties of space-time, but can we say they are significant in relation to the objective reality?

183   Albert Einstein, author, Alan Harris, transl., "On the Method of Theoretical Physics", *Einstein's Essays in Science* (Dover Publications Inc., 2009), pp.15–16.

184 This quotation, taken slightly out of context here, is widely attributed to Einstein from 1954. In 1972, it was quoted in fuller form as a reply from a 70-year-old Einstein to an ordained rabbi who had tried to console his daughter over the death of her sister; source: Walter Sullivan "Einstein Papers. A Man of Many Parts", *The New York Times* (29 March 1972). In 2005, though, this was claimed to be an elaborated misquote, and his briefer words actually appearing in a letter dated 12 February 1950 to a Robert S. Marcus, a man distraught over the death of his young son from polio; source: Alice Calaprice, *The New Quotable Einstein* (Princeton University Press, 2005). An analysis and summary can be found at https://www.thymindoman.com/einsteins-misquote-on-the-illusion-of-feeling-separate-from-the-whole/ (accessed 17 October 2019).

185 Albert Einstein, "Science and Religion", *Out of my later years* (London: Thames and Hudson, 1950), p.22.

186 Ronald William Clark, *Einstein: The Life and Times* (1971; reprint Harper Paperbacks, 2011), p.243.

187 Immanuel Kant, author, William Hastie, ed. and transl., *Kant's Cosmogony* (Glasgow: James Maclehose & Sons, 1900), p.27; Immanuel Kant, *Universal Natural History and Theory of the Heavens* (1755).

188 The term 'anthropic' should relate to human beings but we are taking it for granted that the implications of the SAP, WAP, and TAP, relate to all conscious life, whether earthly or not.

189 John D. Barrow, *The World Within the World* (Oxford University Press, 1988), p.360.

190 Sabine Hossenfelder, "Is the Anthropic Principle scientific?", blogspot.com, *BackReAction*, posted 6 December 2019 (https://backreaction.blogspot.com/2019/12/is-anthropic-principle-scientific.html : accessed 9 December 2019).

191 Sabine Hossenfelder, *Lost in Math: How Beauty Leads Physics Astray* (New York: Basic Books, 2018), p.241.

192 *Kant-Critique-Pure-Reason*, "Preface".

193 Albert Einstein, et al., *Living Philosophies* (New York: Simon and Schuster, 1931), p.6; note that the word "rapt" (as in rapture) is very often appears mis-transcribed as "wrapped", and the commonality of this on the Internet suggests that they were all originally copied from one erroneous transcription.

APPENDIX

194 There is another form of *time dilation* called *gravitational time dilation*, but that is not discussed in this section.

Glossary

Some of the terms used in this work may be unfamiliar, or may have different semantics from their usage elsewhere. They are collected together here as they have been purposely selected or fashioned to make the arguments clearer.

Algorithmic Steps. In general, an algorithm is a branching network of decisions and actions, defined and constrained by some set of rules. It is a directed network, which allows it to be expressed using any sequential medium, but it has no fundamental temporal basis and does not mandate physical processes. The implicit dependencies of the branching is asymmetric and as a consequence irreversible. Whether the inputs are initial (as with mathematical derivation), continuous (as with the computer processing of a file or database), or real-time (as with our mind), this generality still holds. The specific case of computer software is covered in Chapter 9. We have used the term to describe our own thought processes, despite the associated rules no longer being discrete or representable in any symbolic fashion. See also note 17.

Causal Asymmetry. The phenomenon that in every pair of cause and effect that we identify, the cause is deemed to precede the effect (using the direction of subjective time). Also, that more than one effect may be attributed to the same cause. The distinction between cause and effect is a subjective one that rests on our identification of causal entities (§8.2), but we also carry this notion down to the physical level where we can connect it to the gradient of usable energy in the universe: to effect a change from the normal paths or state of a system, you need usable energy, and the utilisation of energy in that respect is deemed to constitute a physical cause, despite the fact that the laws of physics are time-symmetric.

Cohesive Influences. The tendency of the universe to leave stable and semi-stable structures and forms as its usable energy diminishes and it approaches a state of *thermodynamic equilibrium*. These include atoms, molecules and molecular chains, crystals, stars and planets, galaxies and galaxy clusters, organic life forms that grow and reproduce, and the endeavours of such life forms.

Consciousness. The total of all the '*now*' moments of our experience, streamed in the direction of our subjective time (see TAP). It is, then, a one-dimensional (temporal) state of an active mind that is aware of subjective time, of a changing environment, and possessing a notion that future '*now*' moments (moments beyond any given '*now*' moment) can be orchestrated or adjusted based on the collected experience of prior '*now*' moments.

Determinate Pattern Conjecture (DPC). The state of the *block universe* at any point in time has a strict relation to that either side of it in time. Furthermore, each state will be finite, and relations within a state or between states will be continuous. Hence, the pattern of change between states can be fully modelled by sets of consistent mathematical structures and axioms that are finite, deterministic, and continuous (§10.3). The implication of this is that all measurable quantities in our subjective reality must be finite, non-random, and with no discontinuities or singularities.

Existence (capitalised). All space, all time, and everything that appears to persist or act within their bounds. As well as the contents of the objective reality, though, this term also embraces emergent concepts such as the conscious mind and our subjective reality; effectively the contents of Fig. 5-1 in its entirety.

Mind. The conscious mind is an emergent non-physical entity that is here deemed to encompass the cognitive faculties of qualia, emotions, world-view, creativity, planning, pattern recognition, memory, and the executive. The mind, as distinct from the brain, has its own elements of causation that supervene on the brain, and the interface between the two allows physical cause to produce mental effect, and mental cause to produce physical effect (Chapter 6).

Objective Reality. The universe as it is in the absence of any conscious observer. This is here deemed to be static with the 'fabric' of that reality exhibiting a mathematically deterministic pattern of change over time (see DPC). It is proposed that this 'fabric' is dimensional, and hence describing a *block universe*, since our concept of measurement (§5.4) is dependent upon space and time; and our concept of the measurable world (Fig. 5-1) then has a justifiable relationship to the objective reality. This assumes that space-time is not emergent (§11.5). See also 'quantum block universe'.

Objective Time. Time as it is in the absence of any conscious observer. This is here deemed to be a static dimension, differing from the spatial ones only in the extents and relative orientations of world-lines hosted by the associated *block universe*.

Persistence of Form. The phenomenon of our subjective reality that presents us with distinct objects that may change continuously over time and yet allow us to associate unique identities with them. Objects are self-same if they have no distinctness in their form, position, or provenance (§2.1).

Quantum Block Universe. An interpretation of *quantum mechanics*, presented in §7.6, that is consistent with a *block universe*. This is proposed as a first step to understanding the full objective reality as the effects are already manifest and testable.

Subjective Reality. The reality inferred from the direct experience of our environment. This includes its structure (space and subjective time) together with the rules that appear govern the evolvement of its changes (e.g. mechanics and causality). It is shared between conscious entities of the same and different (higher) species, and this remarkable fact suggests that consciousness emerges naturally from the objective reality, and that the path to that emergence (through lower species) would be the same, or very similar, everywhere that the evolution of life is possible.

Subjective Time. Time as experienced by a conscious observer. This includes the difference between past and future (we remember one but not the other), the '*now*' moment that separates them (and which is effectively an instant of consciousness), and the apparent flow of changes from past to future. This experience of flow arises because the temporal sense

Temporal Anthropic Principle (TAP). Consciousness and subjective time cannot exist without each other; they are bound as part of the same emergent phenomenon (§6.3).

Temporal Sense. Term used to describe the fact that the sensory inputs of conscious entities are processed instant-by-instant rather than as a block. This underpins our awareness of moment-to-moment changes, and hence of a flowing subjective time. An explanation is advanced in §10.3

World-view. The mental faculty associated with an internal model of both the structure of our environment (i.e. space, time, and objects within them) and the rules by which it evolves (e.g. change, movement, and causality). The faculty can creatively vary aspects of that internal model, and so can imagine people and places that we have never seen, and fantasy worlds that look nothing likes ours or follow quite different rules.

Connections

In order to make it clearer why these specific terms were coined, the following diagram illustrates the connections between them in the context of the different levels of reality depicted in Fig. 4-3 and Fig. 5-1. Note in particular that the static 'fabric' of the objective reality is taken to be dimensional, and that the associated spatio-temporal dimensions are mathematically the same. Our perceived, subjective reality is different in that space is implied by the separation of material objects, and these objects and separations both change over time. In the mind, we have a mental model (the world-view faculty) which embraces environmental representations (both recollected and created), and the temporal rules that appear to govern their changes.

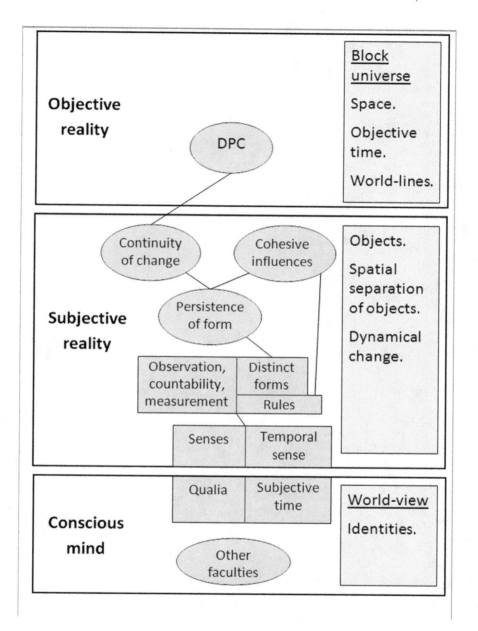

Fig. G- 1, Connections between collected terms.

Index

CPSIA information can be obtained
at www.ICGtesting.com
Printed in the USA
LVHW021105030222
710078LV00002B/112